Mastering Linux - Storage

A catalogue record for this book is available from the Hong Kong Public Libraries.

Published in Hong Kong by Samurai Media Limited.

Email: info@samuraimedia.org

ISBN 978-988-8406-19-7

Table of Contents

List of Tables

Part I. file security

Table of Contents

Chapter 1. standard file permissions

This chapter contains details about basic file security through **file ownership** and **file permissions**.

1.1. file ownership

1.1.1. user owner and group owner

The **users** and **groups** of a system can be locally managed in **/etc/passwd** and **/etc/group**, or they can be in a NIS, LDAP, or Samba domain. These users and groups can **own** files. Actually, every file has a **user owner** and a **group owner**, as can be seen in the following screenshot.

```
paul@rhel65:~/owners$ ls -lh
total 636K
-rw-r--r--. 1 paul  snooker 1.1K Apr  8 18:47 data.odt
-rw-r--r--. 1 paul  paul    626K Apr  8 18:46 file1
-rw-r--r--. 1 root  tennis   185 Apr  8 18:46 file2
-rw-rw-r--. 1 root  root       0 Apr  8 18:47 stuff.txt
paul@rhel65:~/owners$
```

User paul owns three files; file1 has paul as **user owner** and has the group paul as **group owner**, data.odt is **group owned** by the group snooker, file2 by the group tennis.

The last file is called stuff.txt and is owned by the root user and the root group.

1.1.2. listing user accounts

You can use the following command to list all local user accounts.

```
paul@debian7~$ cut -d: -f1 /etc/passwd | column
root           ntp          sam          bert         naomi
daemon         mysql        tom          rino         matthias2
bin            paul         wouter       antonio      bram
sys            maarten      robrecht     simon        fabrice
sync           kevin        bilal        sven         chimene
games          yuri         dimitri      wouter2      messagebus
man            william      ahmed        tarik        roger
lp             yves         dylan        jan          frank
mail           kris         robin        ian          toon
news           hamid        matthias     ivan         rinus
uucp           vladimir     ben          azeddine     eddy
proxy          abiy         mike         eric         bram2
www-data       david        kevin2       kamel        keith
backup         chahid       kenzo        ischa        jesse
list           stef         aaron        bart         frederick
irc            joeri        lorenzo      omer         hans
gnats          glenn        jens         kurt         dries
nobody         yannick      ruben        steve        steve2
libuuid        christof     jelle        constantin   tomas
Debian-exim    george       stefaan      sam2         johan
statd          joost        marc         bjorn        tom2
sshd           arno         thomas       ronald
```

1.1.3. chgrp

You can change the group owner of a file using the **chgrp** command.

```
root@rhel65:/home/paul/owners# ls -l file2
-rw-r--r--. 1 root tennis 185 Apr  8 18:46 file2
root@rhel65:/home/paul/owners# chgrp snooker file2
root@rhel65:/home/paul/owners# ls -l file2
-rw-r--r--. 1 root snooker 185 Apr  8 18:46 file2
root@rhel65:/home/paul/owners#
```

1.1.4. chown

The user owner of a file can be changed with **chown** command.

```
root@laika:/home/paul# ls -l FileForPaul
-rw-r--r-- 1 root paul 0 2008-08-06 14:11 FileForPaul
root@laika:/home/paul# chown paul FileForPaul
root@laika:/home/paul# ls -l FileForPaul
-rw-r--r-- 1 paul paul 0 2008-08-06 14:11 FileForPaul
```

You can also use **chown** to change both the user owner and the group owner.

```
root@laika:/home/paul# ls -l FileForPaul
-rw-r--r-- 1 paul paul 0 2008-08-06 14:11 FileForPaul
root@laika:/home/paul# chown root:project42 FileForPaul
root@laika:/home/paul# ls -l FileForPaul
-rw-r--r-- 1 root project42 0 2008-08-06 14:11 FileForPaul
```

1.2. list of special files

When you use **ls -l**, for each file you can see ten characters before the user and group owner. The first character tells us the type of file. Regular files get a **-**, directories get a **d**, symbolic links are shown with an **l**, pipes get a **p**, character devices a **c**, block devices a **b**, and sockets an **s**.

Table 1.1. Unix special files

first character	file type
-	normal file
d	directory
l	symbolic link
p	named pipe
b	block device
c	character device
s	socket

Below a screenshot of a character device (the console) and a block device (the hard disk).

```
paul@debian6lt~$ ls -ld /dev/console /dev/sda
crw-------   1 root root  5, 1 Mar 15 12:45 /dev/console
brw-rw----   1 root disk  8, 0 Mar 15 12:45 /dev/sda
```

And here you can see a directory, a regular file and a symbolic link.

```
paul@debian6lt~$ ls -ld /etc /etc/hosts /etc/motd
drwxr-xr-x 128 root root 12288 Mar 15 18:34 /etc
-rw-r--r--   1 root root   372 Dec 10 17:36 /etc/hosts
lrwxrwxrwx   1 root root    13 Dec  5 10:36 /etc/motd -> /var/run/motd
```

1.3. permissions

1.3.1. rwx

The nine characters following the file type denote the permissions in three triplets. A permission can be **r** for read access, **w** for write access, and **x** for execute. You need the **r** permission to list (ls) the contents of a directory. You need the **x** permission to enter (cd) a directory. You need the **w** permission to create files in or remove files from a directory.

Table 1.2. standard Unix file permissions

permission	on a file	on a directory
r (read)	read file contents (cat)	read directory contents (ls)
w (write)	change file contents (vi)	create files in (touch)
x (execute)	execute the file	enter the directory (cd)

1.3.2. three sets of rwx

We already know that the output of **ls -l** starts with ten characters for each file. This screenshot shows a regular file (because the first character is a -).

```
paul@RHELv4u4:~/test$ ls -l proc42.bash
-rwxr-xr--  1 paul proj 984 Feb  6 12:01 proc42.bash
```

Below is a table describing the function of all ten characters.

Table 1.3. Unix file permissions position

position	characters	function
1	-	this is a regular file
2-4	rwx	permissions for the **user owner**
5-7	r-x	permissions for the **group owner**
8-10	r--	permissions for **others**

When you are the **user owner** of a file, then the **user owner permissions** apply to you. The rest of the permissions have no influence on your access to the file.

When you belong to the **group** that is the **group owner** of a file, then the **group owner permissions** apply to you. The rest of the permissions have no influence on your access to the file.

When you are not the **user owner** of a file and you do not belong to the **group owner**, then the **others permissions** apply to you. The rest of the permissions have no influence on your access to the file.

1.3.3. permission examples

Some example combinations on files and directories are seen in this screenshot. The name of the file explains the permissions.

```
paul@laika:~/perms$ ls -lh
total 12K
drwxr-xr-x 2 paul paul 4.0K 2007-02-07 22:26 AllEnter_UserCreateDelete
-rwxrwxrwx 1 paul paul    0 2007-02-07 22:21 EveryoneFullControl.txt
-r--r----- 1 paul paul    0 2007-02-07 22:21 OnlyOwnersRead.txt
-rwxrwx--- 1 paul paul    0 2007-02-07 22:21 OwnersAll_RestNothing.txt
dr-xr-x--- 2 paul paul 4.0K 2007-02-07 22:25 UserAndGroupEnter
dr-x------ 2 paul paul 4.0K 2007-02-07 22:25 OnlyUserEnter
paul@laika:~/perms$
```

To summarise, the first **rwx** triplet represents the permissions for the **user owner**. The second triplet corresponds to the **group owner**; it specifies permissions for all members of that group. The third triplet defines permissions for all **other** users that are not the user owner and are not a member of the group owner.

1.3.4. setting permissions (chmod)

Permissions can be changed with **chmod**. The first example gives the user owner execute permissions.

```
paul@laika:~/perms$ ls -l permissions.txt
-rw-r--r-- 1 paul paul 0 2007-02-07 22:34 permissions.txt
paul@laika:~/perms$ chmod u+x permissions.txt
paul@laika:~/perms$ ls -l permissions.txt
-rwxr--r-- 1 paul paul 0 2007-02-07 22:34 permissions.txt
```

This example removes the group owners read permission.

```
paul@laika:~/perms$ chmod g-r permissions.txt
paul@laika:~/perms$ ls -l permissions.txt
-rwx---r-- 1 paul paul 0 2007-02-07 22:34 permissions.txt
```

This example removes the others read permission.

```
paul@laika:~/perms$ chmod o-r permissions.txt
paul@laika:~/perms$ ls -l permissions.txt
-rwx------ 1 paul paul 0 2007-02-07 22:34 permissions.txt
```

This example gives all of them the write permission.

```
paul@laika:~/perms$ chmod a+w permissions.txt
paul@laika:~/perms$ ls -l permissions.txt
-rwx-w--w- 1 paul paul 0 2007-02-07 22:34 permissions.txt
```

You don't even have to type the a.

```
paul@laika:~/perms$ chmod +x permissions.txt
paul@laika:~/perms$ ls -l permissions.txt
-rwx-wx-wx 1 paul paul 0 2007-02-07 22:34 permissions.txt
```

You can also set explicit permissions.

```
paul@laika:~/perms$ chmod u=rw permissions.txt
paul@laika:~/perms$ ls -l permissions.txt
-rw--wx-wx 1 paul paul 0 2007-02-07 22:34 permissions.txt
```

Feel free to make any kind of combination.

```
paul@laika:~/perms$ chmod u=rw,g=rw,o=r permissions.txt
paul@laika:~/perms$ ls -l permissions.txt
-rw-rw-r-- 1 paul paul 0 2007-02-07 22:34 permissions.txt
```

Even fishy combinations are accepted by chmod.

```
paul@laika:~/perms$ chmod u=rwx,ug+rw,o=r permissions.txt
paul@laika:~/perms$ ls -l permissions.txt
-rwxrw-r-- 1 paul paul 0 2007-02-07 22:34 permissions.txt
```

1.3.5. setting octal permissions

Most Unix administrators will use the **old school** octal system to talk about and set permissions. Look at the triplet bitwise, equating r to 4, w to 2, and x to 1.

Table 1.4. Octal permissions

binary	octal	permission
000	0	---
001	1	--x
010	2	-w-
011	3	-wx
100	4	r--
101	5	r-x
110	6	rw-
111	7	rwx

This makes **777** equal to rwxrwxrwx and by the same logic, 654 mean rw-r-xr-- . The **chmod** command will accept these numbers.

```
paul@laika:~/perms$ chmod 777 permissions.txt
paul@laika:~/perms$ ls -l permissions.txt
-rwxrwxrwx 1 paul paul 0 2007-02-07 22:34 permissions.txt
paul@laika:~/perms$ chmod 664 permissions.txt
paul@laika:~/perms$ ls -l permissions.txt
-rw-rw-r-- 1 paul paul 0 2007-02-07 22:34 permissions.txt
paul@laika:~/perms$ chmod 750 permissions.txt
paul@laika:~/perms$ ls -l permissions.txt
-rwxr-x--- 1 paul paul 0 2007-02-07 22:34 permissions.txt
```

1.3.6. umask

When creating a file or directory, a set of default permissions are applied. These default permissions are determined by the **umask**. The **umask** specifies permissions that you do not want set on by default. You can display the **umask** with the **umask** command.

```
[Harry@RHEL4b ~]$ umask
0002
[Harry@RHEL4b ~]$ touch test
[Harry@RHEL4b ~]$ ls -l test
-rw-rw-r--  1 Harry Harry 0 Jul 24 06:03 test
[Harry@RHEL4b ~]$
```

As you can also see, the file is also not executable by default. This is a general security feature among Unixes; newly created files are never executable by default. You have to explicitly do a **chmod +x** to make a file executable. This also means that the 1 bit in the **umask** has no meaning--a **umask** of 0022 is the same as 0033.

1.3.7. mkdir -m

When creating directories with **mkdir** you can use the **-m** option to set the **mode**. This screenshot explains.

```
paul@debian5~$ mkdir -m 700 MyDir
paul@debian5~$ mkdir -m 777 Public
paul@debian5~$ ls -dl MyDir/ Public/
drwx------ 2 paul paul 4096 2011-10-16 19:16 MyDir/
drwxrwxrwx 2 paul paul 4096 2011-10-16 19:16 Public/
```

1.3.8. cp -p

To preserve permissions and time stamps from source files, use **cp -p**.

```
paul@laika:~/perms$ cp file* cp
paul@laika:~/perms$ cp -p file* cpp
paul@laika:~/perms$ ll *
-rwx------ 1 paul paul    0 2008-08-25 13:26 file33
-rwxr-x--- 1 paul paul    0 2008-08-25 13:26 file42

cp:
total 0
-rwx------ 1 paul paul 0 2008-08-25 13:34 file33
-rwxr-x--- 1 paul paul 0 2008-08-25 13:34 file42

cpp:
total 0
-rwx------ 1 paul paul 0 2008-08-25 13:26 file33
-rwxr-x--- 1 paul paul 0 2008-08-25 13:26 file42
```

1.4. practice: standard file permissions

1. As normal user, create a directory ~/permissions. Create a file owned by yourself in there.

2. Copy a file owned by root from /etc/ to your permissions dir, who owns this file now ?

3. As root, create a file in the users ~/permissions directory.

4. As normal user, look at who owns this file created by root.

5. Change the ownership of all files in ~/permissions to yourself.

6. Make sure you have all rights to these files, and others can only read.

7. With chmod, is 770 the same as rwxrwx--- ?

8. With chmod, is 664 the same as r-xr-xr-- ?

9. With chmod, is 400 the same as r-------- ?

10. With chmod, is 734 the same as rwxr-xr-- ?

11a. Display the umask in octal and in symbolic form.

11b. Set the umask to 077, but use the symbolic format to set it. Verify that this works.

12. Create a file as root, give only read to others. Can a normal user read this file ? Test writing to this file with vi.

13a. Create a file as normal user, give only read to others. Can another normal user read this file ? Test writing to this file with vi.

13b. Can root read this file ? Can root write to this file with vi ?

14. Create a directory that belongs to a group, where every member of that group can read and write to files, and create files. Make sure that people can only delete their own files.

1.5. solution: standard file permissions

1. As normal user, create a directory ~/permissions. Create a file owned by yourself in there.

```
mkdir ~/permissions ; touch ~/permissions/myfile.txt
```

2. Copy a file owned by root from /etc/ to your permissions dir, who owns this file now ?

```
cp /etc/hosts ~/permissions/
```

The copy is owned by you.

3. As root, create a file in the users ~/permissions directory.

```
(become root)# touch /home/username/permissions/rootfile
```

4. As normal user, look at who owns this file created by root.

```
ls -l ~/permissions
```

The file created by root is owned by root.

5. Change the ownership of all files in ~/permissions to yourself.

```
chown user ~/permissions/*
```

You cannot become owner of the file that belongs to root.

6. Make sure you have all rights to these files, and others can only read.

```
chmod 644 (on files)
```
```
chmod 755 (on directories)
```

7. With chmod, is 770 the same as rwxrwx--- ?

yes

8. With chmod, is 664 the same as r-xr-xr-- ?

No

9. With chmod, is 400 the same as r-------- ?

yes

10. With chmod, is 734 the same as rwxr-xr-- ?

no

11a. Display the umask in octal and in symbolic form.

```
umask ; umask -S
```

11b. Set the umask to 077, but use the symbolic format to set it. Verify that this works.

```
umask -S u=rwx,go=
```

12. Create a file as root, give only read to others. Can a normal user read this file ? Test writing to this file with vi.

```
(become root)

# echo hello > /home/username/root.txt

# chmod 744 /home/username/root.txt

(become user)

vi ~/root.txt
```

13a. Create a file as normal user, give only read to others. Can another normal user read this file ? Test writing to this file with vi.

```
echo hello > file ; chmod 744 file
```

Yes, others can read this file

13b. Can root read this file ? Can root write to this file with vi ?

Yes, root can read and write to this file. Permissions do not apply to root.

14. Create a directory that belongs to a group, where every member of that group can read and write to files, and create files. Make sure that people can only delete their own files.

```
mkdir /home/project42 ; groupadd project42

chgrp project42 /home/project42 ; chmod 775 /home/project42
```

You can not yet do the last part of this exercise...

Chapter 2. advanced file permissions

2.1. sticky bit on directory

You can set the **sticky bit** on a directory to prevent users from removing files that they do not own as a user owner. The sticky bit is displayed at the same location as the x permission for others. The sticky bit is represented by a **t** (meaning x is also there) or a **T** (when there is no x for others).

```
root@RHELv4u4:~# mkdir /project55
root@RHELv4u4:~# ls -ld /project55
drwxr-xr-x  2 root root 4096 Feb  7 17:38 /project55
root@RHELv4u4:~# chmod +t /project55/
root@RHELv4u4:~# ls -ld /project55
drwxr-xr-t  2 root root 4096 Feb  7 17:38 /project55
root@RHELv4u4:~#
```

The **sticky bit** can also be set with octal permissions, it is binary 1 in the first of four triplets.

```
root@RHELv4u4:~# chmod 1775 /project55/
root@RHELv4u4:~# ls -ld /project55
drwxrwxr-t  2 root root 4096 Feb  7 17:38 /project55
root@RHELv4u4:~#
```

You will typically find the **sticky bit** on the **/tmp** directory.

```
root@barry:~# ls -ld /tmp
drwxrwxrwt 6 root root 4096 2009-06-04 19:02 /tmp
```

2.2. setgid bit on directory

setgid can be used on directories to make sure that all files inside the directory are owned by the group owner of the directory. The **setgid** bit is displayed at the same location as the x permission for group owner. The **setgid** bit is represented by an **s** (meaning x is also there) or a **S** (when there is no x for the group owner). As this example shows, even though **root** does not belong to the group proj55, the files created by root in /project55 will belong to proj55 since the **setgid** is set.

```
root@RHELv4u4:~# groupadd proj55
root@RHELv4u4:~# chown root:proj55 /project55/
root@RHELv4u4:~# chmod 2775 /project55/
root@RHELv4u4:~# touch /project55/fromroot.txt
root@RHELv4u4:~# ls -ld /project55/
drwxrwsr-x  2 root proj55 4096 Feb  7 17:45 /project55/
root@RHELv4u4:~# ls -l /project55/
total 4
-rw-r--r--  1 root proj55 0 Feb  7 17:45 fromroot.txt
root@RHELv4u4:~#
```

You can use the **find** command to find all **setgid** directories.

```
paul@laika:~$ find / -type d -perm -2000 2> /dev/null
/var/log/mysql
/var/log/news
/var/local
...
```

2.3. setgid and setuid on regular files

These two permissions cause an executable file to be executed with the permissions of the **file owner** instead of the **executing owner**. This means that if any user executes a program that belongs to the **root user**, and the **setuid** bit is set on that program, then the program runs as **root**. This can be dangerous, but sometimes this is good for security.

Take the example of passwords; they are stored in **/etc/shadow** which is only readable by **root**. (The **root** user never needs permissions anyway.)

```
root@RHELv4u4:~# ls -l /etc/shadow
-r--------  1 root root 1260 Jan 21 07:49 /etc/shadow
```

Changing your password requires an update of this file, so how can normal non-root users do this? Let's take a look at the permissions on the **/usr/bin/passwd**.

```
root@RHELv4u4:~# ls -l /usr/bin/passwd
-r-s--x--x  1 root root 21200 Jun 17  2005 /usr/bin/passwd
```

When running the **passwd** program, you are executing it with **root** credentials.

You can use the **find** command to find all **setuid** programs.

```
paul@laika:~$ find /usr/bin -type f -perm -04000
/usr/bin/arping
/usr/bin/kgrantpty
/usr/bin/newgrp
/usr/bin/chfn
/usr/bin/sudo
/usr/bin/fping6
/usr/bin/passwd
/usr/bin/gpasswd
...
```

In most cases, setting the **setuid** bit on executables is sufficient. Setting the **setgid** bit will result in these programs to run with the credentials of their group owner.

2.4. setuid on sudo

The **sudo** binary has the **setuid** bit set, so any user can run it with the effective userid of root.

```
paul@rhel65:~$ ls -l $(which sudo)
---s--x--x. 1 root root 123832 Oct  7  2013 /usr/bin/sudo
paul@rhel65:~$
```

2.5. practice: sticky, setuid and setgid bits

1a. Set up a directory, owned by the group sports.

1b. Members of the sports group should be able to create files in this directory.

1c. All files created in this directory should be group-owned by the sports group.

1d. Users should be able to delete only their own user-owned files.

1e. Test that this works!

2. Verify the permissions on **/usr/bin/passwd**. Remove the **setuid**, then try changing your password as a normal user. Reset the permissions back and try again.

3. If time permits (or if you are waiting for other students to finish this practice), read about file attributes in the man page of chattr and lsattr. Try setting the i attribute on a file and test that it works.

2.6. solution: sticky, setuid and setgid bits

1a. Set up a directory, owned by the group sports.

```
groupadd sports

mkdir /home/sports

chown root:sports /home/sports
```

1b. Members of the sports group should be able to create files in this directory.

```
chmod 770 /home/sports
```

1c. All files created in this directory should be group-owned by the sports group.

```
chmod 2770 /home/sports
```

1d. Users should be able to delete only their own user-owned files.

```
chmod +t /home/sports
```

1e. Test that this works!

Log in with different users (group members and others and root), create files and watch the permissions. Try changing and deleting files...

2. Verify the permissions on **/usr/bin/passwd**. Remove the **setuid**, then try changing your password as a normal user. Reset the permissions back and try again.

```
root@deb503:~# ls -l /usr/bin/passwd
-rwsr-xr-x 1 root root 31704 2009-11-14 15:41 /usr/bin/passwd
root@deb503:~# chmod 755 /usr/bin/passwd
root@deb503:~# ls -l /usr/bin/passwd
-rwxr-xr-x 1 root root 31704 2009-11-14 15:41 /usr/bin/passwd
```

A normal user cannot change password now.

```
root@deb503:~# chmod 4755 /usr/bin/passwd
root@deb503:~# ls -l /usr/bin/passwd
-rwsr-xr-x 1 root root 31704 2009-11-14 15:41 /usr/bin/passwd
```

3. If time permits (or if you are waiting for other students to finish this practice), read about file attributes in the man page of chattr and lsattr. Try setting the i attribute on a file and test that it works.

```
paul@laika:~$ sudo su -
[sudo] password for paul:
root@laika:~# mkdir attr
root@laika:~# cd attr/
root@laika:~/attr# touch file42
root@laika:~/attr# lsattr
------------------ ./file42
root@laika:~/attr# chattr +i file42
```

```
root@laika:~/attr# lsattr
----i------------- ./file42
root@laika:~/attr# rm -rf file42
rm: cannot remove `file42': Operation not permitted
root@laika:~/attr# chattr -i file42
root@laika:~/attr# rm -rf file42
root@laika:~/attr#
```

Chapter 3. access control lists

Standard Unix permissions might not be enough for some organisations. This chapter introduces **access control lists** or **acl's** to further protect files and directories.

3.1. acl in /etc/fstab

File systems that support **access control lists**, or **acls**, have to be mounted with the **acl** option listed in **/etc/fstab**. In the example below, you can see that the root file system has **acl** support, whereas /home/data does not.

```
root@laika:~# tail -4 /etc/fstab
/dev/sda1          /              ext3    acl,relatime     0  1
/dev/sdb2          /home/data     auto    noacl,defaults   0  0
pasha:/home/r      /home/pasha    nfs     defaults         0  0
wolf:/srv/data     /home/wolf     nfs     defaults         0  0
```

3.2. getfacl

Reading **acls** can be done with **/usr/bin/getfacl**. This screenshot shows how to read the **acl** of **file33** with **getfacl**.

```
paul@laika:~/test$ getfacl file33
# file: file33
# owner: paul
# group: paul
user::rw-
group::r--
mask::rwx
other::r--
```

3.3. setfacl

Writing or changing **acls** can be done with **/usr/bin/setfacl**. These screenshots show how to change the **acl** of **file33** with **setfacl**.

First we add **user sandra** with octal permission **7** to the **acl**.

```
paul@laika:~/test$ setfacl -m u:sandra:7 file33
```

Then we add the **group tennis** with octal permission **6** to the **acl** of the same file.

```
paul@laika:~/test$ setfacl -m g:tennis:6 file33
```

The result is visible with **getfacl**.

```
paul@laika:~/test$ getfacl file33
# file: file33
# owner: paul
# group: paul
user::rw-
user:sandra:rwx
group::r--
group:tennis:rw-
mask::rwx
other::r--
```

3.4. remove an acl entry

The **-x** option of the **setfacl** command will remove an **acl** entry from the targeted file.

```
paul@laika:~/test$ setfacl -m u:sandra:7 file33
paul@laika:~/test$ getfacl file33 | grep sandra
user:sandra:rwx
paul@laika:~/test$ setfacl -x sandra file33
paul@laika:~/test$ getfacl file33 | grep sandra
```

Note that omitting the **u** or **g** when defining the **acl** for an account will default it to a user account.

3.5. remove the complete acl

The **-b** option of the **setfacl** command will remove the **acl** from the targeted file.

```
paul@laika:~/test$ setfacl -b file33
paul@laika:~/test$ getfacl file33
# file: file33
# owner: paul
# group: paul
user::rw-
group::r--
other::r--
```

3.6. the acl mask

The **acl mask** defines the maximum effective permissions for any entry in the **acl**. This **mask** is calculated every time you execute the **setfacl** or **chmod** commands.

You can prevent the calculation by using the **--no-mask** switch.

```
paul@laika:~/test$ setfacl --no-mask -m u:sandra:7 file33
paul@laika:~/test$ getfacl file33
# file: file33
# owner: paul
# group: paul
user::rw-
user:sandra:rwx    #effective:rw-
group::r--
mask::rw-
other::r--
```

3.7. eiciel

Desktop users might want to use **eiciel** to manage **acls** with a graphical tool.

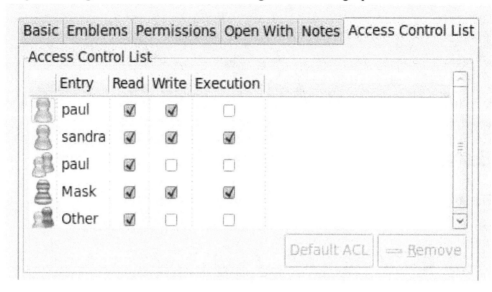

You will need to install **eiciel** and **nautilus-actions** to have an extra tab in **nautilus** to manage **acls**.

```
paul@laika:~$ sudo aptitude install eiciel nautilus-actions
```

Chapter 4. file links

An average computer using Linux has a file system with many **hard links** and **symbolic links**.

To understand links in a file system, you first have to understand what an **inode** is.

4.1. inodes

4.1.1. inode contents

An **inode** is a data structure that contains metadata about a file. When the file system stores a new file on the hard disk, it stores not only the contents (data) of the file, but also extra properties like the name of the file, the creation date, its permissions, the owner of the file, and more. All this information (except the name of the file and the contents of the file) is stored in the **inode** of the file.

The **ls -l** command will display some of the inode contents, as seen in this screenshot.

```
root@rhel53 ~# ls -ld /home/project42/
drwxr-xr-x 4 root pro42 4.0K Mar 27 14:29 /home/project42/
```

4.1.2. inode table

The **inode table** contains all of the **inodes** and is created when you create the file system (with **mkfs**). You can use the **df -i** command to see how many **inodes** are used and free on mounted file systems.

```
root@rhel53 ~# df -i
Filesystem              Inodes    IUsed    IFree IUse% Mounted on
/dev/mapper/VolGroup00-LogVol00
                       4947968   115326  4832642    3% /
/dev/hda1                26104       45    26059    1% /boot
tmpfs                    64417        1    64416    1% /dev/shm
/dev/sda1               262144     2207   259937    1% /home/project42
/dev/sdb1                74400     5519    68881    8% /home/project33
/dev/sdb5                    0        0        0     - /home/sales
/dev/sdb6               100744       11   100733    1% /home/research
```

In the **df -i** screenshot above you can see the **inode** usage for several mounted **file systems**. You don't see numbers for **/dev/sdb5** because it is a **fat** file system.

4.1.3. inode number

Each **inode** has a unique number (the inode number). You can see the **inode** numbers with the **ls -li** command.

```
paul@RHELv4u4:~/test$ touch file1
paul@RHELv4u4:~/test$ touch file2
paul@RHELv4u4:~/test$ touch file3
paul@RHELv4u4:~/test$ ls -li
total 12
817266 -rw-rw-r--  1 paul paul 0 Feb  5 15:38 file1
817267 -rw-rw-r--  1 paul paul 0 Feb  5 15:38 file2
817268 -rw-rw-r--  1 paul paul 0 Feb  5 15:38 file3
paul@RHELv4u4:~/test$
```

These three files were created one after the other and got three different **inodes** (the first column). All the information you see with this **ls** command resides in the **inode**, except for the filename (which is contained in the directory).

4.1.4. inode and file contents

Let's put some data in one of the files.

```
paul@RHELv4u4:~/test$ ls -li
total 16
817266 -rw-rw-r--  1 paul paul  0 Feb  5 15:38 file1
817270 -rw-rw-r--  1 paul paul 92 Feb  5 15:42 file2
817268 -rw-rw-r--  1 paul paul  0 Feb  5 15:38 file3
paul@RHELv4u4:~/test$ cat file2
It is winter now and it is very cold.
We do not like the cold, we prefer hot summer nights.
paul@RHELv4u4:~/test$
```

The data that is displayed by the **cat** command is not in the **inode**, but somewhere else on the disk. The **inode** contains a pointer to that data.

4.2. about directories

4.2.1. a directory is a table

A **directory** is a special kind of file that contains a table which maps filenames to inodes. Listing our current directory with **ls -ali** will display the contents of the directory file.

```
paul@RHELv4u4:~/test$ ls -ali
total 32
817262 drwxrwxr-x   2 paul paul 4096 Feb  5 15:42 .
800768 drwx------  16 paul paul 4096 Feb  5 15:42 ..
817266 -rw-rw-r--   1 paul paul    0 Feb  5 15:38 file1
817270 -rw-rw-r--   1 paul paul   92 Feb  5 15:42 file2
817268 -rw-rw-r--   1 paul paul    0 Feb  5 15:38 file3
paul@RHELv4u4:~/test$
```

4.2.2. . and ..

You can see five names, and the mapping to their five inodes. The dot . is a mapping to itself, and the dotdot .. is a mapping to the parent directory. The three other names are mappings to different inodes.

4.3. hard links

4.3.1. creating hard links

When we create a **hard link** to a file with **ln**, an extra entry is added in the directory. A new file name is mapped to an existing inode.

```
paul@RHELv4u4:~/test$ ln file2 hardlink_to_file2
paul@RHELv4u4:~/test$ ls -li
total 24
817266 -rw-rw-r--  1 paul paul  0 Feb  5 15:38 file1
817270 -rw-rw-r--  2 paul paul 92 Feb  5 15:42 file2
817268 -rw-rw-r--  1 paul paul  0 Feb  5 15:38 file3
817270 -rw-rw-r--  2 paul paul 92 Feb  5 15:42 hardlink_to_file2
paul@RHELv4u4:~/test$
```

Both files have the same inode, so they will always have the same permissions and the same owner. Both files will have the same content. Actually, both files are equal now, meaning you can safely remove the original file, the hardlinked file will remain. The inode contains a counter, counting the number of hard links to itself. When the counter drops to zero, then the inode is emptied.

4.3.2. finding hard links

You can use the **find** command to look for files with a certain inode. The screenshot below shows how to search for all filenames that point to **inode** 817270. Remember that an **inode** number is unique to its partition.

```
paul@RHELv4u4:~/test$ find / -inum 817270 2> /dev/null
/home/paul/test/file2
/home/paul/test/hardlink_to_file2
```

4.4. symbolic links

Symbolic links (sometimes called **soft links**) do not link to inodes, but create a name to name mapping. Symbolic links are created with **ln -s**. As you can see below, the **symbolic link** gets an inode of its own.

```
paul@RHELv4u4:~/test$ ln -s file2 symlink_to_file2
paul@RHELv4u4:~/test$ ls -li
total 32
817273 -rw-rw-r--  1 paul paul  13 Feb  5 17:06 file1
817270 -rw-rw-r--  2 paul paul 106 Feb  5 17:04 file2
817268 -rw-rw-r--  1 paul paul   0 Feb  5 15:38 file3
817270 -rw-rw-r--  2 paul paul 106 Feb  5 17:04 hardlink_to_file2
817267 lrwxrwxrwx  1 paul paul   5 Feb  5 16:55 symlink_to_file2 -> file2
paul@RHELv4u4:~/test$
```

Permissions on a symbolic link have no meaning, since the permissions of the target apply. Hard links are limited to their own partition (because they point to an inode), symbolic links can link anywhere (other file systems, even networked).

4.5. removing links

Links can be removed with **rm**.

```
paul@laika:~$ touch data.txt
paul@laika:~$ ln -s data.txt sl_data.txt
paul@laika:~$ ln data.txt hl_data.txt
paul@laika:~$ rm sl_data.txt
paul@laika:~$ rm hl_data.txt
```

4.6. practice : links

1. Create two files named winter.txt and summer.txt, put some text in them.

2. Create a hard link to winter.txt named hlwinter.txt.

3. Display the inode numbers of these three files, the hard links should have the same inode.

4. Use the find command to list the two hardlinked files

5. Everything about a file is in the inode, except two things : name them!

6. Create a symbolic link to summer.txt called slsummer.txt.

7. Find all files with inode number 2. What does this information tell you ?

8. Look at the directories /etc/init.d/ /etc/rc2.d/ /etc/rc3.d/ ... do you see the links ?

9. Look in /lib with ls -l...

10. Use **find** to look in your home directory for regular files that do not(!) have one hard link.

4.7. solution : links

1. Create two files named winter.txt and summer.txt, put some text in them.

```
echo cold > winter.txt ; echo hot > summer.txt
```

2. Create a hard link to winter.txt named hlwinter.txt.

```
ln winter.txt hlwinter.txt
```

3. Display the inode numbers of these three files, the hard links should have the same inode.

```
ls -li winter.txt summer.txt hlwinter.txt
```

4. Use the find command to list the two hardlinked files

```
find . -inum xyz #replace xyz with the inode number
```

5. Everything about a file is in the inode, except two things : name them!

The name of the file is in a directory, and the contents is somewhere on the disk.

6. Create a symbolic link to summer.txt called slsummer.txt.

```
ln -s summer.txt slsummer.txt
```

7. Find all files with inode number 2. What does this information tell you ?

It tells you there is more than one inode table (one for every formatted partition + virtual file systems)

8. Look at the directories /etc/init.d/ /etc/rc.d/ /etc/rc3.d/ ... do you see the links ?

```
ls -l /etc/init.d
ls -l /etc/rc2.d
ls -l /etc/rc3.d
```

9. Look in /lib with ls -l...

```
ls -l /lib
```

10. Use **find** to look in your home directory for regular files that do not(!) have one hard link.

```
find ~ ! -links 1 -type f
```

Part II. disk management

Table of Contents

Chapter 5. disk devices

This chapter teaches you how to locate and recognise **hard disk devices**. This prepares you for the next chapter, where we put **partitions** on these devices.

5.1. terminology

5.1.1. platter, head, track, cylinder, sector

Data is commonly stored on magnetic or optical **disk platters**. The platters are rotated (at high speeds). Data is read by **heads**, which are very close to the surface of the platter, without touching it! The heads are mounted on an arm (sometimes called a comb or a fork).

Data is written in concentric circles called **tracks**. Track zero is (usually) on the outside. The time it takes to position the head over a certain track is called the **seek time**. Often the platters are stacked on top of each other, hence the set of tracks accessible at a certain position of the comb forms a **cylinder**. Tracks are divided into 512 byte **sectors**, with more unused space (**gap**) between the sectors on the outside of the platter.

When you break down the advertised **access time** of a hard drive, you will notice that most of that time is taken by movement of the heads (about 65%) and **rotational latency** (about 30%).

5.1.2. ide or scsi

Actually, the title should be **ata** or **scsi**, since ide is an ata compatible device. Most desktops use **ata devices**, most servers use **scsi**.

5.1.3. ata

An **ata controller** allows two devices per bus, one **master** and one **slave**. Unless your controller and devices support **cable select**, you have to set this manually with jumpers.

With the introduction of **sata** (serial ata), the original ata was renamed to **parallel ata**. Optical drives often use **atapi**, which is an ATA interface using the SCSI communication protocol.

5.1.4. scsi

A **scsi controller** allows more than two devices. When using **SCSI (small computer system interface)**, each device gets a unique **scsi id**. The **scsi controller** also needs a **scsi id**, do not use this id for a scsi-attached device.

Older 8-bit SCSI is now called **narrow**, whereas 16-bit is **wide**. When the bus speeds was doubled to 10Mhz, this was known as **fast SCSI**. Doubling to 20Mhz made it **ultra SCSI**. Take a look at http://en.wikipedia.org/wiki/SCSI for more SCSI standards.

5.1.5. block device

Random access hard disk devices have an abstraction layer called **block device** to enable formatting in fixed-size (usually 512 bytes) blocks. Blocks can be accessed independent of access to other blocks.

```
[root@centos65 ~]# lsblk
NAME                       MAJ:MIN RM   SIZE RO TYPE MOUNTPOINT
sda                          8:0    0    40G  0 disk
--sda1                       8:1    0   500M  0 part /boot
--sda2                       8:2    0  39.5G  0 part
  --VolGroup-lv_root (dm-0) 253:0   0  38.6G  0 lvm  /
  --VolGroup-lv_swap (dm-1) 253:1   0   928M  0 lvm  [SWAP]
sdb                          8:16   0    72G  0 disk
sdc                          8:32   0   144G  0 disk
```

A block device has the letter b to denote the file type in the output of **ls -l**.

```
[root@centos65 ~]# ls -l /dev/sd*
brw-rw----. 1 root disk 8,  0 Apr 19 10:12 /dev/sda
brw-rw----. 1 root disk 8,  1 Apr 19 10:12 /dev/sda1
brw-rw----. 1 root disk 8,  2 Apr 19 10:12 /dev/sda2
brw-rw----. 1 root disk 8, 16 Apr 19 10:12 /dev/sdb
brw-rw----. 1 root disk 8, 32 Apr 19 10:12 /dev/sdc
```

Note that a **character device** is a constant stream of characters, being denoted by a c in **ls -l**. Note also that the **ISO 9660** standard for cdrom uses a **2048 byte** block size.

Old hard disks (and floppy disks) use **cylinder-head-sector** addressing to access a sector on the disk. Most current disks use **LBA (Logical Block Addressing)**.

5.1.6. solid state drive

A **solid state drive** or **ssd** is a block device without moving parts. It is comparable to **flash memory**. An **ssd** is more expensive than a hard disk, but it typically has a much faster access time.

In this book we will use the following pictograms for **spindle disks** (in brown) and **solid state disks** (in blue).

5.2. device naming

5.2.1. ata (ide) device naming

All **ata** drives on your system will start with **/dev/hd** followed by a unit letter. The master hdd on the first **ata controller** is /dev/hda, the slave is /dev/hdb. For the second controller, the names of the devices are /dev/hdc and /dev/hdd.

Table 5.1. ide device naming

controller	connection	device name
ide0	master	/dev/hda
	slave	/dev/hdb
ide1	master	/dev/hdc
	slave	/dev/hdd

It is possible to have only **/dev/hda** and **/dev/hdd**. The first one is a single ata hard disk, the second one is the cdrom (by default configured as slave).

5.2.2. scsi device naming

scsi drives follow a similar scheme, but all start with **/dev/sd**. When you run out of letters (after /dev/sdz), you can continue with /dev/sdaa and /dev/sdab and so on. (We will see later on that **lvm** volumes are commonly seen as /dev/md0, /dev/md1 etc.)

Below a **sample** of how scsi devices on a Linux can be named. Adding a scsi disk or raid controller with a lower scsi address will change the naming scheme (shifting the higher scsi addresses one letter further in the alphabet).

Table 5.2. scsi device naming

device	scsi id	device name
disk 0	0	/dev/sda
disk 1	1	/dev/sdb
raid controller 0	5	/dev/sdc
raid controller 1	6	/dev/sdd

A modern Linux system will use **/dev/sd*** for scsi and sata devices, and also for sd-cards, usb-sticks, (legacy) ATA/IDE devices and solid state drives.

5.3. discovering disk devices

5.3.1. fdisk

You can start by using **/sbin/fdisk** to find out what kind of disks are seen by the kernel. Below the result on old Debian desktop, with two **ata-ide disks** present.

```
root@barry:~# fdisk -l | grep Disk
Disk /dev/hda: 60.0 GB, 60022480896 bytes
Disk /dev/hdb: 81.9 GB, 81964302336 bytes
```

And here an example of **sata and scsi disks** on a server with CentOS. Remember that **sata** disks are also presented to you with the **scsi** /dev/sd* notation.

```
[root@centos65 ~]# fdisk -l | grep 'Disk /dev/sd'
Disk /dev/sda: 42.9 GB, 42949672960 bytes
Disk /dev/sdb: 77.3 GB, 77309411328 bytes
Disk /dev/sdc: 154.6 GB, 154618822656 bytes
Disk /dev/sdd: 154.6 GB, 154618822656 bytes
```

Here is an overview of disks on a RHEL4u3 server with two real 72GB **scsi disks**. This server is attached to a **NAS** with four **NAS disks** of half a terabyte. On the NAS disks, four LVM (/dev/mdx) software RAID devices are configured.

```
[root@tsvt11 ~]# fdisk -l | grep Disk
Disk /dev/sda: 73.4 GB, 73407488000 bytes
Disk /dev/sdb: 73.4 GB, 73407488000 bytes
Disk /dev/sdc: 499.0 GB, 499036192768 bytes
Disk /dev/sdd: 499.0 GB, 499036192768 bytes
Disk /dev/sde: 499.0 GB, 499036192768 bytes
Disk /dev/sdf: 499.0 GB, 499036192768 bytes
Disk /dev/md0: 271 MB, 271319040 bytes
Disk /dev/md2: 21.4 GB, 21476081664 bytes
Disk /dev/md3: 21.4 GB, 21467889664 bytes
Disk /dev/md1: 21.4 GB, 21476081664 bytes
```

You can also use **fdisk** to obtain information about one specific hard disk device.

```
[root@centos65 ~]# fdisk -l /dev/sdc

Disk /dev/sdc: 154.6 GB, 154618822656 bytes
255 heads, 63 sectors/track, 18798 cylinders
Units = cylinders of 16065 * 512 = 8225280 bytes
Sector size (logical/physical): 512 bytes / 512 bytes
I/O size (minimum/optimal): 512 bytes / 512 bytes
Disk identifier: 0x00000000
```

Later we will use fdisk to do dangerous stuff like creating and deleting partitions.

5.3.2. dmesg

Kernel boot messages can be seen after boot with **dmesg**. Since hard disk devices are detected by the kernel during boot, you can also use dmesg to find information about disk devices.

```
[root@centos65 ~]# dmesg | grep 'sd[a-z]' | head
sd 0:0:0:0: [sda] 83886080 512-byte logical blocks: (42.9 GB/40.0 GiB)
sd 0:0:0:0: [sda] Write Protect is off
sd 0:0:0:0: [sda] Mode Sense: 00 3a 00 00
sd 0:0:0:0: [sda] Write cache: enabled, read cache: enabled, doesn't support \
DPO or FUA
sda: sda1 sda2
sd 0:0:0:0: [sda] Attached SCSI disk
sd 3:0:0:0: [sdb] 150994944 512-byte logical blocks: (77.3 GB/72.0 GiB)
sd 3:0:0:0: [sdb] Write Protect is off
sd 3:0:0:0: [sdb] Mode Sense: 00 3a 00 00
sd 3:0:0:0: [sdb] Write cache: enabled, read cache: enabled, doesn't support \
DPO or FUA
```

Here is another example of **dmesg** on a computer with a 200GB ata disk.

```
paul@barry:~$ dmesg | grep -i "ata disk"
[    2.624149] hda: ST360021A, ATA DISK drive
[    2.904150] hdb: Maxtor 6Y080L0, ATA DISK drive
[    3.472148] hdd: WDC WD2000BB-98DWA0, ATA DISK drive
```

Third and last example of **dmesg** running on RHEL5.3.

```
root@rhel53 ~# dmesg | grep -i "scsi disk"
sd 0:0:2:0: Attached scsi disk sda
sd 0:0:3:0: Attached scsi disk sdb
sd 0:0:6:0: Attached scsi disk sdc
```

5.3.3. /sbin/lshw

The **lshw** tool will **list hardware**. With the right options **lshw** can show a lot of information about disks (and partitions).

Below a truncated screenshot on Debian 6:

```
root@debian6~# lshw -class volume | grep -A1 -B2 scsi
      description: Linux raid autodetect partition
      physical id: 1
      bus info: scsi@1:0.0.0,1
      logical name: /dev/sdb1
--
      description: Linux raid autodetect partition
      physical id: 1
      bus info: scsi@2:0.0.0,1
      logical name: /dev/sdc1
--
      description: Linux raid autodetect partition
      physical id: 1
      bus info: scsi@3:0.0.0,1
      logical name: /dev/sdd1
--
      description: Linux raid autodetect partition
      physical id: 1
      bus info: scsi@4:0.0.0,1
      logical name: /dev/sde1
--
      vendor: Linux
      physical id: 1
      bus info: scsi@0:0.0.0,1
      logical name: /dev/sda1
--
      vendor: Linux
      physical id: 2
      bus info: scsi@0:0.0.0,2
      logical name: /dev/sda2
--
      description: Extended partition
      physical id: 3
      bus info: scsi@0:0.0.0,3
      logical name: /dev/sda3
```

Redhat and CentOS do not have this tool (unless you add a repository).

5.3.4. /sbin/lsscsi

The **lsscsi** command provides a nice readable output of all scsi (and scsi emulated devices). This first screenshot shows **lsscsi** on a SPARC system.

```
root@shaka:~# lsscsi
[0:0:0:0]    disk    Adaptec  RAID5           V1.0   /dev/sda
[1:0:0:0]    disk    SEAGATE  ST336605FSUN36G 0438   /dev/sdb
root@shaka:~#
```

Below a screenshot of **lsscsi** on a QNAP NAS (which has four 750GB disks and boots from a usb stick).

```
lroot@debian6~# lsscsi
[0:0:0:0]    disk    SanDisk  Cruzer Edge     1.19   /dev/sda
[1:0:0:0]    disk    ATA      ST3750330AS     SD04   /dev/sdb
[2:0:0:0]    disk    ATA      ST3750330AS     SD04   /dev/sdc
[3:0:0:0]    disk    ATA      ST3750330AS     SD04   /dev/sdd
[4:0:0:0]    disk    ATA      ST3750330AS     SD04   /dev/sde
```

This screenshot shows the classic output of **lsscsi**.

```
root@debian6~# lsscsi -c
Attached devices:
Host: scsi0 Channel: 00 Target: 00 Lun: 00
  Vendor: SanDisk  Model: Cruzer Edge     Rev: 1.19
  Type:   Direct-Access               ANSI SCSI revision: 02
Host: scsi1 Channel: 00 Target: 00 Lun: 00
  Vendor: ATA      Model: ST3750330AS     Rev: SD04
  Type:   Direct-Access               ANSI SCSI revision: 05
Host: scsi2 Channel: 00 Target: 00 Lun: 00
  Vendor: ATA      Model: ST3750330AS     Rev: SD04
  Type:   Direct-Access               ANSI SCSI revision: 05
Host: scsi3 Channel: 00 Target: 00 Lun: 00
  Vendor: ATA      Model: ST3750330AS     Rev: SD04
  Type:   Direct-Access               ANSI SCSI revision: 05
Host: scsi4 Channel: 00 Target: 00 Lun: 00
  Vendor: ATA      Model: ST3750330AS     Rev: SD04
  Type:   Direct-Access               ANSI SCSI revision: 05
```

5.3.5. /proc/scsi/scsi

Another way to locate **scsi** (or sd) devices is via **/proc/scsi/scsi**.

This screenshot is from a **sparc** computer with adaptec RAID5.

```
root@shaka:~# cat /proc/scsi/scsi
Attached devices:
Host: scsi0 Channel: 00 Id: 00 Lun: 00
  Vendor: Adaptec  Model: RAID5          Rev: V1.0
  Type:   Direct-Access                  ANSI SCSI revision: 02
Host: scsi1 Channel: 00 Id: 00 Lun: 00
  Vendor: SEAGATE  Model: ST336605FSUN36G Rev: 0438
  Type:   Direct-Access                  ANSI SCSI revision: 03
root@shaka:~#
```

Here we run **cat /proc/scsi/scsi** on the QNAP from above (with Debian Linux).

```
root@debian6~# cat /proc/scsi/scsi
Attached devices:
Host: scsi0 Channel: 00 Id: 00 Lun: 00
  Vendor: SanDisk  Model: Cruzer Edge    Rev: 1.19
  Type:   Direct-Access                  ANSI  SCSI revision: 02
Host: scsi1 Channel: 00 Id: 00 Lun: 00
  Vendor: ATA      Model: ST3750330AS    Rev: SD04
  Type:   Direct-Access                  ANSI  SCSI revision: 05
Host: scsi2 Channel: 00 Id: 00 Lun: 00
  Vendor: ATA      Model: ST3750330AS    Rev: SD04
  Type:   Direct-Access                  ANSI  SCSI revision: 05
Host: scsi3 Channel: 00 Id: 00 Lun: 00
  Vendor: ATA      Model: ST3750330AS    Rev: SD04
  Type:   Direct-Access                  ANSI  SCSI revision: 05
Host: scsi4 Channel: 00 Id: 00 Lun: 00
  Vendor: ATA      Model: ST3750330AS    Rev: SD04
  Type:   Direct-Access                  ANSI  SCSI revision: 05
```

Note that some recent versions of Debian have this disabled in the kernel. You can enable it (after a kernel compile) using this entry:

```
# CONFIG_SCSI_PROC_FS is not set
```

Redhat and CentOS have this by default (if there are scsi devices present).

```
[root@centos65 ~]# cat /proc/scsi/scsi
Attached devices:
Host: scsi0 Channel: 00 Id: 00 Lun: 00
  Vendor: ATA      Model: VBOX HARDDISK  Rev: 1.0
  Type:   Direct-Access                  ANSI  SCSI revision: 05
Host: scsi3 Channel: 00 Id: 00 Lun: 00
  Vendor: ATA      Model: VBOX HARDDISK  Rev: 1.0
  Type:   Direct-Access                  ANSI  SCSI revision: 05
Host: scsi4 Channel: 00 Id: 00 Lun: 00
  Vendor: ATA      Model: VBOX HARDDISK  Rev: 1.0
  Type:   Direct-Access                  ANSI  SCSI revision: 05
```

5.4. erasing a hard disk

Before selling your old hard disk on the internet, it may be a good idea to erase it. By simply repartitioning, or by using the Microsoft Windows format utility, or even after an **mkfs** command, some people will still be able to read most of the data on the disk.

```
root@debian6~# aptitude search foremost autopsy sleuthkit | tr -s ' '
p autopsy - graphical interface to SleuthKit
p foremost - Forensics application to recover data
p sleuthkit - collection of tools for forensics analysis
```

Although technically the **/sbin/badblocks** tool is meant to look for bad blocks, you can use it to completely erase all data from a disk. Since this is really writing to every sector of the disk, it can take a long time!

```
root@RHELv4u2:~# badblocks -ws /dev/sdb
Testing with pattern 0xaa: done
Reading and comparing: done
Testing with pattern 0x55: done
Reading and comparing: done
Testing with pattern 0xff: done
Reading and comparing: done
Testing with pattern 0x00: done
Reading and comparing: done
```

The previous screenshot overwrites every sector of the disk **four times**. Erasing **once** with a tool like **dd** is enough to destroy all data.

Warning, this screenshot shows how to permanently destroy all data on a block device.

```
[root@rhel65 ~]# dd if=/dev/zero of=/dev/sdb
```

5.5. advanced hard disk settings

Tweaking of hard disk settings (dma, gap, ...) are not covered in this course. Several tools exists, **hdparm** and **sdparm** are two of them.

hdparm can be used to display or set information and parameters about an ATA (or SATA) hard disk device. The -i and -I options will give you even more information about the physical properties of the device.

```
root@laika:~# hdparm /dev/sdb

/dev/sdb:
 IO_support   =  0 (default 16-bit)
 readonly     =  0 (off)
 readahead    = 256 (on)
 geometry     = 12161/255/63, sectors = 195371568, start = 0
```

Below **hdparm** info about a 200GB IDE disk.

```
root@barry:~# hdparm /dev/hdd

/dev/hdd:
 multcount     =  0 (off)
 IO_support    =  0 (default)
 unmaskirq     =  0 (off)
 using_dma     =  1 (on)
 keepsettings  =  0 (off)
 readonly      =  0 (off)
 readahead     = 256 (on)
 geometry      = 24321/255/63, sectors = 390721968, start = 0
```

Here a screenshot of **sdparm** on Ubuntu 10.10.

```
root@ubu1010:~# aptitude install sdparm
...
root@ubu1010:~# sdparm /dev/sda | head -1
    /dev/sda: ATA       FUJITSU MJA2160B  0081
root@ubu1010:~# man sdparm
```

Use **hdparm** and **sdparm** with care.

5.6. practice: hard disk devices

About this lab: To practice working with hard disks, you will need some hard disks. When there are no physical hard disk available, you can use virtual disks in **vmware** or **VirtualBox**. The teacher will help you in attaching a couple of ATA and/or SCSI disks to a virtual machine. The results of this lab can be used in the next three labs (partitions, file systems, mounting).

It is adviced to attach three 1GB disks and three 2GB disks to the virtual machine. This will allow for some freedom in the practices of this chapter as well as the next chapters (raid, lvm, iSCSI).

1. Use **dmesg** to make a list of hard disk devices detected at boot-up.

2. Use **fdisk** to find the total size of all hard disk devices on your system.

3. Stop a virtual machine, add three virtual 1 gigabyte **scsi** hard disk devices and one virtual 400 megabyte **ide** hard disk device. If possible, also add another virtual 400 megabyte **ide** disk.

4. Use **dmesg** to verify that all the new disks are properly detected at boot-up.

5. Verify that you can see the disk devices in **/dev**.

6. Use **fdisk** (with **grep** and **/dev/null**) to display the total size of the new disks.

7. Use **badblocks** to completely erase one of the smaller hard disks.

8. Look at **/proc/scsi/scsi**.

9. If possible, install **lsscsi**, **lshw** and use them to list the disks.

5.7. solution: hard disk devices

1. Use **dmesg** to make a list of hard disk devices detected at boot-up.

```
Some possible answers...

dmesg | grep -i disk

Looking for ATA disks: dmesg | grep hd[abcd]

Looking for ATA disks: dmesg | grep -i "ata disk"

Looking for SCSI disks: dmesg | grep sd[a-f]

Looking for SCSI disks: dmesg | grep -i "scsi disk"
```

2. Use **fdisk** to find the total size of all hard disk devices on your system.

```
fdisk -l
```

3. Stop a virtual machine, add three virtual 1 gigabyte **scsi** hard disk devices and one virtual 400 megabyte **ide** hard disk device. If possible, also add another virtual 400 megabyte **ide** disk.

```
This exercise happens in the settings of vmware or VirtualBox.
```

4. Use **dmesg** to verify that all the new disks are properly detected at boot-up.

```
See 1.
```

5. Verify that you can see the disk devices in **/dev**.

```
SCSI+SATA: ls -l /dev/sd*

ATA: ls -l /dev/hd*
```

6. Use **fdisk** (with **grep** and **/dev/null**) to display the total size of the new disks.

```
root@rhel53 ~# fdisk -l 2>/dev/null | grep [MGT]B
Disk /dev/hda: 21.4 GB, 21474836480 bytes
Disk /dev/hdb: 1073 MB, 1073741824 bytes
Disk /dev/sda: 2147 MB, 2147483648 bytes
Disk /dev/sdb: 2147 MB, 2147483648 bytes
Disk /dev/sdc: 2147 MB, 2147483648 bytes
```

7. Use **badblocks** to completely erase one of the smaller hard disks.

```
#Verify the device (/dev/sdc??) you want to erase before typing this.
#
root@rhel53 ~# badblocks -ws /dev/sdc
Testing with pattern 0xaa: done
Reading and comparing: done
Testing with pattern 0x55: done
Reading and comparing: done
Testing with pattern 0xff: done
Reading and comparing: done
Testing with pattern 0x00: done
Reading and comparing: done
```

8. Look at **/proc/scsi/scsi**.

```
root@rhel53 ~# cat /proc/scsi/scsi
```

```
Attached devices:
Host: scsi0 Channel: 00 Id: 02 Lun: 00
  Vendor: VBOX       Model: HARDDISK          Rev: 1.0
  Type:    Direct-Access                      ANSI SCSI revision: 05
Host: scsi0 Channel: 00 Id: 03 Lun: 00
  Vendor: VBOX       Model: HARDDISK          Rev: 1.0
  Type:    Direct-Access                      ANSI SCSI revision: 05
Host: scsi0 Channel: 00 Id: 06 Lun: 00
  Vendor: VBOX       Model: HARDDISK          Rev: 1.0
  Type:    Direct-Access                      ANSI SCSI revision: 05
```

9. If possible, install **lsscsi**, **lshw** and use them to list the disks.

```
Debian,Ubuntu: aptitude install lsscsi lshw

Fedora: yum install lsscsi lshw

root@rhel53 ~# lsscsi
[0:0:2:0]    disk    VBOX    HARDDISK          1.0    /dev/sda
[0:0:3:0]    disk    VBOX    HARDDISK          1.0    /dev/sdb
[0:0:6:0]    disk    VBOX    HARDDISK          1.0    /dev/sdc
```

Chapter 6. disk partitions

This chapter continues on the **hard disk devices** from the previous one. Here we will put **partitions** on those devices.

This chapter prepares you for the next chapter, where we put **file systems** on our partitions.

6.1. about partitions

6.1.1. primary, extended and logical

Linux requires you to create one or more **partitions**. The next paragraphs will explain how to create and use partitions.

A partition's **geometry** and size is usually defined by a starting and ending cylinder (sometimes by sector). Partitions can be of type **primary** (maximum four), **extended** (maximum one) or **logical** (contained within the extended partition). Each partition has a **type field** that contains a code. This determines the computers operating system or the partitions file system.

Table 6.1. primary, extended and logical partitions

Partition Type	naming
Primary (max 4)	1-4
Extended (max 1)	1-4
Logical	5-

6.1.2. partition naming

We saw before that hard disk devices are named /dev/hdx or /dev/sdx with x depending on the hardware configuration. Next is the partition number, starting the count at 1. Hence the four (possible) primary partitions are numbered 1 to 4. Logical partition counting always starts at 5. Thus /dev/hda2 is the second partition on the first ATA hard disk device, and /dev/hdb5 is the first logical partition on the second ATA hard disk device. Same for SCSI, /dev/sdb3 is the third partition on the second SCSI disk.

Table 6.2. Partition naming

partition	device
/dev/hda1	first primary partition on /dev/hda
/dev/hda2	second primary or extended partition on /dev/hda
/dev/sda5	first logical drive on /dev/sda
/dev/sdb6	second logical on /dev/sdb

The picture below shows two (spindle) disks with partitions. Note that an extended partition is a container holding logical drives.

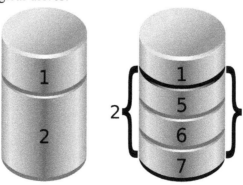

6.2. discovering partitions

6.2.1. fdisk -l

In the **fdisk -l** example below you can see that two partitions exist on **/dev/sdb**. The first partition spans 31 cylinders and contains a Linux swap partition. The second partition is much bigger.

```
root@laika:~# fdisk -l /dev/sdb

Disk /dev/sdb: 100.0 GB, 100030242816 bytes
255 heads, 63 sectors/track, 12161 cylinders
Units = cylinders of 16065 * 512 = 8225280 bytes

   Device Boot      Start         End      Blocks   Id  System
/dev/sdb1               1          31      248976   82  Linux swap / Solaris
/dev/sdb2              32       12161    97434225   83  Linux
root@laika:~#
```

6.2.2. /proc/partitions

The **/proc/partitions** file contains a table with major and minor number of partitioned devices, their number of blocks and the device name in **/dev**. Verify with **/proc/devices** to link the major number to the proper device.

```
paul@RHELv4u4:~$ cat /proc/partitions
major minor  #blocks  name

   3     0    524288 hda
   3    64    734003 hdb
   8     0   8388608 sda
   8     1    104391 sda1
   8     2   8281507 sda2
   8    16   1048576 sdb
   8    32   1048576 sdc
   8    48   1048576 sdd
 253     0   7176192 dm-0
 253     1   1048576 dm-1
```

The **major** number corresponds to the device type (or driver) and can be found in **/proc/devices**. In this case 3 corresponds to **ide** and 8 to **sd**. The **major** number determines the **device driver** to be used with this device.

The **minor** number is a unique identification of an instance of this device type. The **devices.txt** file in the kernel tree contains a full list of major and minor numbers.

6.2.3. parted and others

You may be interested in alternatives to **fdisk** like **parted**, **cfdisk**, **sfdisk** and **gparted**. This course mainly uses **fdisk** to partition hard disks.

parted is recommended by some Linux distributions for handling storage with **gpt** instead of **mbr**.

Below a screenshot of **parted** on CentOS.

```
[root@centos65 ~]# rpm -q parted
parted-2.1-21.el6.x86_64
[root@centos65 ~]# parted /dev/sda
GNU Parted 2.1
Using /dev/sda
Welcome to GNU Parted! Type 'help' to view a list of commands.
(parted) print
Model: ATA VBOX HARDDISK (scsi)
Disk /dev/sda: 42.9GB
Sector size (logical/physical): 512B/512B
Partition Table: msdos

Number  Start   End     Size    Type     File system  Flags
 1      1049kB  525MB   524MB   primary  ext4         boot
 2      525MB   42.9GB  42.4GB  primary               lvm

(parted)
```

6.3. partitioning new disks

In the example below, we bought a new disk for our system. After the new hardware is properly attached, you can use **fdisk** and **parted** to create the necessary partition(s). This example uses **fdisk**, but there is nothing wrong with using **parted**.

6.3.1. recognising the disk

First, we check with **fdisk -l** whether Linux can see the new disk. Yes it does, the new disk is seen as /dev/sdb, but it does not have any partitions yet.

```
root@RHELv4u2:~# fdisk -l

Disk /dev/sda: 12.8 GB, 12884901888 bytes
255 heads, 63 sectors/track, 1566 cylinders
Units = cylinders of 16065 * 512 = 8225280 bytes

Device Boot      Start         End      Blocks   Id  System
/dev/sda1   *        1          13      104391   83  Linux
/dev/sda2           14        1566    12474472+  8e  Linux LVM

Disk /dev/sdb: 1073 MB, 1073741824 bytes
255 heads, 63 sectors/track, 130 cylinders
Units = cylinders of 16065 * 512 = 8225280 bytes

Disk /dev/sdb doesn't contain a valid partition table
```

6.3.2. opening the disk with fdisk

Then we create a partition with fdisk on /dev/sdb. First we start the fdisk tool with /dev/sdb as argument. Be very very careful not to partition the wrong disk!!

```
root@RHELv4u2:~# fdisk /dev/sdb
Device contains neither a valid DOS partition table, nor Sun, SGI...
Building a new DOS disklabel. Changes will remain in memory only,
until you decide to write them. After that, of course, the previous
content won't be recoverable.

Warning: invalid flag 0x0000 of partition table 4 will be corrected...
```

6.3.3. empty partition table

Inside the fdisk tool, we can issue the **p** command to see the current disks partition table.

```
Command (m for help): p

Disk /dev/sdb: 1073 MB, 1073741824 bytes
255 heads, 63 sectors/track, 130 cylinders
Units = cylinders of 16065 * 512 = 8225280 bytes

Device Boot      Start         End      Blocks   Id  System
```

6.3.4. create a new partition

No partitions exist yet, so we issue **n** to create a new partition. We choose p for primary, 1 for the partition number, 1 for the start cylinder and 14 for the end cylinder.

```
Command (m for help): n
Command action
e   extended
p   primary partition (1-4)
p
Partition number (1-4): 1
First cylinder (1-130, default 1):
Using default value 1
Last cylinder or +size or +sizeM or +sizeK (1-130, default 130): 14
```

We can now issue p again to verify our changes, but they are not yet written to disk. This means we can still cancel this operation! But it looks good, so we use **w** to write the changes to disk, and then quit the fdisk tool.

```
Command (m for help): p

Disk /dev/sdb: 1073 MB, 1073741824 bytes
255 heads, 63 sectors/track, 130 cylinders
Units = cylinders of 16065 * 512 = 8225280 bytes

Device Boot      Start         End      Blocks   Id  System
/dev/sdb1            1          14      112423+  83  Linux

Command (m for help): w
The partition table has been altered!

Calling ioctl() to re-read partition table.
Syncing disks.
root@RHELv4u2:~#
```

6.3.5. display the new partition

Let's verify again with **fdisk -l** to make sure reality fits our dreams. Indeed, the screenshot below now shows a partition on /dev/sdb.

```
root@RHELv4u2:~# fdisk -l

Disk /dev/sda: 12.8 GB, 12884901888 bytes
255 heads, 63 sectors/track, 1566 cylinders
Units = cylinders of 16065 * 512 = 8225280 bytes

Device Boot      Start         End      Blocks   Id  System
/dev/sda1   *        1          13      104391   83  Linux
/dev/sda2           14        1566    12474472+  8e  Linux LVM

Disk /dev/sdb: 1073 MB, 1073741824 bytes
255 heads, 63 sectors/track, 130 cylinders
Units = cylinders of 16065 * 512 = 8225280 bytes

Device Boot      Start         End      Blocks   Id  System
/dev/sdb1            1          14      112423+  83  Linux
root@RHELv4u2:~#
```

6.4. about the partition table

6.4.1. master boot record

The **partition table** information (primary and extended partitions) is written in the **master boot record** or **mbr**. You can use **dd** to copy the mbr to a file.

This example copies the master boot record from the first SCSI hard disk.

```
dd if=/dev/sda of=/SCSIdisk.mbr bs=512 count=1
```

The same tool can also be used to wipe out all information about partitions on a disk. This example writes zeroes over the master boot record.

```
dd if=/dev/zero of=/dev/sda bs=512 count=1
```

Or to wipe out the whole partition or disk.

```
dd if=/dev/zero of=/dev/sda
```

6.4.2. partprobe

Don't forget that after restoring a **master boot record** with **dd**, that you need to force the kernel to reread the partition table with **partprobe**. After running **partprobe**, the partitions can be used again.

```
[root@RHEL5 ~]# partprobe
[root@RHEL5 ~]#
```

6.4.3. logical drives

The **partition table** does not contain information about **logical drives**. So the **dd** backup of the **mbr** only works for primary and extended partitions. To backup the partition table including the logical drives, you can use **sfdisk**.

This example shows how to backup all partition and logical drive information to a file.

```
sfdisk -d /dev/sda > parttable.sda.sfdisk
```

The following example copies the **mbr** and all **logical drive** info from /dev/sda to /dev/sdb.

```
sfdisk -d /dev/sda | sfdisk /dev/sdb
```

6.5. GUID partition table

gpt was developed because of the limitations of the 1980s **mbr** partitioning scheme (for example only four partitions can be defined, and they have a maximum size two terabytes).

Since 2010 **gpt** is a part of the **uefi** specification, but it is also used on **bios** systems.

Newer versions of **fdisk** work fine with **gpt**, but most production servers today (mid 2015) still have an older **fdisk..** You can use **parted** instead.

6.6. labeling with parted

parted is an interactive tool, just like **fdisk**. Type **help** in **parted** for a list of commands and options.

This screenshot shows how to start **parted** to manage partitions on **/dev/sdb**.

```
[root@rhel71 ~]# parted /dev/sdb
GNU Parted 3.1
Using /dev/sdb
Welcome to GNU Parted! Type 'help' to view a list of commands.
(parted)
```

Each command also has built-in help. For example **help mklabel** will list all supported labels. Note that we only discussed **mbr**(msdos) and **gpt** in this book.

```
(parted) help mklabel
 mklabel,mktable LABEL-TYPE                create a new disklabel (partition table)

    LABEL-TYPE is one of: aix, amiga, bsd, dvh, gpt, mac, msdos, pc98, sun, loop
(parted)
```

We create an **mbr** label.

```
(parted) mklabel msdos>
Warning: The existing disk label on /dev/sdb will be destroyed and all data on
this disk will be lost. Do you want to continue?
Yes/No? yes
(parted) mklabel gpt
Warning: The existing disk label on /dev/sdb will be destroyed and all data on
this disk will be lost. Do you want to continue?
Yes/No? Y
(parted)
```

6.6.1. partitioning with parted

Once labeled it is easy to create partitions with **parted**. This screenshot starts with an unpartitioned (but **gpt** labeled) disk.

```
(parted) print
Model: ATA VBOX HARDDISK (scsi)
Disk /dev/sdb: 8590MB
Sector size (logical/physical): 512B/512B
Partition Table: gpt
Disk Flags:

Number  Start  End  Size  File system  Name  Flags

(parted)
```

This example shows how to create two primary partitions of equal size.

```
(parted) mkpart primary 0 50%
Warning: The resulting partition is not properly aligned for best performance.
Ignore/Cancel? I
(parted) mkpart primary 50% 100%
(parted)
```

Verify with **print** and exit with **quit**. Since **parted** works directly on the disk, there is no need to **w(rite)** like in **fdisk**.

```
(parted) print
Model: ATA VBOX HARDDISK (scsi)
Disk /dev/sdb: 8590MB
Sector size (logical/physical): 512B/512B
Partition Table: gpt
Disk Flags:

Number  Start   End     Size    File system  Name     Flags
 1      17.4kB  4295MB  4295MB                primary
 2      4295MB  8589MB  4294MB                primary

(parted) quit
Information: You may need to update /etc/fstab.

[root@rhel71 ~]#
```

6.7. practice: partitions

1. Use **fdisk -l** to display existing partitions and sizes.

2. Use **df -h** to display existing partitions and sizes.

3. Compare the output of **fdisk** and **df**.

4. Create a 200MB primary partition on a small disk.

5. Create a 400MB primary partition and two 300MB logical drives on a big disk.

6. Use **df -h** and **fdisk -l** to verify your work.

7. Compare the output again of **fdisk** and **df**. Do both commands display the new partitions ?

8. Create a backup with **dd** of the **mbr** that contains your 200MB primary partition.

9. Take a backup of the **partition table** containing your 400MB primary and 300MB logical drives. Make sure the logical drives are in the backup.

10. (optional) Remove all your partitions with fdisk. Then restore your backups.

6.8. solution: partitions

1. Use **fdisk -l** to display existing partitions and sizes.

```
as root: # fdisk -l
```

2. Use **df -h** to display existing partitions and sizes.

```
df -h
```

3. Compare the output of **fdisk** and **df**.

```
Some partitions will be listed in both outputs (maybe /dev/sda1 or /dev/hda1).
```

4. Create a 200MB primary partition on a small disk.

```
Choose one of the disks you added (this example uses /dev/sdc).
root@rhel53 ~# fdisk /dev/sdc
...
Command (m for help): n
Command action
   e   extended
   p   primary partition (1-4)
p
Partition number (1-4): 1
First cylinder (1-261, default 1): 1
Last cylinder or +size or +sizeM or +sizeK (1-261, default 261): +200m
Command (m for help): w
The partition table has been altered!
Calling ioctl() to re-read partition table.
Syncing disks.
```

5. Create a 400MB primary partition and two 300MB logical drives on a big disk.

```
Choose one of the disks you added (this example uses /dev/sdb)

fdisk /dev/sdb

inside fdisk : n p 1 +400m enter --- n e 2 enter enter --- n l +300m (twice)
```

6. Use **df -h** and **fdisk -l** to verify your work.

```
fdisk -l ; df -h
```

7. Compare the output again of **fdisk** and **df**. Do both commands display the new partitions ?

```
The newly created partitions are visible with fdisk.

But they are not displayed by df.
```

8. Create a backup with **dd** of the **mbr** that contains your 200MB primary partition.

```
dd if=/dev/sdc of=bootsector.sdc.dd count=1 bs=512
```

9. Take a backup of the **partition table** containing your 400MB primary and 300MB logical drives. Make sure the logical drives are in the backup.

```
sfdisk -d /dev/sdb > parttable.sdb.sfdisk
```

Chapter 7. file systems

When you are finished partitioning the hard disk, you can put a **file system** on each partition.

This chapter builds on the **partitions** from the previous chapter, and prepares you for the next one where we will **mount** the filesystems.

7.1. about file systems

A file system is a way of organizing files on your partition. Besides file-based storage, file systems usually include **directories** and **access control**, and contain meta information about files like access times, modification times and file ownership.

The properties (length, character set, ...) of filenames are determined by the file system you choose. Directories are usually implemented as files, you will have to learn how this is implemented! Access control in file systems is tracked by user ownership (and group owner- and membership) in combination with one or more access control lists.

7.1.1. man fs

The manual page about filesystems is accessed by typing **man fs**.

```
[root@rhel65 ~]# man fs
```

7.1.2. /proc/filesystems

The Linux kernel will inform you about currently loaded file system drivers in **/proc/filesystems**.

```
root@rhel53 ~# cat /proc/filesystems  | grep -v nodev
 ext2
 iso9660
 ext3
```

7.1.3. /etc/filesystems

The **/etc/filesystems** file contains a list of autodetected filesystems (in case the **mount** command is used without the **-t** option.

Help for this file is provided by **man mount**.

```
[root@rhel65 ~]# man mount
```

7.2. common file systems

7.2.1. ext2 and ext3

Once the most common Linux file systems is the **ext2** (the second extended) file system. A disadvantage is that file system checks on ext2 can take a long time.

ext2 was being replaced by **ext3** on most Linux machines. They are essentially the same, except for the **journaling** which is only present in ext3.

Journaling means that changes are first written to a journal on the disk. The journal is flushed regularly, writing the changes in the file system. Journaling keeps the file system in a consistent state, so you don't need a file system check after an unclean shutdown or power failure.

7.2.2. creating ext2 and ext3

You can create these file systems with the **/sbin/mkfs** or **/sbin/mke2fs** commands. Use **mke2fs -j** to create an **ext3** file system.

You can convert an ext2 to ext3 with **tune2fs -j**. You can mount an ext3 file system as ext2, but then you lose the journaling. Do not forget to run **mkinitrd** if you are booting from this device.

7.2.3. ext4

The newest incarnation of the ext file system is named **ext4** and is available in the Linux kernel since 2008. **ext4** supports larger files (up to 16 terabyte) and larger file systems than **ext3** (and many more features).

Development started by making **ext3** fully capable for 64-bit. When it turned out the changes were significant, the developers decided to name it **ext4**.

7.2.4. xfs

Redhat Enterprise Linux 7 will have **XFS** as the default file system. This is a highly scalable high-performance file system.

xfs was created for **Irix** and for a couple of years it was also used in **FreeBSD**. It is supported by the Linux kernel, but rarely used in dsitributions outside of the Redhat/CentOS realm.

7.2.5. vfat

The **vfat** file system exists in a couple of forms : **fat12** for floppy disks, **fat16** on **ms-dos**, and **fat32** for larger disks. The Linux **vfat** implementation supports all of these, but vfat lacks a lot of features like security and links. **fat** disks can be read by every operating system, and are used a lot for digital cameras, **usb** sticks and to exchange data between different OS'ses on a home user's computer.

7.2.6. iso 9660

iso 9660 is the standard format for cdroms. Chances are you will encounter this file system also on your hard disk in the form of images of cdroms (often with the .iso extension). The **iso 9660** standard limits filenames to the 8.3 format. The Unix world didn't like this, and thus added the **rock ridge** extensions, which allows for filenames up to 255 characters and Unix-style file-modes, ownership and symbolic links. Another extensions to **iso 9660** is **joliet**, which adds 64 unicode characters to the filename. The **el torito** standard extends **iso 9660** to be able to boot from CD-ROM's.

7.2.7. udf

Most optical media today (including cd's and dvd's) use **udf**, the Universal Disk Format.

7.2.8. swap

All things considered, swap is not a file system. But to use a partition as a **swap partition** it must be formatted and mounted as swap space.

7.2.9. gfs

Linux clusters often use a dedicated cluster filesystem like GFS, GFS2, ClusterFS, ...

7.2.10. and more...

You may encounter **reiserfs** on older Linux systems. Maybe you will see Sun's **zfs** or the open source **btrfs**. This last one requires a chapter on itself.

7.2.11. /proc/filesystems

The **/proc/filesystems** file displays a list of supported file systems. When you mount a file system without explicitly defining one, then mount will first try to probe **/etc/filesystems** and then probe **/proc/filesystems** for all the filesystems without the **nodev** label. If **/etc/filesystems** ends with a line containing only an asterisk (*) then both files are probed.

```
paul@RHELv4u4:~$ cat /proc/filesystems
nodev    sysfs
nodev    rootfs
nodev    bdev
nodev    proc
nodev    sockfs
nodev    binfmt_misc
nodev    usbfs
nodev    usbdevfs
nodev    futexfs
nodev    tmpfs
nodev    pipefs
nodev    eventpollfs
nodev    devpts
         ext2
nodev    ramfs
nodev    hugetlbfs
         iso9660
nodev    relayfs
nodev    mqueue
nodev    selinuxfs
         ext3
nodev    rpc_pipefs
nodev    vmware-hgfs
nodev    autofs
paul@RHELv4u4:~$
```

7.3. putting a file system on a partition

We now have a fresh partition. The system binaries to make file systems can be found with ls.

```
[root@RHEL4b ~]# ls -lS /sbin/mk*
-rwxr-xr-x  3 root root 34832 Apr 24  2006 /sbin/mke2fs
-rwxr-xr-x  3 root root 34832 Apr 24  2006 /sbin/mkfs.ext2
-rwxr-xr-x  3 root root 34832 Apr 24  2006 /sbin/mkfs.ext3
-rwxr-xr-x  3 root root 28484 Oct 13  2004 /sbin/mkdosfs
-rwxr-xr-x  3 root root 28484 Oct 13  2004 /sbin/mkfs.msdos
-rwxr-xr-x  3 root root 28484 Oct 13  2004 /sbin/mkfs.vfat
-rwxr-xr-x  1 root root 20313 Apr 10  2006 /sbin/mkinitrd
-rwxr-x---  1 root root 15444 Oct  5  2004 /sbin/mkzonedb
-rwxr-xr-x  1 root root 15300 May 24  2006 /sbin/mkfs.cramfs
-rwxr-xr-x  1 root root 13036 May 24  2006 /sbin/mkswap
-rwxr-xr-x  1 root root  6912 May 24  2006 /sbin/mkfs
-rwxr-xr-x  1 root root  5905 Aug  3  2004 /sbin/mkbootdisk
[root@RHEL4b ~]#
```

It is time for you to read the manual pages of **mkfs** and **mke2fs**. In the example below, you see the creation of an **ext2 file system** on /dev/sdb1. In real life, you might want to use options like -m0 and -j.

```
root@RHELv4u2:~# mke2fs /dev/sdb1
mke2fs 1.35 (28-Feb-2004)
Filesystem label=
OS type: Linux
Block size=1024 (log=0)
Fragment size=1024 (log=0)
28112 inodes, 112420 blocks
5621 blocks (5.00%) reserved for the super user
First data block=1
Maximum filesystem blocks=67371008
14 block groups
8192 blocks per group, 8192 fragments per group
2008 inodes per group
Superblock backups stored on blocks:
8193, 24577, 40961, 57345, 73729

Writing inode tables: done
Writing superblocks and filesystem accounting information: done

This filesystem will be automatically checked every 37 mounts or
180 days, whichever comes first.  Use tune2fs -c or -i to override.
```

7.4. tuning a file system

You can use **tune2fs** to list and set file system settings. The first screenshot lists the reserved space for root (which is set at five percent).

```
[root@rhel4 ~]# tune2fs -l /dev/sda1 | grep -i "block count"
Block count:            104388
Reserved block count:   5219
[root@rhel4 ~]#
```

This example changes this value to ten percent. You can use tune2fs while the file system is active, even if it is the root file system (as in this example).

```
[root@rhel4 ~]# tune2fs -m10 /dev/sda1
tune2fs 1.35 (28-Feb-2004)
Setting reserved blocks percentage to 10 (10430 blocks)
[root@rhel4 ~]# tune2fs -l /dev/sda1 | grep -i "block count"
Block count:            104388
Reserved block count:   10430
[root@rhel4 ~]#
```

7.5. checking a file system

The **fsck** command is a front end tool used to check a file system for errors.

```
[root@RHEL4b ~]# ls /sbin/*fsck*
/sbin/dosfsck  /sbin/fsck         /sbin/fsck.ext2  /sbin/fsck.msdos
/sbin/e2fsck   /sbin/fsck.cramfs  /sbin/fsck.ext3  /sbin/fsck.vfat
[root@RHEL4b ~]#
```

The last column in **/etc/fstab** is used to determine whether a file system should be checked at boot-up.

```
[paul@RHEL4b ~]$ grep ext /etc/fstab
/dev/VolGroup00/LogVol00  /            ext3    defaults      1 1
LABEL=/boot               /boot        ext3    defaults      1 2
[paul@RHEL4b ~]$
```

Manually checking a mounted file system results in a warning from fsck.

```
[root@RHEL4b ~]# fsck /boot
fsck 1.35 (28-Feb-2004)
e2fsck 1.35 (28-Feb-2004)
/dev/sda1 is mounted.

WARNING!!!  Running e2fsck on a mounted filesystem may cause
SEVERE filesystem damage.

Do you really want to continue (y/n)? no

check aborted.
```

But after unmounting fsck and **e2fsck** can be used to check an ext2 file system.

```
[root@RHEL4b ~]# fsck  /boot
fsck 1.35 (28-Feb-2004)
e2fsck 1.35 (28-Feb-2004)
/boot: clean, 44/26104 files, 17598/104388 blocks
[root@RHEL4b ~]# fsck -p /boot
fsck 1.35 (28-Feb-2004)
/boot: clean, 44/26104 files, 17598/104388 blocks
[root@RHEL4b ~]# e2fsck -p /dev/sda1
/boot: clean, 44/26104 files, 17598/104388 blocks
```

7.6. practice: file systems

1. List the filesystems that are known by your system.

2. Create an **ext2** filesystem on the 200MB partition.

3. Create an **ext3** filesystem on one of the 300MB logical drives.

4. Create an **ext4** on the 400MB partition.

5. Set the reserved space for root on the ext3 filesystem to 0 percent.

6. Verify your work with **fdisk** and **df**.

7. Perform a file system check on all the new file systems.

7.7. solution: file systems

1. List the filesystems that are known by your system.

```
man fs
```

```
cat /proc/filesystems
```

```
cat /etc/filesystems (not on all Linux distributions)
```

2. Create an **ext2** filesystem on the 200MB partition.

```
mke2fs /dev/sdc1 (replace sdc1 with the correct partition)
```

3. Create an **ext3** filesystem on one of the 300MB logical drives.

```
mke2fs -j /dev/sdb5 (replace sdb5 with the correct partition)
```

4. Create an **ext4** on the 400MB partition.

```
mkfs.ext4 /dev/sdb1 (replace sdb1 with the correct partition)
```

5. Set the reserved space for root on the ext3 filesystem to 0 percent.

```
tune2fs -m 0 /dev/sdb5
```

6. Verify your work with **fdisk** and **df**.

```
mkfs (mke2fs) makes no difference in the output of these commands
```

```
The big change is in the next topic: mounting
```

7. Perform a file system check on all the new file systems.

```
fsck /dev/sdb1
fsck /dev/sdc1
fsck /dev/sdb5
```

Chapter 8. mounting

Once you've put a file system on a partition, you can **mount** it. Mounting a file system makes it available for use, usually as a directory. We say **mounting a file system** instead of mounting a partition because we will see later that we can also mount file systems that do not exists on partitions.

On all **Unix** systems, every file and every directory is part of one big file tree. To access a file, you need to know the full path starting from the root directory. When adding a **file system** to your computer, you need to make it available somewhere in the file tree. The directory where you make a file system available is called a **mount point**.

8.1. mounting local file systems

8.1.1. mkdir

This example shows how to create a new **mount point** with **mkdir**.

```
root@RHELv4u2:~# mkdir /home/project42
```

8.1.2. mount

When the **mount point** is created, and a **file system** is present on the partition, then **mount** can **mount** the **file system** on the **mount point directory**.

```
root@RHELv4u2:~# mount -t ext2 /dev/sdb1 /home/project42/
```

Once mounted, the new file system is accessible to users.

8.1.3. /etc/filesystems

Actually the explicit **-t ext2** option to set the file system is not always necessary. The **mount** command is able to automatically detect a lot of file systems.

When mounting a file system without specifying explicitly the file system, then **mount** will first probe **/etc/filesystems**. Mount will skip lines with the **nodev** directive.

```
paul@RHELv4u4:~$ cat /etc/filesystems
ext3
ext2
nodev proc
nodev devpts
iso9660
vfat
hfs
```

8.1.4. /proc/filesystems

When **/etc/filesystems** does not exist, or ends with a single * on the last line, then **mount** will read **/proc/filesystems**.

```
[root@RHEL52 ~]# cat /proc/filesystems | grep -v ^nodev
 ext2
 iso9660
 ext3
```

8.1.5. umount

You can **unmount** a mounted file system using the **umount** command.

```
root@pasha:~# umount /home/reet
```

8.2. displaying mounted file systems

To display all mounted file systems, issue the **mount** command. Or look at the files **/proc/mounts** and **/etc/mtab**.

8.2.1. mount

The simplest and most common way to view all mounts is by issuing the **mount** command without any arguments.

```
root@RHELv4u2:~# mount | grep /dev/sdb
/dev/sdb1 on /home/project42 type ext2 (rw)
```

8.2.2. /proc/mounts

The kernel provides the info in **/proc/mounts** in file form, but **/proc/mounts** does not exist as a file on any hard disk. Looking at **/proc/mounts** is looking at information that comes directly from the kernel.

```
root@RHELv4u2:~# cat /proc/mounts | grep /dev/sdb
/dev/sdb1 /home/project42 ext2 rw 0 0
```

8.2.3. /etc/mtab

The **/etc/mtab** file is not updated by the kernel, but is maintained by the **mount** command. Do not edit **/etc/mtab** manually.

```
root@RHELv4u2:~# cat /etc/mtab | grep /dev/sdb
/dev/sdb1 /home/project42 ext2 rw 0 0
```

8.2.4. df

A more user friendly way to look at mounted file systems is **df**. The **df (diskfree)** command has the added benefit of showing you the free space on each mounted disk. Like a lot of Linux commands, **df** supports the **-h** switch to make the output more **human readable**.

```
root@RHELv4u2:~# df
Filesystem            1K-blocks       Used Available Use% Mounted on
/dev/mapper/VolGroup00-LogVol00
11707972   6366996   4746240   58% /
/dev/sda1             101086     9300     86567   10% /boot
none                 127988        0    127988    0% /dev/shm
/dev/sdb1            108865     1550    101694    2% /home/project42
root@RHELv4u2:~# df -h
Filesystem            Size  Used Avail Use% Mounted on
/dev/mapper/VolGroup00-LogVol00
12G  6.1G  4.6G   58% /
/dev/sda1              99M  9.1M    85M   10% /boot
none                 125M     0    125M    0% /dev/shm
/dev/sdb1           107M  1.6M    100M    2% /home/project42
```

8.2.5. df -h

In the **df -h** example below you can see the size, free space, used gigabytes and percentage and mount point of a partition.

```
root@laika:~# df -h | egrep -e "(sdb2|File)"
Filesystem            Size Used Avail Use% Mounted on
/dev/sdb2             92G   83G  8.6G  91% /media/sdb2
```

8.2.6. du

The **du** command can summarize **disk usage** for files and directories. By using **du** on a mount point you effectively get the disk space used on a file system.

While **du** can go display each subdirectory recursively, the **-s** option will give you a total summary for the parent directory. This option is often used together with **-h**. This means **du -sh** on a mount point gives the total amount used by the file system in that partition.

```
root@debian6~# du -sh /boot /srv/wolf
6.2M /boot
1.1T /srv/wolf
```

8.3. from start to finish

Below is a screenshot that show a summary roadmap starting with detection of the hardware (/dev/sdb) up until mounting on **/mnt**.

```
[root@centos65 ~]# dmesg | grep '\[sdb\]'
sd 3:0:0:0: [sdb] 150994944 512-byte logical blocks: (77.3 GB/72.0 GiB)
sd 3:0:0:0: [sdb] Write Protect is off
sd 3:0:0:0: [sdb] Mode Sense: 00 3a 00 00
sd 3:0:0:0: [sdb] Write cache: enabled, read cache: enabled, doesn't support \
DPO or FUA
sd 3:0:0:0: [sdb] Attached SCSI disk

[root@centos65 ~]# parted /dev/sdb

(parted) mklabel msdos
(parted) mkpart primary ext4 1 77000
(parted) print
Model: ATA VBOX HARDDISK (scsi)
Disk /dev/sdb: 77.3GB
Sector size (logical/physical): 512B/512B
Partition Table: msdos

Number  Start    End     Size    Type     File system  Flags
 1      1049kB   77.0GB  77.0GB  primary

(parted) quit
[root@centos65 ~]# mkfs.ext4 /dev/sdb1
mke2fs 1.41.12 (17-May-2010)
Filesystem label=
OS type: Linux
Block size=4096 (log=2)
Fragment size=4096 (log=2)
Stride=0 blocks, Stripe width=0 blocks
4702208 inodes, 18798592 blocks
939929 blocks (5.00%) reserved for the super user
First data block=0
Maximum filesystem blocks=4294967296
574 block groups
32768 blocks per group, 32768 fragments per group
8192 inodes per group
( output truncated )
...
[root@centos65 ~]# mount /dev/sdb1 /mnt
[root@centos65 ~]# mount | grep mnt
/dev/sdb1 on /mnt type ext4 (rw)
[root@centos65 ~]# df -h | grep mnt
/dev/sdb1              71G   180M   67G   1% /mnt
[root@centos65 ~]# du -sh /mnt
20K      /mnt
[root@centos65 ~]# umount /mnt
```

8.4. permanent mounts

Until now, we performed all mounts manually. This works nice, until the next reboot. Luckily there is a way to tell your computer to automatically mount certain file systems during boot.

8.4.1. /etc/fstab

The file system table located in **/etc/fstab** contains a list of file systems, with an option to automtically mount each of them at boot time.

Below is a sample **/etc/fstab** file.

```
root@RHELv4u2:~# cat /etc/fstab
/dev/VolGroup00/LogVol00 /              ext3    defaults         1 1
LABEL=/boot              /boot          ext3    defaults         1 2
none                     /dev/pts       devpts  gid=5,mode=620   0 0
none                     /dev/shm       tmpfs   defaults         0 0
none                     /proc          proc    defaults         0 0
none                     /sys           sysfs   defaults         0 0
/dev/VolGroup00/LogVol01 swap           swap    defaults         0 0
```

By adding the following line, we can automate the mounting of a file system.

```
/dev/sdb1                /home/project42   ext2    defaults     0 0
```

8.4.2. mount /mountpoint

Adding an entry to **/etc/fstab** has the added advantage that you can simplify the **mount** command. The command in the screenshot below forces **mount** to look for the partition info in **/etc/fstab**.

```
root@rhel65:~# mount /home/project42
```

8.5. securing mounts

File systems can be secured with several **mount options**. Here are some examples.

8.5.1. ro

The **ro** option will mount a file system as read only, preventing anyone from writing.

```
root@rhel53 ~# mount -t ext2 -o ro /dev/hdb1 /home/project42
root@rhel53 ~# touch /home/project42/testwrite
touch: cannot touch `/home/project42/testwrite': Read-only file system
```

8.5.2. noexec

The **noexec** option will prevent the execution of binaries and scripts on the mounted file system.

```
root@rhel53 ~# mount -t ext2 -o noexec /dev/hdb1 /home/project42
root@rhel53 ~# cp /bin/cat /home/project42
root@rhel53 ~# /home/project42/cat /etc/hosts
-bash: /home/project42/cat: Permission denied
root@rhel53 ~# echo echo hello > /home/project42/helloscript
root@rhel53 ~# chmod +x /home/project42/helloscript
root@rhel53 ~# /home/project42/helloscript
-bash: /home/project42/helloscript: Permission denied
```

8.5.3. nosuid

The **nosuid** option will ignore **setuid** bit set binaries on the mounted file system.

Note that you can still set the **setuid** bit on files.

```
root@rhel53 ~# mount -o nosuid /dev/hdb1 /home/project42
root@rhel53 ~# cp /bin/sleep /home/project42/
root@rhel53 ~# chmod 4555 /home/project42/sleep
root@rhel53 ~# ls -l /home/project42/sleep
-r-sr-xr-x 1 root root 19564 Jun 24 17:57 /home/project42/sleep
```

But users cannot exploit the **setuid** feature.

```
root@rhel53 ~# su - paul
[paul@rhel53 ~]$ /home/project42/sleep 500 &
[1] 2876
[paul@rhel53 ~]$ ps -f 2876
UID        PID  PPID  C STIME TTY      STAT   TIME CMD
paul      2876  2853  0 17:58 pts/0    S      0:00 /home/project42/sleep 500
[paul@rhel53 ~]$
```

8.5.4. noacl

To prevent cluttering permissions with **acl's**, use the **noacl** option.

```
root@rhel53 ~# mount -o noacl /dev/hdb1 /home/project42
```

More **mount options** can be found in the manual page of **mount**.

8.6. mounting remote file systems

8.6.1. smb/cifs

The Samba team (samba.org) has a Unix/Linux service that is compatible with the SMB/CIFS protocol. This protocol is mainly used by networked Microsoft Windows computers.

Connecting to a Samba server (or to a Microsoft computer) is also done with the mount command.

This example shows how to connect to the **10.0.0.42** server, to a share named **data2**.

```
[root@centos65 ~]# mount -t cifs -o user=paul //10.0.0.42/data2 /home/data2
Password:
[root@centos65 ~]# mount | grep cifs
//10.0.0.42/data2 on /home/data2 type cifs (rw)
```

The above requires **yum install cifs-client**.

8.6.2. nfs

Unix servers often use **nfs** (aka the network file system) to share directories over the network. Setting up an nfs server is discussed later. Connecting as a client to an nfs server is done with **mount**, and is very similar to connecting to local storage.

This command shows how to connect to the nfs server named **server42**, which is sharing the directory **/srv/data**. The **mount point** at the end of the command (**/home/data**) must already exist.

```
[root@centos65 ~]# mount -t nfs server42:/srv/data /home/data
[root@centos65 ~]#
```

If this **server42** has ip-address **10.0.0.42** then you can also write:

```
[root@centos65 ~]# mount -t nfs 10.0.0.42:/srv/data /home/data
[root@centos65 ~]# mount | grep data
10.0.0.42:/srv/data on /home/data type nfs (rw,vers=4,addr=10.0.0.42,clienta\
ddr=10.0.0.33)
```

8.6.3. nfs specific mount options

```
bg If mount fails, retry in background.
fg (default)If mount fails, retry in foreground.
soft Stop trying to mount after X attempts.
hard (default)Continue trying to mount.
```

The **soft+bg** options combined guarantee the fastest client boot if there are NFS problems.

```
retrans=X Try X times to connect (over udp).
tcp Force tcp (default and supported)
udp Force udp (unsupported)
```

8.7. practice: mounting file systems

1. Mount the small 200MB partition on /home/project22.

2. Mount the big 400MB primary partition on /mnt, the copy some files to it (everything in /etc). Then umount, and mount the file system as read only on /srv/nfs/salesnumbers. Where are the files you copied ?

3. Verify your work with **fdisk**, **df** and **mount**. Also look in **/etc/mtab** and **/proc/mounts**.

4. Make both mounts permanent, test that it works.

5. What happens when you mount a file system on a directory that contains some files ?

6. What happens when you mount two file systems on the same mount point ?

7. (optional) Describe the difference between these commands: find, locate, updatedb, makewhatis, whereis, apropos, which and type.

8. (optional) Perform a file system check on the partition mounted at /srv/nfs/salesnumbers.

8.8. solution: mounting file systems

1. Mount the small 200MB partition on /home/project22.

```
mkdir /home/project22
mount /dev/sdc1 /home/project22
```

2. Mount the big 400MB primary partition on /mnt, the copy some files to it (everything in /
etc). Then umount, and mount the file system as read only on /srv/nfs/salesnumbers. Where
are the files you copied ?

```
mount /dev/sdb1 /mnt
cp -r /etc /mnt
ls -l /mnt

umount /mnt
ls -l /mnt

mkdir -p /srv/nfs/salesnumbers
mount /dev/sdb1 /srv/nfs/salesnumbers

You see the files in /srv/nfs/salenumbers now...

But physically they are on ext3 on partition /dev/sdb1
```

3. Verify your work with **fdisk**, **df** and **mount**. Also look in **/etc/mtab** and **/proc/mounts**.

```
fdisk -l
df -h
mount

All three the above commands should show your mounted partitions.

grep project22 /etc/mtab
grep project22 /proc/mounts
```

4. Make both mounts permanent, test that it works.

```
add the following lines to /etc/fstab

/dev/sdc1 /home/project22 auto defaults 0 0
/dev/sdb1 /srv/nfs/salesnumbers auto defaults 0 0
```

5. What happens when you mount a file system on a directory that contains some files ?

```
The files are hidden until umount.
```

6. What happens when you mount two file systems on the same mount point ?

```
Only the last mounted fs is visible.
```

7. (optional) Describe the difference between these commands: find, locate, updatedb, makewhatis, whereis, apropos, which and type.

```
man find
man locate
...
```

8. (optional) Perform a file system check on the partition mounted at /srv/nfs/salesnumbers.

```
# umount /srv/nfs/salesnumbers (optional but recommended)
# fsck /dev/sdb1
```

Chapter 9. troubleshooting tools

This chapter introduces some tools that go beyond **df -h** and **du -sh**. Tools that will enable you to troubleshoot a variety of issues with **file systems** and storage.

9.1. lsof

List open files with **lsof**.

When invoked without options, **lsof** will list all open files. You can see the command (init in this case), its PID (1) and the user (root) has openend the root directory and **/sbin/init**. The FD (file descriptor) columns shows that / is both the root directory (rtd) and current working directory (cwd) for the /sbin/init command. The FD column displays **rtd** for root directory, **cwd** for current directory and **txt** for text (both including data and code).

```
root@debian7:~# lsof | head -4
COMMAND PID TID   USER   FD     TYPE     DEVICE SIZE/OFF   NODE NAME
init    1          root   cwd    DIR      254,0    4096        2 /
init    1          root   rtd    DIR      254,0    4096        2 /
init    1          root   txt    REG      254,0    36992  130856 /sbin/init
```

Other options in the FD column besides w for writing, are r for reading and u for both reading and writing. You can look at open files for a process id by typing **lsof -p PID**. For **init** this would look like this:

```
lsof -p 1
```

The screenshot below shows basic use of **lsof** to prove that **vi** keeps a **.swp** file open (even when stopped in background) on our freshly mounted file system.

```
[root@RHEL65 ~]# df -h | grep sdb
/dev/sdb1                   541M   17M  497M   4% /srv/project33
[root@RHEL65 ~]# vi /srv/project33/busyfile.txt
[1]+  Stopped                 vi /srv/project33/busyfile.txt
[root@RHEL65 ~]# lsof /srv/*
COMMAND   PID USER  FD   TYPE DEVICE SIZE/OFF NODE NAME
vi       3243 root   3u  REG   8,17    4096    12 /srv/project33/.busyfile.txt.swp
```

Here we see that **rsyslog** has a couple of log files open for writing (the FD column).

```
root@debian7:~# lsof /var/log/*
COMMAND    PID USER    FD    TYPE DEVICE SIZE/OFF    NODE NAME
rsyslogd  2013 root    1w    REG   254,0   454297 1308187 /var/log/syslog
rsyslogd  2013 root    2w    REG   254,0   419328 1308189 /var/log/kern.log
rsyslogd  2013 root    5w    REG   254,0   116725 1308200 /var/log/debug
rsyslogd  2013 root    6w    REG   254,0   309847 1308201 /var/log/messages
rsyslogd  2013 root    7w    REG   254,0    17591 1308188 /var/log/daemon.log
rsyslogd  2013 root    8w    REG   254,0   101768 1308186 /var/log/auth.log
```

You can specify a specific user with **lsof -u**. This example shows the current working directory for a couple of command line programs.

```
[paul@RHEL65 ~]$ lsof -u paul | grep home
bash     3302 paul  cwd    DIR  253,0    4096   788024 /home/paul
lsof     3329 paul  cwd    DIR  253,0    4096   788024 /home/paul
grep     3330 paul  cwd    DIR  253,0    4096   788024 /home/paul
lsof     3331 paul  cwd    DIR  253,0    4096   788024 /home/paul
```

The -u switch of **lsof** also supports the ^ character meaning 'not'. To see all open files, but not those open by root:

```
lsof -u^root
```

9.2. fuser

The **fuser** command will display the 'user' of a file system.

In this example we still have a vi process in background and we use **fuser** to find the process id of the process using this file system.

```
[root@RHEL65 ~]# jobs
[1]+  Stopped                 vi /srv/project33/busyfile.txt
[root@RHEL65 ~]# fuser -m /srv/project33/
/srv/project33/:     3243
```

Adding the **-u** switch will also display the user name.

```
[root@RHEL65 ~]# fuser -m -u /srv/project33/
/srv/project33/:     3243(root)
```

You can quickly kill all processes that are using a specific file (or directory) with the -k switch.

```
[root@RHEL65 ~]# fuser -m -k -u /srv/project33/
/srv/project33/:     3243(root)
[1]+  Killed                  vi /srv/project33/busyfile.txt
[root@RHEL65 ~]# fuser -m -u /srv/project33/
[root@RHEL65 ~]#
```

This example shows all processes that are using the current directory (bash and vi in this case).

```
root@debian7:~/test42# vi file42

[1]+  Stopped                 vi file42
root@debian7:~/test42# fuser -v .
                    USER        PID ACCESS COMMAND
/root/test42:       root       2909 ..c.. bash
                    root       3113 ..c.. vi
```

This example shows that the **vi** command actually accesses **/usr/bin/vim.basic** as an **executable** file.

```
root@debian7:~/test42# fuser -v $(which vi)
                    USER        PID ACCESS COMMAND
/usr/bin/vim.basic: root       3113 ...e. vi
```

The last example shows how to find the process that is accessing a specific file.

```
[root@RHEL65 ~]# vi /srv/project33/busyfile.txt

[1]+  Stopped                 vi /srv/project33/busyfile.txt
[root@RHEL65 ~]# fuser -v -m /srv/project33/busyfile.txt
                    USER        PID ACCESS COMMAND
/srv/project33/busyfile.txt:
                    root      13938 F.... vi
[root@RHEL65 ~]# ps -fp 13938
UID        PID  PPID  C STIME TTY          TIME CMD
root     13938  3110  0 15:47 pts/0    00:00:00 vi /srv/project33/busyfile.txt
```

9.3. chroot

The **chroot** command creates a shell with an alternate root directory. It effectively hides anything outside of this directory.

In the example below we assume that our system refuses to start (maybe because there is a problem with **/etc/fstab** or the mounting of the root file system).

We start a live system (booted from cd/dvd/usb) to troubleshoot our server. The live system will not use our main hard disk as root device

```
root@livecd:~# df -h | grep root
rootfs          186M   11M  175M   6% /
/dev/loop0      807M  807M      0 100% /lib/live/mount/rootfs/filesystem.squashfs
root@livecd:~# mount | grep root
/dev/loop0 on /lib/live/mount/rootfs/filesystem.squashfs type squashfs (ro)
```

We create some test file on the current rootfs.

```
root@livecd:~# touch /file42
root@livecd:~# mkdir /dir42
root@livecd:~# ls /
bin    dir42   home         lib64   opt    run       srv   usr
boot   etc     initrd.img   media   proc   sbin      sys   var
dev    file42  lib          mnt     root   selinux   tmp   vmlinuz
```

First we mount the root file system from the disk (which is on **lvm** so we use **/dev/mapper** instead of **/dev/sda5**).

```
root@livecd:~# mount /dev/mapper/packer--debian--7-root /mnt
```

We are now ready to **chroot** into the rootfs on disk.

```
root@livecd:~# cd /mnt
root@livecd:/mnt# chroot /mnt
root@livecd:/# ls /
bin    dev    initrd.img   lost+found   opt    run       srv   usr       vmlinuz
boot   etc    lib          media        proc   sbin      sys   vagrant
data   home   lib64        mnt          root   selinux   tmp   var
```

Our test files (file42 and dir42) are not visible because they are out of the **chrooted** environment.

Note that the **hostname** of the chrooted environment is identical to the existing hostname.

To exit the **chrooted** file system:

```
root@livecd:/# exit
exit
root@livecd:~# ls /
bin    dir42   home         lib64   opt    run       srv   usr
boot   etc     initrd.img   media   proc   sbin      sys   var
dev    file42  lib          mnt     root   selinux   tmp   vmlinuz
```

9.4. iostat

iostat reports IO statitics every given period of time. It also includes a small cpu usage summary. This example shows **iostat** running every ten seconds with **/dev/sdc** and **/dev/sde** showing a lot of write activity.

```
[root@RHEL65 ~]# iostat 10 3
Linux 2.6.32-431.el6.x86_64 (RHEL65)  06/16/2014   _x86_64_    (1 CPU)

avg-cpu:  %user   %nice %system %iowait  %steal   %idle
          5.81    0.00    3.15    0.18    0.00   90.85

Device:            tps    Blk_read/s    Blk_wrtn/s    Blk_read    Blk_wrtn
sda              42.08       1204.10       1634.88     1743708     2367530
sdb               1.20          7.69         45.78       11134       66292
sdc               0.92          5.30         45.82        7672       66348
sdd               0.91          5.29         45.78        7656       66292
sde               1.04          6.28         91.49        9100      132496
sdf               0.70          3.40         91.46        4918      132440
sdg               0.69          3.40         91.46        4918      132440
dm-0            191.68       1045.78       1362.30     1514434     1972808
dm-1             49.26        150.54        243.55      218000      352696

avg-cpu:  %user   %nice %system %iowait  %steal   %idle
         56.11    0.00   16.83    0.10    0.00   26.95

Device:            tps    Blk_read/s    Blk_wrtn/s    Blk_read    Blk_wrtn
sda             257.01      10185.97         76.95      101656         768
sdb               0.00          0.00          0.00           0           0
sdc               3.81          1.60       2953.11          16       29472
sdd               0.00          0.00          0.00           0           0
sde               4.91          1.60       4813.63          16       48040
sdf               0.00          0.00          0.00           0           0
sdg               0.00          0.00          0.00           0           0
dm-0            283.77      10185.97         76.95      101656         768
dm-1              0.00          0.00          0.00           0           0

avg-cpu:  %user   %nice %system %iowait  %steal   %idle
         67.65    0.00   31.11    0.11    0.00    1.13

Device:            tps    Blk_read/s    Blk_wrtn/s    Blk_read    Blk_wrtn
sda             466.86      26961.09        178.28      238336        1576
sdb               0.00          0.00          0.00           0           0
sdc              31.45          0.90      24997.29           8      220976
sdd               0.00          0.00          0.00           0           0
sde               0.34          0.00          5.43           0          48
sdf               0.00          0.00          0.00           0           0
sdg               0.00          0.00          0.00           0           0
dm-0            503.62      26938.46        178.28      238136        1576
dm-1              2.83         22.62          0.00         200           0

[root@RHEL65 ~]#
```

Other options are to specify the disks you want to monitor (every 5 seconds here):

```
iostat sdd sde sdf 5
```

Or to show statistics per partition:

```
iostat -p sde -p sdf 5
```

9.5. iotop

iotop works like the **top** command but orders processes by input/output instead of by CPU.

By default **iotop** will show all processes. This example uses **iotop -o** to only display processes with actual I/O.

```
[root@RHEL65 ~]# iotop -o

Total DISK READ: 8.63 M/s | Total DISK WRITE: 0.00 B/s
   TID PRIO  USER   DISK READ  DISK WRITE  SWAPIN     IO>    COMMAND
 15000 be/4 root     2.43 M/s    0.00 B/s  0.00 % 14.60 % tar cjf /srv/di...
 25000 be/4 root     6.20 M/s    0.00 B/s  0.00 %  6.15 % tar czf /srv/di...
 24988 be/4 root     0.00 B/s    7.21 M/s  0.00 %  0.00 % gzip
 25003 be/4 root     0.00 B/s 1591.19 K/s  0.00 %  0.00 % gzip
 25004 be/4 root     0.00 B/s  193.51 K/s  0.00 %  0.00 % bzip2
```

Use the **-b** switch to create a log of **iotop** output (instead of the default interactive view).

```
[root@RHEL65 ~]# iotop -bod 10
Total DISK READ: 12.82 M/s | Total DISK WRITE: 5.69 M/s
   TID PRIO  USER   DISK READ  DISK WRITE  SWAPIN     IO    COMMAND
 25153 be/4 root     2.05 M/s    0.00 B/s  0.00 %  7.81 % tar cjf /srv/di...
 25152 be/4 root    10.77 M/s    0.00 B/s  0.00 %  2.94 % tar czf /srv/di...
 25144 be/4 root   408.54 B/s    0.00 B/s  0.00 %  0.05 % python /usr/sbi...
 12516 be/3 root     0.00 B/s 1491.33 K/s  0.00 %  0.04 % [jbd2/sdc1-8]
 12522 be/3 root     0.00 B/s   45.48 K/s  0.00 %  0.01 % [jbd2/sde1-8]
 25158 be/4 root     0.00 B/s    0.00 B/s  0.00 %  0.00 % [flush-8:64]
 25155 be/4 root     0.00 B/s  493.12 K/s  0.00 %  0.00 % bzip2
 25156 be/4 root     0.00 B/s    2.81 M/s  0.00 %  0.00 % gzip
 25159 be/4 root     0.00 B/s  528.63 K/s  0.00 %  0.00 % [flush-8:32]
```

This is an example of **iotop** to track disk I/O every ten seconds for one user named **vagrant** (and only one process of this user, but this can be omitted). The **-a** switch accumulates I/O over time.

```
[root@RHEL65 ~]# iotop -q -a -u vagrant -b -p 5216 -d 10 -n 10
Total DISK READ: 0.00 B/s | Total DISK WRITE: 0.00 B/s
   TID PRIO  USER      DISK READ  DISK WRITE  SWAPIN     IO    COMMAND
  5216 be/4 vagrant       0.00 B      0.00 B  0.00 %  0.00 % gzip
Total DISK READ: 818.22 B/s | Total DISK WRITE: 20.78 M/s
  5216 be/4 vagrant       0.00 B    213.89 M  0.00 %  0.00 % gzip
Total DISK READ: 2045.95 B/s | Total DISK WRITE: 23.16 M/s
  5216 be/4 vagrant       0.00 B    430.70 M  0.00 %  0.00 % gzip
Total DISK READ: 1227.50 B/s | Total DISK WRITE: 22.37 M/s
  5216 be/4 vagrant       0.00 B    642.02 M  0.00 %  0.00 % gzip
Total DISK READ: 818.35 B/s | Total DISK WRITE: 16.44 M/s
  5216 be/4 vagrant       0.00 B    834.09 M  0.00 %  0.00 % gzip
Total DISK READ: 6.95 M/s | Total DISK WRITE: 8.74 M/s
  5216 be/4 vagrant       0.00 B    920.69 M  0.00 %  0.00 % gzip
Total DISK READ: 21.71 M/s | Total DISK WRITE: 11.99 M/s
```

9.6. vmstat

While **vmstat** is mainly a memory monitoring tool, it is worth mentioning here for its reporting on summary I/O data for block devices and swap space.

This example shows some disk activity (underneath the **-----io----** column), without swapping.

```
[root@RHEL65 ~]# vmstat 5 10
procs ----------memory---------- ---swap-- -----io---- --system-- -----cpu-----
 r  b   swpd   free   buff  cache   si   so    bi    bo   in    cs us sy id wa st
 0  0   5420   9092  14020 340876    7   12   235   252   77   100  2  1 98  0  0
 2  0   5420   6104  13840 338176    0    0  7401  7812  747  1887 38 12 50  0  0
 2  0   5420  10136  13696 336012    0    0 11334    14 1725  4036 76 24  0  0  0
 0  0   5420  14160  13404 341552    0    0 10161  9914 1174  1924 67 15 18  0  0
 0  0   5420  14300  13420 341564    0    0     0    16   28    18  0  0 100 0  0
 0  0   5420  14300  13420 341564    0    0     0     0   22    16  0  0 100 0  0
...
[root@RHEL65 ~]#
```

You can benefit from **vmstat**'s ability to display memory in kilobytes, megabytes or even kibibytes and mebibytes using -S (followed by k K m or M).

```
[root@RHEL65 ~]# vmstat -SM 5 10
procs ----------memory---------- ---swap-- -----io---- --system-- -----cpu-----
 r  b   swpd   free   buff  cache   si   so    bi    bo   in    cs us sy id wa st
 0  0      5     14     11   334     0    0   259   255   79   107  2  1 97  0  0
 0  0      5     14     11   334     0    0     0     2   21    18  0  0 100 0  0
 0  0      5     15     11   334     0    0     6     0   35    31  0  0 100 0  0
 2  0      5      6     11   336     0    0 17100  7814 1378  2945 48 21 31  0  0
 2  0      5      6     11   336     0    0 13193    14 1662  3343 78 22  0  0  0
 2  0      5     13     11   330     0    0 11656  9781 1419  2642 82 18  0  0  0
 2  0      5      9     11   334     0    0 10705  2716 1504  2657 81 19  0  0  0
 1  0      5     14     11   336     0    0  6467  3788  765  1384 43  9 48  0  0
 0  0      5     14     11   336     0    0     0    13   28    24  0  0 100 0  0
 0  0      5     14     11   336     0    0     0     0   20    15  0  0 100 0  0
[root@RHEL65 ~]#
```

vmstat is also discussed in other chapters.

9.7. practice: troubleshooting tools

0. It is imperative that you practice these tools **before** trouble arises. It will help you get familiar with the tools and allow you to create a base line of normal behaviour for your systems.

1. Read the theory on **fuser** and explore its man page. Use this command to find files that you open yourself.

2. Read the theory on **lsof** and explore its man page. Use this command to find files that you open yourself.

3. Boot a live image on an existing computer (virtual or real) and **chroot** into to it.

4. Start one or more disk intensive jobs and monitor them with **iostat** and **iotop** (compare to **vmstat**).

9.8. solution: troubleshooting tools

0. It is imperative that you practice these tools **before** trouble arises. It will help you get familiar with the tools and allow you to create a base line of normal behaviour for your systems.

1. Read the theory on **fuser** and explore its man page. Use this command to find files that you open yourself.

2. Read the theory on **lsof** and explore its man page. Use this command to find files that you open yourself.

3. Boot a live image on an existing computer (virtual or real) and **chroot** into to it.

4. Start one or more disk intensive jobs and monitor them with **iostat** and **iotop** (compare to **vmstat**).

Chapter 10. introduction to uuid's

A **uuid** or **universally unique identifier** is used to uniquely identify objects. This 128bit standard allows anyone to create a unique **uuid**.

This chapter takes a brief look at **uuid's**.

10.1. about unique objects

Older versions of Linux have a **vol_id** utility to display the **uuid** of a file system.

```
root@debian5:~# vol_id --uuid /dev/sda1
193c3c9b-2c40-9290-8b71-4264ee4d4c82
```

Red Hat Enterprise Linux 5 puts **vol_id** in **/lib/udev/vol_id**, which is not in the $PATH. The syntax is also a bit different from Debian/Ubuntu/Mint.

```
root@rhel53 ~# /lib/udev/vol_id -u /dev/hda1
48a6a316-9ca9-4214-b5c6-e7b33a77e860
```

This utility is not available in standard installations of RHEL6 or Debian6.

10.2. tune2fs

Use **tune2fs** to find the **uuid** of a file system.

```
[root@RHEL5 ~]# tune2fs -l /dev/sda1 | grep UUID
Filesystem UUID:          11cfc8bc-07c0-4c3f-9f64-78422ef1dd5c
[root@RHEL5 ~]# /lib/udev/vol_id -u /dev/sda1
11cfc8bc-07c0-4c3f-9f64-78422ef1dd5c
```

10.3. uuid

There is more information in the manual of **uuid**, a tool that can generate uuid's.

```
[root@rhel65 ~]# yum install uuid
(output truncated)
[root@rhel65 ~]# man uuid
```

10.4. uuid in /etc/fstab

You can use the **uuid** to make sure that a volume is universally uniquely identified in **/etc/fstab**. The device name can change depending on the disk devices that are present at boot time, but a **uuid** never changes.

First we use **tune2fs** to find the **uuid**.

```
[root@RHEL5 ~]# tune2fs -l /dev/sdc1 | grep UUID
Filesystem UUID:          7626d73a-2bb6-4937-90ca-e451025d64e8
```

Then we check that it is properly added to **/etc/fstab**, the **uuid** replaces the variable devicename /dev/sdc1.

```
[root@RHEL5 ~]# grep UUID /etc/fstab
UUID=7626d73a-2bb6-4937-90ca-e451025d64e8 /home/pro42 ext3 defaults 0 0
```

Now we can mount the volume using the mount point defined in **/etc/fstab**.

```
[root@RHEL5 ~]# mount /home/pro42
[root@RHEL5 ~]# df -h | grep 42
/dev/sdc1              397M   11M  366M   3% /home/pro42
```

The real test now, is to remove **/dev/sdb** from the system, reboot the machine and see what happens. After the reboot, the disk previously known as **/dev/sdc** is now **/dev/sdb**.

```
[root@RHEL5 ~]# tune2fs -l /dev/sdb1 | grep UUID
Filesystem UUID:          7626d73a-2bb6-4937-90ca-e451025d64e8
```

And thanks to the **uuid** in **/etc/fstab**, the mountpoint is mounted on the same disk as before.

```
[root@RHEL5 ~]# df -h | grep sdb
/dev/sdb1              397M   11M  366M   3% /home/pro42
```

10.5. uuid as a boot device

Recent Linux distributions (Debian, Ubuntu, ...) use **grub** with a **uuid** to identify the root file system.

This example shows how a **root=/dev/sda1** is replaced with a **uuid**.

```
title           Ubuntu 9.10, kernel 2.6.31-19-generic
uuid            f001ba5d-9077-422a-9634-8d23d57e782a
kernel          /boot/vmlinuz-2.6.31-19-generic \
root=UUID=f001ba5d-9077-422a-9634-8d23d57e782a ro quiet splash
initrd          /boot/initrd.img-2.6.31-19-generic
```

The screenshot above contains only four lines. The line starting with **root=** is the continuation of the **kernel** line.

RHEL and CentOS boot from LVM after a default install.

10.6. practice: uuid and filesystems

1. Find the **uuid** of one of your **ext3** partitions with **tune2fs** (and **vol_id** if you are on RHEL5).

2. Use this **uuid** in **/etc/fstab** and test that it works with a simple **mount**.

3. (optional) Test it also by removing a disk (so the device name is changed). You can edit settings in vmware/Virtualbox to remove a hard disk.

4. Display the **root=** directive in **/boot/grub/menu.lst**. (We see later in the course how to maintain this file.)

5. (optional on ubuntu) Replace the **/dev/xxx** in **/boot/grub/menu.lst** with a **uuid** (use an extra stanza for this). Test that it works.

10.7. solution: uuid and filesystems

1. Find the **uuid** of one of your **ext3** partitions with **tune2fs** (and **vol_id** if you are on RHEL5).

```
root@rhel55:~# /lib/udev/vol_id -u /dev/hda1
60926898-2c78-49b4-a71d-c1d6310c87cc

root@ubu1004:~# tune2fs -l /dev/sda2 | grep UUID
Filesystem UUID:         3007b743-1dce-2d62-9a59-cf25f85191b7
```

2. Use this **uuid** in **/etc/fstab** and test that it works with a simple **mount**.

```
tail -1 /etc/fstab
UUID=60926898-2c78-49b4-a71d-c1d6310c87cc /home/pro42 ext3 defaults 0 0
```

3. (optional) Test it also by removing a disk (so the device name is changed). You can edit settings in vmware/Virtualbox to remove a hard disk.

4. Display the **root=** directive in **/boot/grub/menu.lst**. (We see later in the course how to maintain this file.)

```
paul@deb503:~$ grep ^[^#] /boot/grub/menu.lst | grep root=
kernel        /boot/vmlinuz-2.6.26-2-686 root=/dev/hda1 ro selinux=1 quiet
kernel        /boot/vmlinuz-2.6.26-2-686 root=/dev/hda1 ro selinux=1 single
```

5. (optional on ubuntu) Replace the **/dev/xxx** in **/boot/grub/menu.lst** with a **uuid** (use an extra stanza for this). Test that it works.

Chapter 11. introduction to raid

11.1. hardware or software

Redundant Array of Independent (originally Inexpensive) Disks or **RAID** can be set up using hardware or software. Hardware RAID is more expensive, but offers better performance. Software RAID is cheaper and easier to manage, but it uses your CPU and your memory.

Where ten years ago nobody was arguing about the best choice being hardware RAID, this has changed since technologies like mdadm, lvm and even zfs focus more on managability. The workload on the cpu for software RAID used to be high, but cpu's have gotten a lot faster.

11.2. raid levels

11.2.1. raid 0

raid 0 uses two or more disks, and is often called **striping** (or stripe set, or striped volume). Data is divided in **chunks**, those chunks are evenly spread across every disk in the array. The main advantage of **raid 0** is that you can create **larger drives**. **raid 0** is the only **raid** without redundancy.

11.2.2. jbod

jbod uses two or more disks, and is often called **concatenating** (spanning, spanned set, or spanned volume). Data is written to the first disk, until it is full. Then data is written to the second disk... The main advantage of **jbod** (Just a Bunch of Disks) is that you can create **larger drives**. JBOD offers no redundancy.

11.2.3. raid 1

raid 1 uses exactly two disks, and is often called **mirroring** (or mirror set, or mirrored volume). All data written to the array is written on each disk. The main advantage of raid 1 is **redundancy**. The main disadvantage is that you lose at least half of your available disk space (in other words, you at least double the cost).

11.2.4. raid 2, 3 and 4 ?

raid 2 uses bit level striping, **raid 3** byte level, and **raid 4** is the same as **raid 5**, but with a dedicated parity disk. This is actually slower than **raid 5**, because every write would have to write parity to this one (bottleneck) disk. It is unlikely that you will ever see these **raid** levels in production.

11.2.5. raid 5

raid 5 uses **three** or more disks, each divided into chunks. Every time chunks are written to the array, one of the disks will receive a **parity** chunk. Unlike **raid 4**, the parity chunk will alternate between all disks. The main advantage of this is that **raid 5** will allow for full data recovery in case of **one** hard disk failure.

11.2.6. raid 6

raid 6 is very similar to **raid 5**, but uses two parity chunks. **raid 6** protects against two hard disk failures. Oracle Solaris **zfs** calls this **raidz2** (and also had **raidz3** with triple parity).

11.2.7. raid 0+1

raid 0+1 is a mirror(1) of stripes(0). This means you first create two **raid 0 stripe** sets, and then you set them up as a mirror set. For example, when you have six 100GB disks, then the stripe sets are each 300GB. Combined in a mirror, this makes 300GB total. **raid 0+1** will survive one disk failure. It will only survive the second disk failure if this disk is in the same stripe set as the previous failed disk.

11.2.8. raid 1+0

raid 1+0 is a stripe(0) of mirrors(1). For example, when you have six 100GB disks, then you first create three mirrors of 100GB each. You then stripe them together into a 300GB drive. In this example, as long as not all disks in the same mirror fail, it can survive up to three hard disk failures.

11.2.9. raid 50

raid 5+0 is a stripe(0) of **raid 5** arrays. Suppose you have nine disks of 100GB, then you can create three **raid 5** arrays of 200GB each. You can then combine them into one large stripe set.

11.2.10. many others

There are many other nested **raid** combinations, like **raid** 30, 51, 60, 100, 150, ...

11.3. building a software raid5 array

11.3.1. do we have three disks?

First, you have to attach some disks to your computer. In this scenario, three brand new disks of eight gigabyte each are added. Check with **fdisk -l** that they are connected.

```
[root@rhel6c ~]# fdisk -l 2> /dev/null | grep MB
Disk /dev/sdb: 8589 MB, 8589934592 bytes
Disk /dev/sdc: 8589 MB, 8589934592 bytes
Disk /dev/sdd: 8589 MB, 8589934592 bytes
```

11.3.2. fd partition type

The next step is to create a partition of type **fd** on every disk. The **fd** type is to set the partition as **Linux RAID autodetect**. See this (truncated) screenshot:

```
[root@rhel6c ~]# fdisk /dev/sdd
...
Command (m for help): n
Command action
   e   extended
   p   primary partition (1-4)
p
Partition number (1-4): 1
First cylinder (1-1044, default 1):
Using default value 1
Last cylinder, +cylinders or +size{K,M,G} (1-1044, default 1044):
Using default value 1044

Command (m for help): t
Selected partition 1
Hex code (type L to list codes): fd
Changed system type of partition 1 to fd (Linux raid autodetect)

Command (m for help): w
The partition table has been altered!

Calling ioctl() to re-read partition table.
Syncing disks.
```

11.3.3. verify all three partitions

Now all three disks are ready for **raid 5**, so we have to tell the system what to do with these disks.

```
[root@rhel6c ~]# fdisk -l 2> /dev/null | grep raid
/dev/sdb1        1        1044      8385898+  fd  Linux raid autodetect
/dev/sdc1        1        1044      8385898+  fd  Linux raid autodetect
/dev/sdd1        1        1044      8385898+  fd  Linux raid autodetect
```

11.3.4. create the raid5

The next step used to be *create the **raid table** in /etc/raidtab*. Nowadays, you can just issue the command **mdadm** with the correct parameters.

The command below is split on two lines to fit this print, but you should type it on one line, without the backslash (\).

```
[root@rhel6c ~]# mdadm --create /dev/md0 --chunk=64 --level=5 --raid-\
devices=3 /dev/sdb1 /dev/sdc1 /dev/sdd1
mdadm: Defaulting to version 1.2 metadata
mdadm: array /dev/md0 started.
```

Below a partial screenshot how fdisk -l sees the **raid 5**.

```
[root@rhel6c ~]# fdisk -l /dev/md0

Disk /dev/md0: 17.2 GB, 17172135936 bytes
2 heads, 4 sectors/track, 4192416 cylinders
Units = cylinders of 8 * 512 = 4096 bytes
Sector size (logical/physical): 512 bytes / 512 bytes
I/O size (minimum/optimal): 65536 bytes / 131072 bytes
Disk identifier: 0x00000000

Disk /dev/md0 doesn't contain a valid partition table
```

We could use this software **raid 5** array in the next topic: **lvm**.

11.3.5. /proc/mdstat

The status of the raid devices can be seen in **/proc/mdstat**. This example shows a **raid 5** in the process of rebuilding.

```
[root@rhel6c ~]# cat /proc/mdstat
Personalities : [raid6] [raid5] [raid4]
md0 : active raid5 sdd1[3] sdc1[1] sdb1[0]
      16769664 blocks super 1.2 level 5, 64k chunk, algorithm 2 [3/2] [UU_]
      [============>........]  recovery = 62.8% (5266176/8384832) finish=0\
.3min speed=139200K/sec
```

This example shows an active software **raid 5**.

```
[root@rhel6c ~]# cat /proc/mdstat
Personalities : [raid6] [raid5] [raid4]
md0 : active raid5 sdd1[3] sdc1[1] sdb1[0]
    16769664 blocks super 1.2 level 5, 64k chunk, algorithm 2 [3/3] [UUU]
```

11.3.6. mdadm --detail

Use **mdadm --detail** to get information on a raid device.

```
[root@rhel6c ~]# mdadm --detail /dev/md0
/dev/md0:
          Version : 1.2
    Creation Time : Sun Jul 17 13:48:41 2011
       Raid Level : raid5
       Array Size : 16769664 (15.99 GiB 17.17 GB)
    Used Dev Size : 8384832 (8.00 GiB 8.59 GB)
     Raid Devices : 3
    Total Devices : 3
      Persistence : Superblock is persistent

      Update Time : Sun Jul 17 13:49:43 2011
            State : clean
   Active Devices : 3
  Working Devices : 3
   Failed Devices : 0
    Spare Devices : 0

           Layout : left-symmetric
       Chunk Size : 64K

             Name : rhel6c:0  (local to host rhel6c)
             UUID : c10fd9c3:08f9a25f:be913027:999c8e1f
           Events : 18

    Number   Major   Minor   RaidDevice State
       0       8       17        0      active sync   /dev/sdb1
       1       8       33        1      active sync   /dev/sdc1
       3       8       49        2      active sync   /dev/sdd1
```

11.3.7. removing a software raid

The software raid is visible in **/proc/mdstat** when active. To remove the raid completely so you can use the disks for other purposes, you stop (de-activate) it with **mdadm**.

```
[root@rhel6c ~]# mdadm --stop /dev/md0
mdadm: stopped /dev/md0
```

The disks can now be repartitioned.

11.3.8. further reading

Take a look at the man page of **mdadm** for more information. Below an example command to add a new partition while removing a faulty one.

```
mdadm /dev/md0 --add /dev/sdd1 --fail /dev/sdb1 --remove /dev/sdb1
```

11.4. practice: raid

1. Add three virtual disks of 1GB each to a virtual machine.

2. Create a software **raid 5** on the three disks. (It is not necessary to put a filesystem on it)

3. Verify with **fdisk** and in **/proc** that the **raid 5** exists.

4. Stop and remove the **raid 5**.

5. Create a **raid 1** to mirror two disks.

11.5. solution: raid

1. Add three virtual disks of 1GB each to a virtual machine.

2. Create a software **raid 5** on the three disks. (It is not necessary to put a filesystem on it)

3. Verify with **fdisk** and in **/proc** that the **raid 5** exists.

4. Stop and remove the **raid 5**.

5. Create a **raid 1** to mirror two disks.

```
[root@rhel6c ~]# mdadm --create /dev/md0 --level=1 --raid-devices=2 \
/dev/sdb1 /dev/sdc1
mdadm: Defaulting to version 1.2 metadata
mdadm: array /dev/md0 started.
[root@rhel6c ~]# cat /proc/mdstat
Personalities : [raid6] [raid5] [raid4] [raid1]
md0 : active raid1 sdc1[1] sdb1[0]
      8384862 blocks super 1.2 [2/2] [UU]
      [====>................]  resync = 20.8% (1745152/8384862) \
finish=0.5min speed=218144K/sec
```

Chapter 12. logical volume management

Most **lvm** implementations support **physical storage grouping**, **logical volume resizing** and **data migration**.

Physical storage grouping is a fancy name for grouping multiple block devices (hard disks, but also iSCSI etc) into a logical mass storage device. To enlarge this physical group, block devices (including partitions) can be added at a later time.

The size of **lvm volumes** on this **physical group** is independent of the individual size of the components. The total size of the group is the limit.

One of the nice features of **lvm** is the logical volume resizing. You can increase the size of an **lvm volume**, sometimes even without any downtime. Additionally, you can migrate data away from a failing hard disk device, create mirrors and create snapshots.

12.1. introduction to lvm

12.1.1. problems with standard partitions

There are some problems when working with hard disks and standard partitions. Consider a system with a small and a large hard disk device, partitioned like this. The first disk (/dev/sda) is partitioned in two, the second disk (/dev/sdb) has two partitions and some empty space.

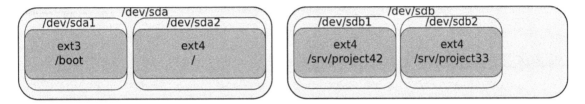

In the example above, consider the options when you want to enlarge the space available for **/srv/project42**. What can you do ? The solution will always force you to unmount the file system, take a backup of the data, remove and recreate partitions, and then restore the data and remount the file system.

12.1.2. solution with lvm

Using **lvm** will create a virtual layer between the mounted file systems and the hardware devices. This virtual layer will allow for an administrator to enlarge a mounted file system in use. When **lvm** is properly used, then there is no need to unmount the file system to enlarge it.

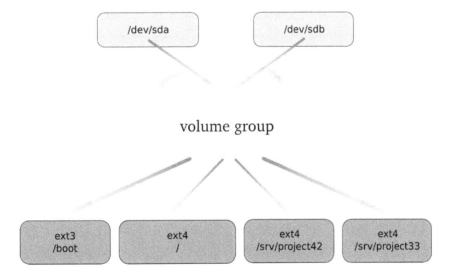

12.2. lvm terminology

12.2.1. physical volume (pv)

A **physical volume** is any block device (a disk, a partition, a RAID device or even an iSCSI device). All these devices can become a member of a **volume group**.

The commands used to manage a **physical volume** start with pv.

```
[root@centos65 ~]# pv
pvchange    pvck       pvcreate    pvdisplay  pvmove     pvremove
pvresize    pvs        pvscan
```

12.2.2. volume group (vg)

A **volume group** is an abstraction layer between **block devices** and **logical volumes**.

The commands used to manage a **volume group** start with vg.

```
[root@centos65 ~]# vg
vgcfgbackup    vgconvert    vgextend        vgmknodes    vgs
vgcfgrestore   vgcreate     vgimport        vgreduce     vgscan
vgchange       vgdisplay    vgimportclone   vgremove     vgsplit
vgck           vgexport     vgmerge         vgrename
```

12.2.3. logical volume (lv)

A **logical volume** is created in a **volume group**. Logical volumes that contain a file system can be mounted. The use of **logical volumes** is similar to the use of **partitions** and is accomplished with the same standard commands (mkfs, mount, fsck, df, ...).

The commands used to manage a **logical volume** start with lv.

```
[root@centos65 ~]# lv
lvchange    lvextend     lvmdiskscan  lvmsar     lvresize
lvconvert   lvm          lvmdump      lvreduce   lvs
lvcreate    lvmchange    lvmetad      lvremove   lvscan
lvdisplay   lvmconf      lvmsadc      lvrename
```

12.3. example: using lvm

This example shows how you can use a device (in this case /dev/sdc, but it could have been /dev/sdb or any other disk or partition) with lvm, how to create a volume group (vg) and how to create and use a logical volume (vg/lvol0).

First thing to do, is create physical volumes that can join the volume group with **pvcreate**. This command makes a disk or partition available for use in Volume Groups. The screenshot shows how to present the SCSI Disk device to LVM.

```
root@RHEL4:~# pvcreate /dev/sdc
Physical volume "/dev/sdc" successfully created
```

*Note: lvm **will** work fine when using the complete device, but another operating system on the same computer (or on the same SAN) will not recognize lvm and will mark the block device as being empty! You can avoid this by creating a partition that spans the whole device, then run **pvcreate** on the partition instead of the disk.*

Then **vgcreate** creates a volume group using one device. Note that more devices could be added to the volume group.

```
root@RHEL4:~# vgcreate vg /dev/sdc
Volume group "vg" successfully created
```

The last step **lvcreate** creates a logical volume.

```
root@RHEL4:~# lvcreate --size 500m vg
Logical volume "lvol0" created
```

The logical volume /dev/vg/lvol0 can now be formatted with ext3, and mounted for normal use.

```
root@RHELv4u2:~# mke2fs -m0 -j /dev/vg/lvol0
mke2fs 1.35 (28-Feb-2004)
Filesystem label=
OS type: Linux
Block size=1024 (log=0)
Fragment size=1024 (log=0)
128016 inodes, 512000 blocks
0 blocks (0.00%) reserved for the super user
First data block=1
Maximum filesystem blocks=67633152
63 block groups
8192 blocks per group, 8192 fragments per group
2032 inodes per group
Superblock backups stored on blocks:
8193, 24577, 40961, 57345, 73729, 204801, 221185, 401409

Writing inode tables: done
Creating journal (8192 blocks): done
Writing superblocks and filesystem accounting information: done

This filesystem will be automatically checked every 37 mounts or
180 days, whichever comes first.  Use tune2fs -c or -i to override.
root@RHELv4u2:~# mkdir /home/project10
root@RHELv4u2:~# mount /dev/vg/lvol0 /home/project10/
root@RHELv4u2:~# df -h | grep proj
/dev/mapper/vg-lvol0  485M   11M  474M   3% /home/project10
```

A logical volume is very similar to a partition, it can be formatted with a file system, and can be mounted so users can access it.

12.4. example: extend a logical volume

A logical volume can be extended without unmounting the file system. Whether or not a volume can be extended depends on the file system it uses. Volumes that are mounted as vfat or ext2 cannot be extended, so in the example here we use the ext3 file system.

The fdisk command shows us newly added scsi-disks that will serve our lvm volume. This volume will then be extended. First, take a look at these disks.

```
[root@RHEL5 ~]# fdisk -l | grep sd[bc]
Disk /dev/sdb doesn't contain a valid partition table
Disk /dev/sdc doesn't contain a valid partition table
Disk /dev/sdb: 1181 MB, 1181115904 bytes
Disk /dev/sdc: 429 MB, 429496320 bytes
```

You already know how to partition a disk, below the first disk is partitioned (in one big primary partition), the second disk is left untouched.

```
[root@RHEL5 ~]# fdisk -l | grep sd[bc]
Disk /dev/sdc doesn't contain a valid partition table
Disk /dev/sdb: 1181 MB, 1181115904 bytes
/dev/sdb1               1          143        1148616   83   Linux
Disk /dev/sdc: 429 MB, 429496320 bytes
```

You also know how to prepare disks for lvm with **pvcreate**, and how to create a volume group with **vgcreate**. This example adds both the partitioned disk and the untouched disk to the volume group named **vg2**.

```
[root@RHEL5 ~]# pvcreate /dev/sdb1
  Physical volume "/dev/sdb1" successfully created
[root@RHEL5 ~]# pvcreate /dev/sdc
  Physical volume "/dev/sdc" successfully created
[root@RHEL5 ~]# vgcreate vg2 /dev/sdb1 /dev/sdc
  Volume group "vg2" successfully created
```

You can use **pvdisplay** to verify that both the disk and the partition belong to the volume group.

```
[root@RHEL5 ~]# pvdisplay | grep -B1 vg2
  PV Name               /dev/sdb1
  VG Name               vg2
  --
  PV Name               /dev/sdc
  VG Name               vg2
```

And you are familiar both with the **lvcreate** command to create a small logical volume and the **mke2fs** command to put ext3 on it.

```
[root@RHEL5 ~]# lvcreate --size 200m vg2
  Logical volume "lvol0" created
[root@RHEL5 ~]# mke2fs -m20 -j /dev/vg2/lvol0
...
```

As you see, we end up with a mounted logical volume that according to **df** is almost 200 megabyte in size.

```
[root@RHEL5 ~]# mkdir /home/resizetest
[root@RHEL5 ~]# mount /dev/vg2/lvol0 /home/resizetest/
[root@RHEL5 ~]# df -h | grep resizetest
                 194M  5.6M  149M   4% /home/resizetest
```

Extending the volume is easy with **lvextend**.

```
[root@RHEL5 ~]# lvextend -L +100 /dev/vg2/lvol0
  Extending logical volume lvol0 to 300.00 MB
  Logical volume lvol0 successfully resized
```

But as you can see, there is a small problem: it appears that df is not able to display the extended volume in its full size. This is because the filesystem is only set for the size of the volume before the extension was added.

```
[root@RHEL5 ~]# df -h | grep resizetest
                 194M  5.6M  149M   4% /home/resizetest
```

With **lvdisplay** however we can see that the volume is indeed extended.

```
[root@RHEL5 ~]# lvdisplay /dev/vg2/lvol0 | grep Size
  LV Size              300.00 MB
```

To finish the extension, you need **resize2fs** to span the filesystem over the full size of the logical volume.

```
[root@RHEL5 ~]# resize2fs /dev/vg2/lvol0
resize2fs 1.39 (29-May-2006)
Filesystem at /dev/vg2/lvol0 is mounted on /home/resizetest; on-line re\
sizing required
Performing an on-line resize of /dev/vg2/lvol0 to 307200 (1k) blocks.
The filesystem on /dev/vg2/lvol0 is now 307200 blocks long.
```

Congratulations, you just successfully expanded a logical volume.

```
[root@RHEL5 ~]# df -h | grep resizetest
                 291M  6.1M  225M   3% /home/resizetest
[root@RHEL5 ~]#
```

12.5. example: resize a physical Volume

This is a humble demonstration of how to resize a physical Volume with lvm (after you resize it with fdisk). The demonstration starts with a 100MB partition named /dev/sde1. We used fdisk to create it, and to verify the size.

```
[root@RHEL5 ~]# fdisk -l 2>/dev/null | grep sde1
/dev/sde1               1         100      102384   83  Linux
[root@RHEL5 ~]#
```

Now we can use pvcreate to create the Physical Volume, followed by pvs to verify the creation.

```
[root@RHEL5 ~]# pvcreate /dev/sde1
  Physical volume "/dev/sde1" successfully created
[root@RHEL5 ~]# pvs | grep sde1
  /dev/sde1             lvm2 --    99.98M  99.98M
[root@RHEL5 ~]#
```

The next step is to use fdisk to enlarge the partition (actually deleting it and then recreating /dev/sde1 with more cylinders).

```
[root@RHEL5 ~]# fdisk /dev/sde

Command (m for help): p

Disk /dev/sde: 858 MB, 858993152 bytes
64 heads, 32 sectors/track, 819 cylinders
Units = cylinders of 2048 * 512 = 1048576 bytes

   Device Boot      Start         End      Blocks   Id  System
/dev/sde1               1         100      102384   83  Linux

Command (m for help): d
Selected partition 1

Command (m for help): n
Command action
   e   extended
   p   primary partition (1-4)
p
Partition number (1-4):
Value out of range.
Partition number (1-4): 1
First cylinder (1-819, default 1):
Using default value 1
Last cylinder or +size or +sizeM or +sizeK (1-819, default 819): 200

Command (m for help): w
The partition table has been altered!

Calling ioctl() to re-read partition table.
Syncing disks.
[root@RHEL5 ~]#
```

111

When we now use fdisk and pvs to verify the size of the partition and the Physical Volume, then there is a size difference. LVM is still using the old size.

```
[root@RHEL5 ~]# fdisk -1 2>/dev/null | grep sde1
/dev/sde1               1         200       204784     83  Linux
[root@RHEL5 ~]# pvs | grep sde1
  /dev/sde1             lvm2 --     99.98M  99.98M
[root@RHEL5 ~]#
```

Executing pvresize on the Physical Volume will make lvm aware of the size change of the partition. The correct size can be displayed with pvs.

```
[root@RHEL5 ~]# pvresize /dev/sde1
  Physical volume "/dev/sde1" changed
  1 physical volume(s) resized / 0 physical volume(s) not resized
[root@RHEL5 ~]# pvs | grep sde1
  /dev/sde1             lvm2 --    199.98M 199.98M
[root@RHEL5 ~]#
```

12.6. example: mirror a logical volume

We start by creating three physical volumes for lvm. Then we verify the creation and the size with pvs. Three physical disks because lvm uses two disks for the mirror and a third disk for the mirror log!

```
[root@RHEL5 ~]# pvcreate /dev/sdb /dev/sdc /dev/sdd
  Physical volume "/dev/sdb" successfully created
  Physical volume "/dev/sdc" successfully created
  Physical volume "/dev/sdd" successfully created
[root@RHEL5 ~]# pvs
  PV         VG         Fmt  Attr PSize   PFree
  /dev/sdb              lvm2 --   409.60M 409.60M
  /dev/sdc              lvm2 --   409.60M 409.60M
  /dev/sdd              lvm2 --   409.60M 409.60M
```

Then we create the Volume Group and verify again with pvs. Notice how the three physical volumes now belong to vg33, and how the size is rounded down (in steps of the extent size, here 4MB).

```
[root@RHEL5 ~]# vgcreate vg33 /dev/sdb /dev/sdc /dev/sdd
  Volume group "vg33" successfully created
[root@RHEL5 ~]# pvs
  PV         VG         Fmt  Attr PSize   PFree
  /dev/sda2  VolGroup00 lvm2 a-    15.88G       0
  /dev/sdb   vg33       lvm2 a-   408.00M 408.00M
  /dev/sdc   vg33       lvm2 a-   408.00M 408.00M
  /dev/sdd   vg33       lvm2 a-   408.00M 408.00M
[root@RHEL5 ~]#
```

The last step is to create the Logical Volume with **lvcreate**. Notice the **-m 1** switch to create one mirror. Notice also the change in free space in all three Physical Volumes!

```
[root@RHEL5 ~]# lvcreate --size 300m -n lvmir -m 1 vg33
  Logical volume "lvmir" created
[root@RHEL5 ~]# pvs
  PV         VG         Fmt  Attr PSize   PFree
  /dev/sda2  VolGroup00 lvm2 a-    15.88G       0
  /dev/sdb   vg33       lvm2 a-   408.00M 108.00M
  /dev/sdc   vg33       lvm2 a-   408.00M 108.00M
  /dev/sdd   vg33       lvm2 a-   408.00M 404.00M
```

You can see the copy status of the mirror with lvs. It currently shows a 100 percent copy.

```
[root@RHEL5 ~]# lvs vg33/lvmir
  LV    VG   Attr   LSize   Origin Snap% Move Log        Copy%
  lvmir vg33 mwi-ao 300.00M                   lvmir_mlog 100.00
```

12.7. example: snapshot a logical volume

A snapshot is a virtual copy of all the data at a point in time on a volume. A snapshot Logical Volume will retain a copy of all changed files of the snapshotted Logical Volume.

The example below creates a snapshot of the bigLV Logical Volume.

```
[root@RHEL5 ~]# lvcreate -L100M -s -n snapLV vg42/bigLV
  Logical volume "snapLV" created
[root@RHEL5 ~]#
```

You can see with lvs that the snapshot snapLV is indeed a snapshot of bigLV. Moments after taking the snapshot, there are few changes to bigLV (0.02 percent).

```
[root@RHEL5 ~]# lvs
  LV        VG         Attr    LSize    Origin Snap% Move Log Copy%
  bigLV     vg42       owi-a- 200.00M
  snapLV    vg42       swi-a- 100.00M bigLV   0.02
[root@RHEL5 ~]#
```

But after using bigLV for a while, more changes are done. This means the snapshot volume has to keep more original data (10.22 percent).

```
[root@RHEL5 ~]# lvs | grep vg42
  bigLV     vg42       owi-ao 200.00M
  snapLV    vg42       swi-a- 100.00M bigLV   10.22
[root@RHEL5 ~]#
```

You can now use regular backup tools (dump, tar, cpio, ...) to take a backup of the snapshot Logical Volume. This backup will contain all data as it existed on bigLV at the time the snapshot was taken. When the backup is done, you can remove the snapshot.

```
[root@RHEL5 ~]# lvremove vg42/snapLV
Do you really want to remove active logical volume "snapLV"? [y/n]: y
  Logical volume "snapLV" successfully removed
[root@RHEL5 ~]#
```

12.8. verifying existing physical volumes

12.8.1. lvmdiskscan

To get a list of block devices that can be used with LVM, use **lvmdiskscan**. The example below uses grep to limit the result to SCSI devices.

```
[root@RHEL5 ~]# lvmdiskscan | grep sd
  /dev/sda1                    [      101.94 MB]
  /dev/sda2                    [       15.90 GB] LVM physical volume
  /dev/sdb                     [      409.60 MB]
  /dev/sdc                     [      409.60 MB]
  /dev/sdd                     [      409.60 MB] LVM physical volume
  /dev/sde1                    [       95.98 MB]
  /dev/sde5                    [      191.98 MB]
  /dev/sdf                     [      819.20 MB] LVM physical volume
  /dev/sdg1                    [      818.98 MB]
[root@RHEL5 ~]#
```

12.8.2. pvs

The easiest way to verify whether devices are known to lvm is with the **pvs** command. The screenshot below shows that only /dev/sda2 is currently known for use with LVM. It shows that /dev/sda2 is part of Volgroup00 and is almost 16GB in size. It also shows /dev/sdc and /dev/sdd as part of vg33. The device /dev/sdb is knwon to lvm, but not linked to any Volume Group.

```
[root@RHEL5 ~]# pvs
  PV           VG         Fmt  Attr PSize    PFree
  /dev/sda2    VolGroup00 lvm2 a-    15.88G        0
  /dev/sdb                lvm2 --   409.60M 409.60M
  /dev/sdc     vg33       lvm2 a-   408.00M 408.00M
  /dev/sdd     vg33       lvm2 a-   408.00M 408.00M
[root@RHEL5 ~]#
```

12.8.3. pvscan

The **pvscan** command will scan all disks for existing Physical Volumes. The information is similar to pvs, plus you get a line with total sizes.

```
[root@RHEL5 ~]# pvscan
  PV /dev/sdc   VG vg33        lvm2 [408.00 MB / 408.00 MB free]
  PV /dev/sdd   VG vg33        lvm2 [408.00 MB / 408.00 MB free]
  PV /dev/sda2  VG VolGroup00  lvm2 [15.88 GB / 0     free]
  PV /dev/sdb                  lvm2 [409.60 MB]
  Total: 4 [17.07 GB] / in use: 3 [16.67 GB] / in no VG: 1 [409.60 MB]
[root@RHEL5 ~]#
```

12.8.4. pvdisplay

Use **pvdisplay** to get more information about physical volumes. You can also use **pvdisplay** without an argument to display information about all physical (lvm) volumes.

```
[root@RHEL5 ~]# pvdisplay /dev/sda2
  --- Physical volume ---
  PV Name               /dev/sda2
  VG Name               VolGroup00
  PV Size               15.90 GB / not usable 20.79 MB
  Allocatable           yes (but full)
  PE Size (KByte)       32768
  Total PE              508
  Free PE               0
  Allocated PE          508
  PV UUID               TobYfp-Ggg0-Rf8r-xtLd-5XgN-RSPc-8vkTHD

[root@RHEL5 ~]#
```

12.9. verifying existing volume groups

12.9.1. vgs

Similar to **pvs** is the use of **vgs** to display a quick overview of all volume groups. There is only one volume group in the screenshot below, it is named VolGroup00 and is almost 16GB in size.

```
[root@RHEL5 ~]# vgs
  VG         #PV #LV #SN Attr   VSize   VFree
  VolGroup00   1   2   0 wz--n- 15.88G    0
[root@RHEL5 ~]#
```

12.9.2. vgscan

The **vgscan** command will scan all disks for existing Volume Groups. It will also update the **/etc/lvm/.cache** file. This file contains a list of all current lvm devices.

```
[root@RHEL5 ~]# vgscan
  Reading all physical volumes.  This may take a while...
  Found volume group "VolGroup00" using metadata type lvm2
[root@RHEL5 ~]#
```

LVM will run the vgscan automatically at boot-up, so if you add hot swap devices, then you will need to run vgscan to update /etc/lvm/.cache with the new devices.

12.9.3. vgdisplay

The **vgdisplay** command will give you more detailed information about a volume group (or about all volume groups if you omit the argument).

```
[root@RHEL5 ~]# vgdisplay VolGroup00
  --- Volume group ---
  VG Name               VolGroup00
  System ID
  Format                lvm2
  Metadata Areas        1
  Metadata Sequence No  3
  VG Access             read/write
  VG Status             resizable
  MAX LV                0
  Cur LV                2
  Open LV               2
  Max PV                0
  Cur PV                1
  Act PV                1
  VG Size               15.88 GB
  PE Size               32.00 MB
  Total PE              508
  Alloc PE / Size       508 / 15.88 GB
  Free  PE / Size       0 / 0
  VG UUID               qsXvJb-71qV-917U-ishX-FobM-qptE-VXmKIg

[root@RHEL5 ~]#
```

12.10. verifying existing logical volumes

12.10.1. lvs

Use **lvs** for a quick look at all existing logical volumes. Below you can see two logical volumes named LogVol00 and LogVol01.

```
[root@RHEL5 ~]# lvs
  LV       VG         Attr   LSize  Origin Snap%  Move Log Copy%
  LogVol00 VolGroup00 -wi-ao 14.88G
  LogVol01 VolGroup00 -wi-ao  1.00G
[root@RHEL5 ~]#
```

12.10.2. lvscan

The **lvscan** command will scan all disks for existing Logical Volumes.

```
[root@RHEL5 ~]# lvscan
  ACTIVE               '/dev/VolGroup00/LogVol00' [14.88 GB] inherit
  ACTIVE               '/dev/VolGroup00/LogVol01' [1.00 GB] inherit
[root@RHEL5 ~]#
```

12.10.3. lvdisplay

More detailed information about logical volumes is available through the **lvdisplay(1)** command.

```
[root@RHEL5 ~]# lvdisplay VolGroup00/LogVol01
  --- Logical volume ---
  LV Name                /dev/VolGroup00/LogVol01
  VG Name                VolGroup00
  LV UUID                RnTGK6-xWsi-t530-ksJx-7cax-co5c-A1KlDp
  LV Write Access        read/write
  LV Status              available
  # open                 1
  LV Size                1.00 GB
  Current LE             32
  Segments               1
  Allocation             inherit
  Read ahead sectors     0
  Block device           253:1

[root@RHEL5 ~]#
```

12.11. manage physical volumes

12.11.1. pvcreate

Use the **pvcreate** command to add devices to lvm. This example shows how to add a disk (or hardware RAID device) to lvm.

```
[root@RHEL5 ~]# pvcreate /dev/sdb
  Physical volume "/dev/sdb" successfully created
[root@RHEL5 ~]#
```

This example shows how to add a partition to lvm.

```
[root@RHEL5 ~]# pvcreate /dev/sdc1
  Physical volume "/dev/sdc1" successfully created
[root@RHEL5 ~]#
```

You can also add multiple disks or partitions as target to pvcreate. This example adds three disks to lvm.

```
[root@RHEL5 ~]# pvcreate /dev/sde /dev/sdf /dev/sdg
  Physical volume "/dev/sde" successfully created
  Physical volume "/dev/sdf" successfully created
  Physical volume "/dev/sdg" successfully created
[root@RHEL5 ~]#
```

12.11.2. pvremove

Use the **pvremove** command to remove physical volumes from lvm. The devices may not be in use.

```
[root@RHEL5 ~]# pvremove /dev/sde /dev/sdf /dev/sdg
  Labels on physical volume "/dev/sde" successfully wiped
  Labels on physical volume "/dev/sdf" successfully wiped
  Labels on physical volume "/dev/sdg" successfully wiped
[root@RHEL5 ~]#
```

12.11.3. pvresize

When you used fdisk to resize a partition on a disk, then you must use **pvresize** to make lvm recognize the new size of the physical volume that represents this partition.

```
[root@RHEL5 ~]# pvresize /dev/sde1
  Physical volume "/dev/sde1" changed
  1 physical volume(s) resized / 0 physical volume(s) not resized
```

12.11.4. pvchange

With **pvchange** you can prevent the allocation of a Physical Volume in a new Volume Group or Logical Volume. This can be useful if you plan to remove a Physical Volume.

```
[root@RHEL5 ~]# pvchange -xn /dev/sdd
  Physical volume "/dev/sdd" changed
  1 physical volume changed / 0 physical volumes not changed
[root@RHEL5 ~]#
```

To revert your previous decision, this example shows you how te re-enable the Physical Volume to allow allocation.

```
[root@RHEL5 ~]# pvchange -xy /dev/sdd
  Physical volume "/dev/sdd" changed
  1 physical volume changed / 0 physical volumes not changed
[root@RHEL5 ~]#
```

12.11.5. pvmove

With **pvmove** you can move Logical Volumes from within a Volume Group to another Physical Volume. This must be done before removing a Physical Volume.

```
[root@RHEL5 ~]# pvs | grep vg1
  /dev/sdf    vg1         lvm2 a-   816.00M      0
  /dev/sdg    vg1         lvm2 a-   816.00M 816.00M
[root@RHEL5 ~]# pvmove /dev/sdf
  /dev/sdf: Moved: 70.1%
  /dev/sdf: Moved: 100.0%
[root@RHEL5 ~]# pvs | grep vg1
  /dev/sdf    vg1         lvm2 a-   816.00M 816.00M
  /dev/sdg    vg1         lvm2 a-   816.00M      0
```

12.12. manage volume groups

12.12.1. vgcreate

Use the **vgcreate** command to create a volume group. You can immediately name all the physical volumes that span the volume group.

```
[root@RHEL5 ~]# vgcreate vg42 /dev/sde /dev/sdf
  Volume group "vg42" successfully created
[root@RHEL5 ~]#
```

12.12.2. vgextend

Use the **vgextend** command to extend an existing volume group with a physical volume.

```
[root@RHEL5 ~]# vgextend vg42 /dev/sdg
  Volume group "vg42" successfully extended
[root@RHEL5 ~]#
```

12.12.3. vgremove

Use the **vgremove** command to remove volume groups from lvm. The volume groups may not be in use.

```
[root@RHEL5 ~]# vgremove vg42
  Volume group "vg42" successfully removed
[root@RHEL5 ~]#
```

12.12.4. vgreduce

Use the **vgreduce** command to remove a Physical Volume from the Volume Group.

The following example adds Physical Volume /dev/sdg to the vg1 Volume Group using vgextend. And then removes it again using vgreduce.

```
[root@RHEL5 ~]# pvs | grep sdg
  /dev/sdg                 lvm2 --   819.20M 819.20M
[root@RHEL5 ~]# vgextend vg1 /dev/sdg
  Volume group "vg1" successfully extended
[root@RHEL5 ~]# pvs | grep sdg
  /dev/sdg   vg1         lvm2 a-   816.00M 816.00M
[root@RHEL5 ~]# vgreduce vg1 /dev/sdg
  Removed "/dev/sdg" from volume group "vg1"
[root@RHEL5 ~]# pvs | grep sdg
  /dev/sdg                 lvm2 --   819.20M 819.20M
```

12.12.5. vgchange

Use the **vgchange** command to change parameters of a Volume Group.

This example shows how to prevent Physical Volumes from being added or removed to the Volume Group vg1.

```
[root@RHEL5 ~]# vgchange -xn vg1
  Volume group "vg1" successfully changed
[root@RHEL5 ~]# vgextend vg1 /dev/sdg
  Volume group vg1 is not resizable.
```

You can also use vgchange to change most other properties of a Volume Group. This example changes the maximum number of Logical Volumes and maximum number of Physical Volumes that vg1 can serve.

```
[root@RHEL5 ~]# vgdisplay vg1 | grep -i max
  MAX LV                 0
  Max PV                 0
[root@RHEL5 ~]# vgchange -l16 vg1
  Volume group "vg1" successfully changed
[root@RHEL5 ~]# vgchange -p8 vg1
  Volume group "vg1" successfully changed
[root@RHEL5 ~]# vgdisplay vg1 | grep -i max
  MAX LV                 16
  Max PV                 8
```

12.12.6. vgmerge

Merging two Volume Groups into one is done with **vgmerge**. The following example merges vg2 into vg1, keeping all the properties of vg1.

```
[root@RHEL5 ~]# vgmerge vg1 vg2
  Volume group "vg2" successfully merged into "vg1"
[root@RHEL5 ~]#
```

12.13. manage logical volumes

12.13.1. lvcreate

Use the **lvcreate** command to create Logical Volumes in a Volume Group. This example creates an 8GB Logical Volume in Volume Group vg42.

```
[root@RHEL5 ~]# lvcreate -L5G vg42
  Logical volume "lvol0" created
[root@RHEL5 ~]#
```

As you can see, lvm automatically names the Logical Volume **lvol0**. The next example creates a 200MB Logical Volume named MyLV in Volume Group vg42.

```
[root@RHEL5 ~]# lvcreate -L200M -nMyLV vg42
  Logical volume "MyLV" created
[root@RHEL5 ~]#
```

The next example does the same thing, but with different syntax.

```
[root@RHEL5 ~]# lvcreate --size 200M -n MyLV vg42
  Logical volume "MyLV" created
[root@RHEL5 ~]#
```

This example creates a Logical Volume that occupies 10 percent of the Volume Group.

```
[root@RHEL5 ~]# lvcreate -l 10%VG -n MyLV2 vg42
  Logical volume "MyLV2" created
[root@RHEL5 ~]#
```

This example creates a Logical Volume that occupies 30 percent of the remaining free space in the Volume Group.

```
[root@RHEL5 ~]# lvcreate -l 30%FREE -n MyLV3 vg42
  Logical volume "MyLV3" created
[root@RHEL5 ~]#
```

12.13.2. lvremove

Use the **lvremove** command to remove Logical Volumes from a Volume Group. Removing a Logical Volume requires the name of the Volume Group.

```
[root@RHEL5 ~]# lvremove vg42/MyLV
Do you really want to remove active logical volume "MyLV"? [y/n]: y
  Logical volume "MyLV" successfully removed
[root@RHEL5 ~]#
```

Removing multiple Logical Volumes will request confirmation for each individual volume.

```
[root@RHEL5 ~]# lvremove vg42/MyLV vg42/MyLV2 vg42/MyLV3
Do you really want to remove active logical volume "MyLV"? [y/n]: y
  Logical volume "MyLV" successfully removed
Do you really want to remove active logical volume "MyLV2"? [y/n]: y
  Logical volume "MyLV2" successfully removed
Do you really want to remove active logical volume "MyLV3"? [y/n]: y
  Logical volume "MyLV3" successfully removed
[root@RHEL5 ~]#
```

12.13.3. lvextend

Extending the volume is easy with **lvextend**. This example extends a 200MB Logical Volume with 100 MB.

```
[root@RHEL5 ~]# lvdisplay /dev/vg2/lvol0 | grep Size
  LV Size                200.00 MB
[root@RHEL5 ~]# lvextend -L +100 /dev/vg2/lvol0
  Extending logical volume lvol0 to 300.00 MB
  Logical volume lvol0 successfully resized
[root@RHEL5 ~]# lvdisplay /dev/vg2/lvol0 | grep Size
  LV Size                300.00 MB
```

The next example creates a 100MB Logical Volume, and then extends it to 500MB.

```
[root@RHEL5 ~]# lvcreate --size 100M -n extLV vg42
  Logical volume "extLV" created
[root@RHEL5 ~]# lvextend -L 500M vg42/extLV
  Extending logical volume extLV to 500.00 MB
  Logical volume extLV successfully resized
[root@RHEL5 ~]#
```

This example doubles the size of a Logical Volume.

```
[root@RHEL5 ~]# lvextend -l+100%LV vg42/extLV
  Extending logical volume extLV to 1000.00 MB
  Logical volume extLV successfully resized
[root@RHEL5 ~]#
```

12.13.4. lvrename

Renaming a Logical Volume is done with **lvrename**. This example renames extLV to bigLV in the vg42 Volume Group.

```
[root@RHEL5 ~]# lvrename vg42/extLV vg42/bigLV
  Renamed "extLV" to "bigLV" in volume group "vg42"
[root@RHEL5 ~]#
```

12.14. practice : lvm

1. Create a volume group that contains a complete disk and a partition on another disk.

2. Create two logical volumes (a small one and a bigger one) in this volumegroup. Format them wih ext3, mount them and copy some files to them.

3. Verify usage with fdisk, mount, pvs, vgs, lvs, pvdisplay, vgdisplay, lvdisplay and df. Does fdisk give you any information about lvm?

4. Enlarge the small logical volume by 50 percent, and verify your work!

5. Take a look at other commands that start with vg* , pv* or lv*.

6. Create a mirror and a striped Logical Volume.

7. Convert a linear logical volume to a mirror.

8. Convert a mirror logical volume to a linear.

9. Create a snapshot of a Logical Volume, take a backup of the snapshot. Then delete some files on the Logical Volume, then restore your backup.

10. Move your volume group to another disk (keep the Logical Volumes mounted).

11. If time permits, split a Volume Group with vgsplit, then merge it again with vgmerge.

12.15. solution : lvm

1. Create a volume group that contains a complete disk and a partition on another disk.

step 1: select disks:

```
root@rhel65:~# fdisk -l | grep Disk
Disk /dev/sda: 8589 MB, 8589934592 bytes
Disk identifier: 0x00055ca0
Disk /dev/sdb: 1073 MB, 1073741824 bytes
Disk identifier: 0x00000000
Disk /dev/sdc: 1073 MB, 1073741824 bytes
Disk identifier: 0x00000000
...
```

I choose /dev/sdb and /dev/sdc for now.

step 2: partition /dev/sdc

```
root@rhel65:~# fdisk /dev/sdc
Device contains neither a valid DOS partition table, nor Sun, SGI or OSF disk\
label
Building a new DOS disklabel with disk identifier 0x94c0e5d5.
Changes will remain in memory only, until you decide to write them.
After that, of course, the previous content won't be recoverable.

Warning: invalid flag 0x0000 of partition table 4 will be corrected by w(rite)

WARNING: DOS-compatible mode is deprecated. It's strongly recommended to
         switch off the mode (command 'c') and change display units to
         sectors (command 'u').

Command (m for help): n
Command action
   e   extended
   p   primary partition (1-4)
p
Partition number (1-4): 1
First cylinder (1-130, default 1):
Using default value 1
Last cylinder, +cylinders or +size{K,M,G} (1-130, default 130):
Using default value 130

Command (m for help): w
The partition table has been altered!

Calling ioctl() to re-read partition table.
Syncing disks.
```

step 3: pvcreate and vgcreate

```
root@rhel65:~# pvcreate /dev/sdb /dev/sdc1
  Physical volume "/dev/sdb" successfully created
  Physical volume "/dev/sdc1" successfully created
root@rhel65:~# vgcreate VG42 /dev/sdb /dev/sdc1
  Volume group "VG42" successfully created
```

2. Create two logical volumes (a small one and a bigger one) in this volumegroup. Format them wih ext3, mount them and copy some files to them.

```
root@rhel65:~# lvcreate --size 200m --name LVsmall VG42
  Logical volume "LVsmall" created
root@rhel65:~# lvcreate --size 600m --name LVbig VG42
  Logical volume "LVbig" created
root@rhel65:~# ls -l /dev/mapper/VG42-LVsmall
lrwxrwxrwx. 1 root root 7 Apr 20 20:41 /dev/mapper/VG42-LVsmall -> ../dm-2
root@rhel65:~# ls -l /dev/VG42/LVsmall
lrwxrwxrwx. 1 root root 7 Apr 20 20:41 /dev/VG42/LVsmall -> ../dm-2
root@rhel65:~# ls -l /dev/dm-2
brw-rw----. 1 root disk 253, 2 Apr 20 20:41 /dev/dm-2

root@rhel65:~# mkfs.ext3 /dev/mapper/VG42-LVsmall
mke2fs 1.41.12 (17-May-2010)
Filesystem label=
OS type: Linux
Block size=1024 (log=0)
Fragment size=1024 (log=0)
Stride=0 blocks, Stripe width=0 blocks
51200 inodes, 204800 blocks
10240 blocks (5.00%) reserved for the super user
First data block=1
Maximum filesystem blocks=67371008
25 block groups
8192 blocks per group, 8192 fragments per group
2048 inodes per group
Superblock backups stored on blocks:
 8193, 24577, 40961, 57345, 73729

Writing inode tables: done
Creating journal (4096 blocks): done
Writing superblocks and filesystem accounting information: done

This filesystem will be automatically checked every 39 mounts or
180 days, whichever comes first.  Use tune2fs -c or -i to override.

root@rhel65:~# mkfs.ext3 /dev/VG42/LVbig
mke2fs 1.41.12 (17-May-2010)
Filesystem label=
OS type: Linux
Block size=4096 (log=2)
Fragment size=4096 (log=2)
Stride=0 blocks, Stripe width=0 blocks
38400 inodes, 153600 blocks
7680 blocks (5.00%) reserved for the super user
First data block=0
Maximum filesystem blocks=159383552
5 block groups
32768 blocks per group, 32768 fragments per group
7680 inodes per group
Superblock backups stored on blocks:
 32768, 98304

Writing inode tables: done
Creating journal (4096 blocks): done
Writing superblocks and filesystem accounting information: done

This filesystem will be automatically checked every 25 mounts or
180 days, whichever comes first.  Use tune2fs -c or -i to override.
```

The mounting and copying of files.

```
root@rhel65:~# mkdir /srv/LVsmall
root@rhel65:~# mkdir /srv/LVbig
root@rhel65:~# mount /dev/mapper/VG42-LVsmall /srv/LVsmall
root@rhel65:~# mount /dev/VG42/LVbig /srv/LVbig
root@rhel65:~# cp -r /etc /srv/LVsmall/
root@rhel65:~# cp -r /var/log /srv/LVbig/
```

3. Verify usage with fdisk, mount, pvs, vgs, lvs, pvdisplay, vgdisplay, lvdisplay and df. Does fdisk give you any information about lvm?

Run all those commands (only two are shown below), then answer 'no'.

```
root@rhel65:~# df -h
Filesystem            Size  Used Avail Use% Mounted on
/dev/mapper/VolGroup-lv_root
                      6.7G  1.4G  5.0G  21% /
tmpfs                 246M     0  246M   0% /dev/shm
/dev/sda1             485M   77M  383M  17% /boot
/dev/mapper/VG42-LVsmall
                      194M   30M  154M  17% /srv/LVsmall
/dev/mapper/VG42-LVbig
                      591M   20M  541M   4% /srv/LVbig
root@rhel65:~# mount | grep VG42
/dev/mapper/VG42-LVsmall on /srv/LVsmall type ext3 (rw)
/dev/mapper/VG42-LVbig on /srv/LVbig type ext3 (rw)
```

4. Enlarge the small logical volume by 50 percent, and verify your work!

```
root@rhel65:~# lvextend VG42/LVsmall -l+50%LV
  Extending logical volume LVsmall to 300.00 MiB
  Logical volume LVsmall successfully resized
root@rhel65:~# resize2fs /dev/mapper/VG42-LVsmall
resize2fs 1.41.12 (17-May-2010)
Filesystem at /dev/mapper/VG42-LVsmall is mounted on /srv/LVsmall; on-line res\
izing required
old desc_blocks = 1, new_desc_blocks = 2
Performing an on-line resize of /dev/mapper/VG42-LVsmall to 307200 (1k) blocks.
The filesystem on /dev/mapper/VG42-LVsmall is now 307200 blocks long.

root@rhel65:~# df -h | grep small
/dev/mapper/VG42-LVsmall
                      291M   31M  246M  12% /srv/LVsmall
root@rhel65:~#
```

5. Take a look at other commands that start with vg* , pv* or lv*.

6. Create a mirror and a striped Logical Volume.

7. Convert a linear logical volume to a mirror.

8. Convert a mirror logical volume to a linear.

9. Create a snapshot of a Logical Volume, take a backup of the snapshot. Then delete some files on the Logical Volume, then restore your backup.

10. Move your volume group to another disk (keep the Logical Volumes mounted).

11. If time permits, split a Volume Group with vgsplit, then merge it again with vgmerge.

Chapter 13. iSCSI devices

This chapter teaches you how to setup an **iSCSI target server** and an **iSCSI initiator client**.

13.1. iSCSI terminology

iSCSI is a protocol that enables SCSI over IP. This means that you can have local SCSI devices (like /dev/sdb) without having the storage hardware in the local computer.

The computer holding the physical storage hardware is called the **iSCSI Target**. Each individual addressable iSCSI device on the target server will get a **LUN number**.

The iSCSI client computer that is connecting to the Target server is called an **Initiator**. An initiator will send SCSI commands over IP instead of directly to the hardware. The Initiator will connect to the Target.

13.2. iSCSI Target in RHEL/CentOS

This section will describe iSCSI Target setup on RHEL6, RHEL7 and CentOS.

Start with installing the **iSCSI Target** package.

```
yum install scsi-target-utils
```

We configure three local disks in **/etc/tgt/targets.conf** to become three LUN's.

```
<target iqn.2008-09.com.example:server.target2>
    direct-store /dev/sdb
    direct-store /dev/sdc
    direct-store /dev/sdd
    incominguser paul hunter2
</target>
```

Restart the service.

```
[root@centos65 ~]# service tgtd start
Starting SCSI target daemon:                               [  OK  ]
```

The standard local port for iSCSI Target is 3260, in case of doubt you can verify this with **netstat**.

```
[root@server1 tgt]# netstat -ntpl | grep tgt
tcp    0    0 0.0.0.0:3260      0.0.0.0:*          LISTEN      1670/tgtd
tcp    0    0 :::3260           :::*               LISTEN      1670/tgtd
```

The **tgt-admin -s** command should now give you a nice overview of the three LUN's (and also LUN 0 for the controller).

```
[root@server1 tgt]# tgt-admin -s
Target 1: iqn.2014-04.be.linux-training:server1.target1
    System information:
        Driver: iscsi
        State: ready
    I_T nexus information:
    LUN information:
        LUN: 0
            Type: controller
            SCSI ID: IET      00010000
            SCSI SN: beaf10
            Size: 0 MB, Block size: 1
            Online: Yes
            Removable media: No
            Prevent removal: No
            Readonly: No
            Backing store type: null
            Backing store path: None
            Backing store flags:
        LUN: 1
            Type: disk
            SCSI ID: IET      00010001
            SCSI SN: VB9f23197b-af6cfb60
            Size: 1074 MB, Block size: 512
            Online: Yes
            Removable media: No
            Prevent removal: No
            Readonly: No
            Backing store type: rdwr
            Backing store path: /dev/sdb
            Backing store flags:
        LUN: 2
            Type: disk
            SCSI ID: IET      00010002
            SCSI SN: VB8f554351-a1410828
            Size: 1074 MB, Block size: 512
            Online: Yes
            Removable media: No
            Prevent removal: No
            Readonly: No
            Backing store type: rdwr
            Backing store path: /dev/sdc
            Backing store flags:
        LUN: 3
            Type: disk
            SCSI ID: IET      00010003
            SCSI SN: VB1035d2f0-7ae90b49
            Size: 1074 MB, Block size: 512
            Online: Yes
            Removable media: No
            Prevent removal: No
            Readonly: No
            Backing store type: rdwr
            Backing store path: /dev/sdd
            Backing store flags:
    Account information:
    ACL information:
        ALL
```

13.3. iSCSI Initiator in RHEL/CentOS

This section will describe iSCSI Initiator setup on RHEL6, RHEL7 and CentOS.

Start with installing the **iSCSI Initiator** package.

```
[root@server2 ~]# yum install iscsi-initiator-utils
```

Then ask the **iSCSI target server** to send you the target names.

```
[root@server2 ~]# iscsiadm -m discovery -t sendtargets -p 192.168.1.95:3260
Starting iscsid:                                    [  OK  ]
192.168.1.95:3260,1 iqn.2014-04.be.linux-training:centos65.target1
```

We received **iqn.2014-04.be.linux-training:centos65.target1**.

We use this iqn to configure the username and the password (paul and hunter2) that we set on the target server.

```
[root@server2 iscsi]# iscsiadm -m node --targetname iqn.2014-04.be.linux-tra\
ining:centos65.target1 --portal "192.168.1.95:3260" --op=update --name node.\
session.auth.username --value=paul
[root@server2 iscsi]# iscsiadm -m node --targetname iqn.2014-04.be.linux-tra\
ining:centos65.target1 --portal "192.168.1.95:3260" --op=update --name node.\
session.auth.password --value=hunter2
[root@server2 iscsi]# iscsiadm -m node --targetname iqn.2014-04.be.linux-tra\
ining:centos65.target1 --portal "192.168.1.95:3260" --op=update --name node.\
session.auth.authmethod --value=CHAP
```

RHEL and CentOS will store these in **/var/lib/iscsi/nodes/**.

```
[root@server2 iscsi]# grep auth /var/lib/iscsi/nodes/iqn.2014-04.be.linux-tr\
aining\:centos65.target1/192.168.1.95\,3260\,1/default
node.session.auth.authmethod = CHAP
node.session.auth.username = paul
node.session.auth.password = hunter2
node.conn[0].timeo.auth_timeout = 45
[root@server2 iscsi]#
```

A restart of the **iscsi** service will add three new devices to our system.

```
[root@server2 iscsi]# fdisk -l | grep Disk
Disk /dev/sda: 42.9 GB, 42949672960 bytes
Disk identifier: 0x0004f229
Disk /dev/sdb: 1073 MB, 1073741824 bytes
Disk identifier: 0x00000000
Disk /dev/sdc: 1073 MB, 1073741824 bytes
Disk identifier: 0x00000000
Disk /dev/sdd: 1073 MB, 1073741824 bytes
Disk identifier: 0x00000000
Disk /dev/sde: 2147 MB, 2147483648 bytes
Disk identifier: 0x00000000
Disk /dev/sdf: 2147 MB, 2147483648 bytes
Disk identifier: 0x00000000
Disk /dev/sdg: 2147 MB, 2147483648 bytes
Disk identifier: 0x00000000
Disk /dev/mapper/VolGroup-lv_root: 41.4 GB, 41448112128 bytes
Disk identifier: 0x00000000
Disk /dev/mapper/VolGroup-lv_swap: 973 MB, 973078528 bytes
Disk identifier: 0x00000000
[root@server2 iscsi]# service iscsi restart
Stopping iscsi:                                          [  OK  ]
Starting iscsi:                                          [  OK  ]
[root@server2 iscsi]# fdisk -l | grep Disk
Disk /dev/sda: 42.9 GB, 42949672960 bytes
Disk identifier: 0x0004f229
Disk /dev/sdb: 1073 MB, 1073741824 bytes
Disk identifier: 0x00000000
Disk /dev/sdc: 1073 MB, 1073741824 bytes
Disk identifier: 0x00000000
Disk /dev/sdd: 1073 MB, 1073741824 bytes
Disk identifier: 0x00000000
Disk /dev/sde: 2147 MB, 2147483648 bytes
Disk identifier: 0x00000000
Disk /dev/sdf: 2147 MB, 2147483648 bytes
Disk identifier: 0x00000000
Disk /dev/sdg: 2147 MB, 2147483648 bytes
Disk identifier: 0x00000000
Disk /dev/mapper/VolGroup-lv_root: 41.4 GB, 41448112128 bytes
Disk identifier: 0x00000000
Disk /dev/mapper/VolGroup-lv_swap: 973 MB, 973078528 bytes
Disk identifier: 0x00000000
Disk /dev/sdh: 1073 MB, 1073741824 bytes
Disk identifier: 0x00000000
Disk /dev/sdi: 1073 MB, 1073741824 bytes
Disk identifier: 0x00000000
Disk /dev/sdj: 1073 MB, 1073741824 bytes
Disk identifier: 0x00000000
```

You can verify iscsi status with:

```
service iscsi status
```

13.4. iSCSI target on Debian

Installing the software for the target server requires **iscsitarget** on Ubuntu and Debian, and an extra **iscsitarget-dkms** for the kernel modules only on Debian.

```
root@debby6:~# aptitude install iscsitarget
The following NEW packages will be installed:
  iscsitarget
0 packages upgraded, 1 newly installed, 0 to remove and 0 not upgraded.
Need to get 69.4 kB of archives. After unpacking 262 kB will be used.
Get:1 http://ftp.belnet.be/debian/ squeeze/main iscsitarget i386 1.4.20.2-1\
 [69.4 kB]
Fetched 69.4 kB in 0s (415 kB/s)
Selecting previously deselected package iscsitarget.
(Reading database ... 36441 files and directories currently installed.)
Unpacking iscsitarget (from .../iscsitarget_1.4.20.2-1_i386.deb) ...
Processing triggers for man-db ...
Setting up iscsitarget (1.4.20.2-1) ...
iscsitarget not enabled in "/etc/default/iscsitarget", not starting...(warning).
```

On Debian 6 you will also need **aptitude install iscsitarget-dkms** for the kernel modules, on Debian 5 this is **aptitude install iscsitarget-modules-`uname -a`**. Ubuntu includes the kernel modules in the main package.

The iSCSI target server is disabled by default, so we enable it.

```
root@debby6:~# cat /etc/default/iscsitarget
ISCSITARGET_ENABLE=false
root@debby6:~# vi /etc/default/iscsitarget
root@debby6:~# cat /etc/default/iscsitarget
ISCSITARGET_ENABLE=true
```

13.5. iSCSI target setup with dd files

You can use LVM volumes (/dev/md0/lvol0), physical partitions (/dev/sda) ,raid devices (/dev/md0) or just plain files for storage. In this demo, we use files created with **dd**.

This screenshot shows how to create three small files (100MB, 200MB and 300MB).

```
root@debby6:~# mkdir /iscsi
root@debby6:~# dd if=/dev/zero of=/iscsi/lun1.img bs=1M count=100
100+0 records in
100+0 records out
104857600 bytes (105 MB) copied, 0.315825 s, 332 MB/s
root@debby6:~# dd if=/dev/zero of=/iscsi/lun2.img bs=1M count=200
200+0 records in
200+0 records out
209715200 bytes (210 MB) copied, 1.08342 s, 194 MB/s
root@debby6:~# dd if=/dev/zero of=/iscsi/lun3.img bs=1M count=300
300+0 records in
300+0 records out
314572800 bytes (315 MB) copied, 1.36209 s, 231 MB/s
```

We need to declare these three files as iSCSI targets in **/etc/iet/ietd.conf** (used to be /etc/ietd.conf).

```
root@debby6:/etc/iet# cp ietd.conf ietd.conf.original
root@debby6:/etc/iet# > ietd.conf
root@debby6:/etc/iet# vi ietd.conf
root@debby6:/etc/iet# cat ietd.conf
Target iqn.2010-02.be.linux-training:storage.lun1
 IncomingUser isuser hunter2
 OutgoingUser
 Lun 0 Path=/iscsi/lun1.img,Type=fileio
 Alias LUN1

Target iqn.2010-02.be.linux-training:storage.lun2
 IncomingUser isuser hunter2
 OutgoingUser
 Lun 0 Path=/iscsi/lun2.img,Type=fileio
 Alias LUN2

Target iqn.2010-02.be.linux-training:storage.lun3
 IncomingUser isuser hunter2
 OutgoingUser
 Lun 0 Path=/iscsi/lun3.img,Type=fileio
 Alias LUN3
```

We also need to add our devices to the **/etc/initiators.allow** file.

```
root@debby6:/etc/iet# cp initiators.allow initiators.allow.original
root@debby6:/etc/iet# >initiators.allow
root@debby6:/etc/iet# vi initiators.allow
root@debby6:/etc/iet# cat initiators.allow
iqn.2010-02.be.linux-training:storage.lun1
iqn.2010-02.be.linux-training:storage.lun2
iqn.2010-02.be.linux-training:storage.lun3
```

Time to start the server now:

```
root@debby6:/etc/iet# /etc/init.d/iscsitarget start
Starting iSCSI enterprise target service:.
.
root@debby6:/etc/iet#
```

Verify activation of the storage devices in **/proc/net/iet**:

```
root@debby6:/etc/iet# cat /proc/net/iet/volume
tid:3 name:iqn.2010-02.be.linux-training:storage.lun3
 lun:0 state:0 iotype:fileio iomode:wt blocks:614400 blocksize:\
512 path:/iscsi/lun3.img
tid:2 name:iqn.2010-02.be.linux-training:storage.lun2
 lun:0 state:0 iotype:fileio iomode:wt blocks:409600 blocksize:\
512 path:/iscsi/lun2.img
tid:1 name:iqn.2010-02.be.linux-training:storage.lun1
 lun:0 state:0 iotype:fileio iomode:wt blocks:204800 blocksize:\
512 path:/iscsi/lun1.img
root@debby6:/etc/iet# cat /proc/net/iet/session
tid:3 name:iqn.2010-02.be.linux-training:storage.lun3
tid:2 name:iqn.2010-02.be.linux-training:storage.lun2
tid:1 name:iqn.2010-02.be.linux-training:storage.lun1
```

13.6. ISCSI initiator on ubuntu

First we install the iSCSi client software (on another computer than the target).

```
root@ubu1104:~# aptitude install open-iscsi
Reading package lists... Done
Building dependency tree
Reading state information... Done
Reading extended state information
Initializing package states... Done
The following NEW packages will be installed:
  open-iscsi open-iscsi-utils{a}
```

Then we set the iSCSI client to start automatically.

```
root@ubu1104:/etc/iscsi# cp iscsid.conf iscsid.conf.original
root@ubu1104:/etc/iscsi# vi iscsid.conf
root@ubu1104:/etc/iscsi# grep ^node.startup iscsid.conf
node.startup = automatic
```

Or you could start it manually.

```
root@ubu1104:/etc/iscsi/nodes# /etc/init.d/open-iscsi start
 * Starting iSCSI initiator service iscsid                        [ OK ]
 * Setting up iSCSI targets                                       [ OK ]
root@ubu1104:/etc/iscsi/nodes#
```

Now we can connect to the Target server and use **iscsiadm** to discover the devices it offers:

```
root@ubu1104:/etc/iscsi# iscsiadm  -m discovery -t st -p 192.168.1.31
192.168.1.31:3260,1 iqn.2010-02.be.linux-training:storage.lun2
192.168.1.31:3260,1 iqn.2010-02.be.linux-training:storage.lun1
192.168.1.31:3260,1 iqn.2010-02.be.linux-training:storage.lun3
```

We can use the same **iscsiadm** to edit the files in **/etc/iscsi/nodes/**.

```
root@ubu1104:/etc/iscsi# iscsiadm -m node --targetname "iqn.2010-02.be.linu\
x-training:storage.lun1" --portal "192.168.1.31:3260" --op=update --name no\
de.session.auth.authmethod --value=CHAP
root@ubu1104:/etc/iscsi# iscsiadm -m node --targetname "iqn.2010-02.be.linu\
x-training:storage.lun1" --portal "192.168.1.31:3260" --op=update --name no\
de.session.auth.username --value=isuser
root@ubu1104:/etc/iscsi# iscsiadm -m node --targetname "iqn.2010-02.be.linu\
x-training:storage.lun1" --portal "192.168.1.31:3260" --op=update --name no\
de.session.auth.password --value=hunter2
```

Repeat the above for the other two devices.

Restart the initiator service to log in to the target.

```
root@ubu1104:/etc/iscsi/nodes# /etc/init.d/open-iscsi restart
 * Disconnecting iSCSI targets                             [ OK ]
 * Stopping iSCSI initiator service                        [ OK ]
 * Starting iSCSI initiator service iscsid                 [ OK ]
 * Setting up iSCSI targets
```

Use **fdisk -l** to enjoy three new iSCSI devices.

```
root@ubu1104:/etc/iscsi/nodes# fdisk -l 2> /dev/null | grep Disk
Disk /dev/sda: 17.2 GB, 17179869184 bytes
Disk identifier: 0x0001983f
Disk /dev/sdb: 209 MB, 209715200 bytes
Disk identifier: 0x00000000
Disk /dev/sdd: 314 MB, 314572800 bytes
Disk identifier: 0x00000000
Disk /dev/sdc: 104 MB, 104857600 bytes
Disk identifier: 0x00000000
```

The Target (the server) now shows active sessions.

```
root@debby6:/etc/iet# cat /proc/net/iet/session
tid:3 name:iqn.2010-02.be.linux-training:storage.lun3
 sid:5348024611832320 initiator:iqn.1993-08.org.debian:01:8983ed2d770
  cid:0 ip:192.168.1.35 state:active hd:none dd:none
tid:2 name:iqn.2010-02.be.linux-training:storage.lun2
 sid:4785074624856576 initiator:iqn.1993-08.org.debian:01:8983ed2d770
  cid:0 ip:192.168.1.35 state:active hd:none dd:none
tid:1 name:iqn.2010-02.be.linux-training:storage.lun1
 sid:5066549618344448 initiator:iqn.1993-08.org.debian:01:8983ed2d770
  cid:0 ip:192.168.1.35 state:active hd:none dd:none
root@debby6:/etc/iet#
```

13.7. using iSCSI devices

There is no difference between using SCSI or iSCSI devices once they are connected : partition, make filesystem, mount.

```
root@ubu1104:/etc/iscsi/nodes# history | tail -13
   94  fdisk /dev/sdc
   95  fdisk /dev/sdd
   96  fdisk /dev/sdb
   97  mke2fs /dev/sdb1
   98  mke2fs -j /dev/sdc1
   99  mkfs.ext4 /dev/sdd1
  100  mkdir /mnt/is1
  101  mkdir /mnt/is2
  102  mkdir /mnt/is3
  103  mount /dev/sdb1 /mnt/is1
  104  mount /dev/sdc1 /mnt/is2
  105  mount /dev/sdd1 /mnt/is3
  106  history | tail -13
root@ubu1104:/etc/iscsi/nodes# mount | grep is
/dev/sdb1 on /mnt/is1 type ext2 (rw)
/dev/sdc1 on /mnt/is2 type ext3 (rw)
/dev/sdd1 on /mnt/is3 type ext4 (rw)
```

13.8. iSCSI Target RHEL7/CentOS7

The prefered tool to setup an iSCSI Target on RHEL is **targetcli**.

```
[root@centos7 ~]# yum install targetcli
Loaded plugins: fastestmirror
...
...
Installed:
  targetcli.noarch 0:2.1.fb37-3.el7

Complete!
[root@centos7 ~]#
```

The **targetcli** tool is interactive and represents the configuration fo the **target** in a structure that resembles a directory tree with several files. Although this is explorable inside **targetcli** with **ls**, **cd** and **pwd**, this are not files on the file system.

This tool also has tab-completion, which is very handy for the **iqn** names.

```
[root@centos7 ~]# targetcli
targetcli shell version 2.1.fb37
Copyright 2011-2013 by Datera, Inc and others.
For help on commands, type 'help'.

/> cd backstores/
/backstores> ls
o- backstores ................................................... [...]
  o- block ............................................. [Storage Objects: 0]
  o- fileio ............................................ [Storage Objects: 0]
  o- pscsi ............................................. [Storage Objects: 0]
  o- ramdisk ........................................... [Storage Objects: 0]
/backstores> cd block
/backstores/block> ls
o- block ............................................. [Storage Objects: 0]
/backstores/block> create server1.disk1 /dev/sdb
Created block storage object server1.disk1 using /dev/sdb.
/backstores/block> ls
o- block ............................................. [Storage Objects: 1]
  o- server1.disk1 .................. [/dev/sdb (2.0GiB) write-thru deactivated]
/backstores/block> cd /iscsi
/iscsi> create iqn.2015-04.be.linux:iscsi1
Created target iqn.2015-04.be.linux:iscsi1.
Created TPG 1.
Global pref auto_add_default_portal=true
Created default portal listening on all IPs (0.0.0.0), port 3260.
/iscsi> cd /iscsi/iqn.2015-04.be.linux:iscsi1/tpg1/acls
/iscsi/iqn.20...si1/tpg1/acls> create iqn.2015-04.be.linux:server2
Created Node ACL for iqn.2015-04.be.linux:server2
/iscsi/iqn.20...si1/tpg1/acls> cd iqn.2015-04.be.linux:server2
/iscsi/iqn.20...linux:server2> set auth userid=paul
Parameter userid is now 'paul'.
/iscsi/iqn.20...linux:server2> set auth password=hunter2
Parameter password is now 'hunter2'.
/iscsi/iqn.20...linux:server2> cd /iscsi/iqn.2015-04.be.linux:iscsi1/tpg1/luns
/iscsi/iqn.20...si1/tpg1/luns> create /backstores/block/server1.disk1
Created LUN 0.
Created LUN 0->0 mapping in node ACL iqn.2015-04.be.linux:server2
s/scsi/iqn.20...si1/tpg1/luns> cd /iscsi/iqn.2015-04.be.linux:iscsi1/tpg1/portals
/iscsi/iqn.20.../tpg1/portals> create 192.168.1.128
Using default IP port 3260
Could not create NetworkPortal in configFS.
```

```
/iscsi/iqn.20.../tpg1/portals> cd /
/> ls
o- / ....................................................... [...]
  o- backstores .............................................. [...]
  | o- block ................................. [Storage Objects: 1]
  | | o- server1.disk1 ............... [/dev/sdb (2.0GiB) write-thru activated]
  | o- fileio ................................ [Storage Objects: 0]
  | o- pscsi ................................. [Storage Objects: 0]
  | o- ramdisk ............................... [Storage Objects: 0]
  o- iscsi ......................................... [Targets: 1]
  | o- iqn.2015-04.be.linux:iscsi1 ...................... [TPGs: 1]
  |   o- tpg1 ............................. [no-gen-acls, no-auth]
  |     o- acls ..................................... [ACLs: 1]
  |     | o- iqn.2015-04.be.linux:server2 ........... [Mapped LUNs: 1]
  |     |   o- mapped_lun0 .............. [lun0 block/server1.disk1 (rw)]
  |     o- luns ..................................... [LUNs: 1]
  |     | o- lun0 ................. [block/server1.disk1 (/dev/sdb)]
  |     o- portals .................................. [Portals: 1]
  |       o- 0.0.0.0:3260 ................................. [OK]
  o- loopback ...................................... [Targets: 0]
/> saveconfig
Last 10 configs saved in /etc/target/backup.
Configuration saved to /etc/target/saveconfig.json
/> exit
Global pref auto_save_on_exit=true
Last 10 configs saved in /etc/target/backup.
Configuration saved to /etc/target/saveconfig.json
[root@centos7 ~]#
```

Use the **systemd** tools to manage the service:

```
[root@centos7 ~]# systemctl enable target
ln -s '/usr/lib/systemd/system/target.service' '/etc/systemd/system/multi-user.target.wants/t
[root@centos7 ~]# systemctl start target
[root@centos7 ~]#
```

Depending on your organisations policy, you may need to configure firewall and SELinux. The screenshot belows adds a firewall rule to allow all traffic over port 3260, and disables SELinux.

```
[root@centos7 ~]# firewall-cmd --permanent --add-port=3260/tcp
[root@centos7 ~]# firewall-cmd --reload
[root@centos7 ~]# setenforce 0
```

The total configuration is visible using **ls** from the root.

```
[root@centos7 ~]# targetcli
targetcli shell version 2.1.fb37
Copyright 2011-2013 by Datera, Inc and others.
For help on commands, type 'help'.

/> ls
o- / ....................................................... [...]
  o- backstores .............................................. [...]
  | o- block ................................. [Storage Objects: 1]
  | | o- server1.disk1 ............... [/dev/sdb (2.0GiB) write-thru activated]
  | o- fileio ................................ [Storage Objects: 0]
  | o- pscsi ................................. [Storage Objects: 0]
  | o- ramdisk ............................... [Storage Objects: 0]
  o- iscsi ......................................... [Targets: 1]
  | o- iqn.2015-04.be.linux:iscsi1 ...................... [TPGs: 1]
  |   o- tpg1 ............................. [no-gen-acls, no-auth]
  |     o- acls ..................................... [ACLs: 1]
```

```
  |       | o- iqn.2015-04.be.linux:server2 .................... [Mapped LUNs: 1]
  |       |   o- mapped_lun0 .................... [lun0 block/server1.disk1 (rw)]
  |       o- luns ........................................................ [LUNs: 1]
  |       | o- lun0 ......................... [block/server1.disk1 (/dev/sdb)]
  |       o- portals ................................................... [Portals: 1]
  |         o- 0.0.0.0:3260 .................................................. [OK]
  o- loopback .................................................. [Targets: 0]
/>
/> exit
Global pref auto_save_on_exit=true
Last 10 configs saved in /etc/target/backup.
Configuration saved to /etc/target/saveconfig.json
[root@centos7 ~]#
```

The iSCSI Target is now ready.

13.9. iSCSI Initiator RHEL7/CentOS7

This is identical to the RHEL6/CentOS6 procedure:

```
[root@centos7 ~]# yum install iscsi-initiator-utils
Loaded plugins: fastestmirror
...
...
Installed:
  iscsi-initiator-utils.x86_64 0:6.2.0.873-29.el7

Dependency Installed:
  iscsi-initiator-utils-iscsiuio.x86_64 0:6.2.0.873-29.el7

Complete!
```

Map your initiator name to the **targetcli** acl.

```
[root@centos7 ~]# cat /etc/iscsi/initiatorname.iscsi
InitiatorName=iqn.2015-04.be.linux:server2
[root@centos7 ~]#
```

Enter the CHAP authentication in **/etc/iscsi/iscsid.conf**.

```
[root@centos7 ~]# vi /etc/iscsi/iscsid.conf
...
[root@centos7 ~]# grep ^node.session.auth /etc/iscsi/iscsid.conf
node.session.auth.authmethod = CHAP
node.session.auth.username = paul
node.session.auth.password = hunter2
[root@centos7 ~]#
```

There are no extra devices yet...

```
[root@centos7 ~]# fdisk -l | grep sd
Disk /dev/sda: 22.0 GB, 22038806528 bytes, 43044544 sectors
/dev/sda1   *        2048     1026047      512000   83  Linux
/dev/sda2         1026048    43042815    21008384   8e  Linux LVM
Disk /dev/sdb: 2147 MB, 2147483648 bytes, 4194304 sectors
```

Enable the service and discover the target.

```
[root@centos7 ~]# systemctl enable iscsid
ln -s '/usr/lib/systemd/system/iscsid.service' '/etc/systemd/system/multi-user.target.wants/is
[root@centos7 ~]# iscsiadm -m discovery -t st -p 192.168.1.128
192.168.1.128:3260,1 iqn.2015-04.be.linux:iscsi1
```

Log into the target and see /dev/sdc appear.

```
[root@centos7 ~]# iscsiadm -m node -T iqn.2015-04.be.linux:iscsi1 -p 192.168.1.128 -l
Logging in to [iface: default, target: iqn.2015-04.be.linux:iscsi1, portal: 192.168.1.128,3260
Login to [iface: default, target: iqn.2015-04.be.linux:iscsi1, portal: 192.168.1.128,3260] suc
[root@centos7 ~]#
[root@centos7 ~]# fdisk -l | grep sd
Disk /dev/sda: 22.0 GB, 22038806528 bytes, 43044544 sectors
/dev/sda1   *        2048     1026047       512000   83  Linux
/dev/sda2         1026048    43042815     21008384   8e  Linux LVM
Disk /dev/sdb: 2147 MB, 2147483648 bytes, 4194304 sectors
Disk /dev/sdc: 2147 MB, 2147483648 bytes, 4194304 sectors
[root@centos7 ~]#
```

13.10. practice: iSCSI devices

1. Set up a target (using an LVM and a SCSI device) and an initiator that connects to both.

2. Set up an iSCSI Target and Initiator on two CentOS7/RHEL7 computers with the following information:

Table 13.1. iSCSI Target and Initiator practice

variable	value
Target Server IP	
shared devices on target	/dev/sd /dev/sd /dev/sd
shared device name sd	
shared device name sd	
shared device name sd	
target iqn	
initiator iqn	
username	
password	

13.11. solution: iSCSI devices

1. Set up a target (using an LVM and a SCSI device) and an initiator that connects to both.

This solution was done on **Debian/ubuntu/Mint**. For RHEL/CentOS check the theory.

Decide (with a partner) on a computer to be the Target and another computer to be the Initiator.

On the Target computer:

First install iscsitarget using the standard tools for installing software in your distribution. Then use your knowledge from the previous chapter to setup a logical volume (/dev/vg/lvol0) and use the RAID chapter to setup /dev/md0. Then perform the following step:

```
vi /etc/default/iscsitarget (set enable to true)
```

Add your devices to /etc/iet/ietf.conf

```
root@debby6:/etc/iet# cat ietd.conf
Target iqn.2010-02.be.linux-training:storage.lun1
 IncomingUser isuser hunter2
 OutgoingUser
 Lun 0 Path=/dev/vg/lvol0,Type=fileio
 Alias LUN1
Target iqn.2010-02.be.linux-training:storage.lun2
 IncomingUser isuser hunter2
 OutgoingUser
 Lun 0 Path=/dev/md0,Type=fileio
 Alias LUN2
```

Add both devices to /etc/iet/initiators.allow

```
root@debby6:/etc/iet# cat initiators.allow
iqn.2010-02.be.linux-training:storage.lun1
iqn.2010-02.be.linux-training:storage.lun2
```

Now start the iscsitarget daemon and move over to the Initiator.

On the Initiator computer:

Install open-iscsi and start the daemon.

Then use **iscsiadm -m discovery -t st -p 'target-ip'** to see the iscsi devices on the Target.

Edit the files **/etc/iscsi/nodes/** as shown in the book. Then restart the iSCSI daemon and rund **fdisk -l** to see the iSCSI devices.

2. Set up an iSCSI Target and Initiator on two CentOS7/RHEL7 computers with the following information:

Table 13.2. iSCSI Target and Initiator practice

variable	value
Target Server IP	192.168.1.143 (Adjust for your subnet!)
shared devices on target	/dev/sdb /dev/sdc /dev/sdd
shared device name sdb	target.disk1
shared device name sdc	target.disk2
shared device name sdd	target.disk3
target iqn	iqn.2015-04.be.linux:target
initiator iqn	iqn.2015-04.be.linux:initiator
username	paul
password	hunter2

On the iSCSI Target server:

```
[root@centos7 ~]# targetcli
targetcli shell version 2.1.fb37
Copyright 2011-2013 by Datera, Inc and others.
For help on commands, type 'help'.

/> cd /backstores/block
/backstores/block> ls
o- block .......................................... [Storage Objects: 0]
/backstores/block> create target.disk1 /dev/sdb
Created block storage object target.disk1 using /dev/sdb.
/backstores/block> create target.disk2 /dev/sdc
Created block storage object target.disk2 using /dev/sdc.
/backstores/block> create target.disk3 /dev/sdd
Created block storage object target.disk3 using /dev/sdd.
/backstores/block> ls
o- block .......................................... [Storage Objects: 3]
  o- target.disk1 ................... [/dev/sdb (8.0GiB) write-thru deactivated]
  o- target.disk2 ................... [/dev/sdc (8.0GiB) write-thru deactivated]
  o- target.disk3 ................... [/dev/sdd (8.0GiB) write-thru deactivated]
/backstores/block> cd /iscsi
/iscsi> create iqn.2015-04.be.linux:target
Created target iqn.2015-04.be.linux:target.
Created TPG 1.
Global pref auto_add_default_portal=true
Created default portal listening on all IPs (0.0.0.0), port 3260.
/iscsi> cd /iscsi/iqn.2015-04.be.linux:target/tpg1/acls
/iscsi/iqn.20...get/tpg1/acls> create iqn.2015-04.be.linux:initiator
Created Node ACL for iqn.2015-04.be.linux:initiator
/iscsi/iqn.20...get/tpg1/acls> cd iqn.2015-04.be.linux:initiator
/iscsi/iqn.20...nux:initiator> pwd
/iscsi/iqn.2015-04.be.linux:target/tpg1/acls/iqn.2015-04.be.linux:initiator
/iscsi/iqn.20...nux:initiator> set auth userid=paul
Parameter userid is now 'paul'.
/iscsi/iqn.20...nux:initiator> set auth password=hunter2
Parameter password is now 'hunter2'.
/iscsi/iqn.20...nux:initiator> cd /iscsi/iqn.2015-04.be.linux:target/tpg1/
/iscsi/iqn.20...x:target/tpg1> ls
o- tpg1 ............................................ [no-gen-acls, no-auth]
  o- acls .......................................................... [ACLs: 1]
  | o- iqn.2015-04.be.linux:initiator ........................ [Mapped LUNs: 0]
```

```
    o- luns ........................................................ [LUNs: 0]
   o- portals ................................................... [Portals: 1]
      o- 0.0.0.0:3260 ............................................. [OK]
/iscsi/iqn.20...x:target/tpg1> cd luns
/iscsi/iqn.20...get/tpg1/luns> create /backstores/block/target.disk1
Created LUN 0.
Created LUN 0->0 mapping in node ACL iqn.2015-04.be.linux:initiator
/iscsi/iqn.20...get/tpg1/luns> create /backstores/block/target.disk2
Created LUN 1.
Created LUN 1->1 mapping in node ACL iqn.2015-04.be.linux:initiator
/iscsi/iqn.20...get/tpg1/luns> create /backstores/block/target.disk3
Created LUN 2.
Created LUN 2->2 mapping in node ACL iqn.2015-04.be.linux:initiator
s/scsi/iqn.20...get/tpg1/luns> cd /iscsi/iqn.2015-04.be.linux:target/tpg1/portals
/iscsi/iqn.20.../tpg1/portals> create 192.168.1.143
Using default IP port 3260
Could not create NetworkPortal in configFS.
/iscsi/iqn.20.../tpg1/portals> cd /
/> ls
o- / ........................................................... [...]
  o- backstores ................................................ [...]
  | o- block ................................... [Storage Objects: 3]
  | | o- target.disk1 ................. [/dev/sdb (8.0GiB) write-thru activated]
  | | o- target.disk2 ................. [/dev/sdc (8.0GiB) write-thru activated]
  | | o- target.disk3 ................. [/dev/sdd (8.0GiB) write-thru activated]
  | o- fileio .................................. [Storage Objects: 0]
  | o- pscsi ................................... [Storage Objects: 0]
  | o- ramdisk ................................. [Storage Objects: 0]
  o- iscsi ....................................... [Targets: 1]
  | o- iqn.2015-04.be.linux:target ...................... [TPGs: 1]
  |   o- tpg1 ........................................ [no-gen-acls, no-auth]
  |     o- acls ...................................... [ACLs: 1]
  |     | o- iqn.2015-04.be.linux:initiator ................. [Mapped LUNs: 3]
  |     |   o- mapped_lun0 ..................... [lun0 block/target.disk1 (rw)]
  |     |   o- mapped_lun1 ..................... [lun1 block/target.disk2 (rw)]
  |     |   o- mapped_lun2 ..................... [lun2 block/target.disk3 (rw)]
  |     o- luns ...................................... [LUNs: 3]
  |     | o- lun0 ........................... [block/target.disk1 (/dev/sdb)]
  |     | o- lun1 ........................... [block/target.disk2 (/dev/sdc)]
  |     | o- lun2 ........................... [block/target.disk3 (/dev/sdd)]
  |     o- portals ................................... [Portals: 1]
  |       o- 0.0.0.0:3260 ............................ [OK]
  o- loopback .................................... [Targets: 0]
/> exit
Global pref auto_save_on_exit=true
Last 10 configs saved in /etc/target/backup.
Configuration saved to /etc/target/saveconfig.json
[root@centos7 ~]# systemctl enable target
ln -s '/usr/lib/systemd/system/target.service' '/etc/systemd/system/multi-user.target.wants/ta
[root@centos7 ~]# systemctl start target
[root@centos7 ~]# setenforce 0
```

On the Initiator:

```
[root@centos7 ~]# cat /etc/iscsi/initiatorname.iscsi
InitiatorName=iqn.2015-04.be.linux:initiator
[root@centos7 ~]# vi /etc/iscsi/iscsid.conf
[root@centos7 ~]# grep ^node.session.au /etc/iscsi/iscsid.conf
node.session.auth.authmethod = CHAP
node.session.auth.username = paul
node.session.auth.password = hunter2
[root@centos7 ~]# fdisk -l 2>/dev/null | grep sd
Disk /dev/sda: 22.0 GB, 22038806528 bytes, 43044544 sectors
/dev/sda1   *        2048     1026047      512000   83  Linux
```

```
/dev/sda2          1026048    43042815    21008384   8e   Linux LVM
Disk /dev/sdb: 8589 MB, 8589934592 bytes, 16777216 sectors
/dev/sdb1               2048      821247      409600   83   Linux
/dev/sdb2             821248     1640447      409600   83   Linux
/dev/sdb3            1640448     2459647      409600   83   Linux
Disk /dev/sdc: 8589 MB, 8589934592 bytes, 16777216 sectors
Disk /dev/sdd: 8589 MB, 8589934592 bytes, 16777216 sectors
Disk /dev/sde: 2147 MB, 2147483648 bytes, 4194304 sectors
Disk /dev/sdf: 2147 MB, 2147483648 bytes, 4194304 sectors
[root@centos7 ~]# systemctl enable iscsid
ln -s '/usr/lib/systemd/system/iscsid.service' '/etc/systemd/system/multi-user.target.wants/is
[root@centos7 ~]# iscsiadm -m node -T iqn.2015-04.be.linux:target -p 192.168.1.143 -l
Logging in to [iface: default, target: iqn.2015-04.be.linux:target, portal: 192.168.1.143,3260
Login to [iface: default, target: iqn.2015-04.be.linux:target, portal: 192.168.1.143,3260] suc

[root@centos7 ~]# fdisk -l 2>/dev/null | grep sd
Disk /dev/sda: 22.0 GB, 22038806528 bytes, 43044544 sectors
/dev/sda1    *          2048     1026047      512000   83   Linux
/dev/sda2             1026048    43042815    21008384   8e   Linux LVM
Disk /dev/sdb: 8589 MB, 8589934592 bytes, 16777216 sectors
/dev/sdb1               2048      821247      409600   83   Linux
/dev/sdb2             821248     1640447      409600   83   Linux
/dev/sdb3            1640448     2459647      409600   83   Linux
Disk /dev/sdc: 8589 MB, 8589934592 bytes, 16777216 sectors
Disk /dev/sdd: 8589 MB, 8589934592 bytes, 16777216 sectors
Disk /dev/sde: 2147 MB, 2147483648 bytes, 4194304 sectors
Disk /dev/sdf: 2147 MB, 2147483648 bytes, 4194304 sectors
Disk /dev/sdg: 8589 MB, 8589934592 bytes, 16777216 sectors
Disk /dev/sdh: 8589 MB, 8589934592 bytes, 16777216 sectors
Disk /dev/sdi: 8589 MB, 8589934592 bytes, 16777216 sectors
[root@centos7 ~]#
```

Chapter 14. introduction to multipathing

14.1. install multipath

RHEL and CentOS need the **device-mapper-multipath** package.

```
yum install device-mapper-multipath
```

This will create a sample multipath.conf in **/usr/share/doc/device-mapper-multipath-0.4.9/multipath.conf**.

There is no **/etc/multipath.conf** until you initialize it with **mpathconf**.

```
[root@server2 ~]# mpathconf --enable --with_multipathd y
Starting multipathd daemon:                              [  OK  ]
[root@server2 ~]# wc -l /etc/multipath.conf
99 /etc/multipath.conf
```

14.2. configure multipath

You can now choose to either edit **/etc/multipath.conf** or use **mpathconf** to change this file for you.

```
[root@server2 ~]# grep user_friendly_names /etc/multipath.conf
 user_friendly_names yes
# user_friendly_names yes
[root@server2 ~]# mpathconf --enable --user_friendly_names n
[root@server2 ~]# grep user_friendly_names /etc/multipath.conf
 user_friendly_names no
# user_friendly_names yes
[root@server2 ~]# mpathconf --enable --user_friendly_names y
[root@server2 ~]# grep user_friendly_names /etc/multipath.conf
 user_friendly_names yes
# user_friendly_names yes
```

14.3. network

This example uses three networks, make sure the iSCSI Target is connected to all three networks.

```
[root@server1 tgt]# ifconfig | grep -B1 192.168
eth1      Link encap:Ethernet  HWaddr 08:00:27:4E:AB:8E
          inet addr:192.168.1.98  Bcast:192.168.1.255  Mask:255.255.255.0
--
eth2      Link encap:Ethernet  HWaddr 08:00:27:3F:A9:D1
          inet addr:192.168.2.98  Bcast:192.168.2.255  Mask:255.255.255.0
--
eth3      Link encap:Ethernet  HWaddr 08:00:27:94:52:26
          inet addr:192.168.3.98  Bcast:192.168.3.255  Mask:255.255.255.0
```

The same must be true for the multipath Initiator:

```
[root@server2 ~]# ifconfig | grep -B1 192.168
eth1      Link encap:Ethernet  HWaddr 08:00:27:A1:43:41
          inet addr:192.168.1.99  Bcast:192.168.1.255  Mask:255.255.255.0
--
eth2      Link encap:Ethernet  HWaddr 08:00:27:12:A8:70
          inet addr:192.168.2.99  Bcast:192.168.2.255  Mask:255.255.255.0
--
eth3      Link encap:Ethernet  HWaddr 08:00:27:6E:99:9B
          inet addr:192.168.3.99  Bcast:192.168.3.255  Mask:255.255.255.0
```

Test the triple discovery in three networks (screenshot newer than above).

```
[root@centos7 ~]# iscsiadm -m discovery -t st -p 192.168.1.150
192.168.1.150:3260,1 iqn.2015-04.be.linux:target1
[root@centos7 ~]# iscsiadm -m discovery -t st -p 192.168.2.150
192.168.2.150:3260,1 iqn.2015-04.be.linux:target1
[root@centos7 ~]# iscsiadm -m discovery -t st -p 192.168.3.150
192.168.3.150:3260,1 iqn.2015-04.be.linux:target1
```

14.4. start multipathd and iscsi

Time to start (or restart) both the multipathd and iscsi services:

```
[root@server2 ~]# service multipathd restart
Stopping multipathd daemon:                              [  OK  ]
Starting multipathd daemon:                              [  OK  ]
[root@server2 ~]# service iscsi restart
Stopping iscsi:                                          [  OK  ]
Starting iscsi:                                          [  OK  ]
```

This shows **fdisk** output when leaving the default friendly_names option to yes. The bottom three are the multipath devices to use.

```
[root@server2 ~]# fdisk -l | grep Disk
Disk /dev/sda: 42.9 GB, 42949672960 bytes
Disk identifier: 0x0004f229
Disk /dev/sdb: 1073 MB, 1073741824 bytes
Disk identifier: 0x00000000
Disk /dev/sdc: 1073 MB, 1073741824 bytes
Disk identifier: 0x00000000
Disk /dev/sdd: 1073 MB, 1073741824 bytes
Disk identifier: 0x00000000
Disk /dev/sde: 2147 MB, 2147483648 bytes
Disk identifier: 0x00000000
Disk /dev/sdf: 2147 MB, 2147483648 bytes
Disk identifier: 0x00000000
Disk /dev/sdg: 2147 MB, 2147483648 bytes
Disk identifier: 0x00000000
Disk /dev/mapper/VolGroup-lv_root: 41.4 GB, 41448112128 bytes
Disk identifier: 0x00000000
Disk /dev/mapper/VolGroup-lv_swap: 973 MB, 973078528 bytes
Disk identifier: 0x00000000
Disk /dev/sdh: 1073 MB, 1073741824 bytes
Disk identifier: 0x00000000
Disk /dev/sdi: 1073 MB, 1073741824 bytes
Disk identifier: 0x00000000
Disk /dev/sdj: 1073 MB, 1073741824 bytes
Disk identifier: 0x00000000
Disk /dev/sdl: 1073 MB, 1073741824 bytes
Disk identifier: 0x00000000
Disk /dev/sdn: 1073 MB, 1073741824 bytes
Disk identifier: 0x00000000
Disk /dev/sdk: 1073 MB, 1073741824 bytes
Disk identifier: 0x00000000
Disk /dev/sdm: 1073 MB, 1073741824 bytes
Disk identifier: 0x00000000
Disk /dev/sdp: 1073 MB, 1073741824 bytes
Disk identifier: 0x00000000
Disk /dev/sdo: 1073 MB, 1073741824 bytes
Disk identifier: 0x00000000
Disk /dev/mapper/mpathh: 1073 MB, 1073741824 bytes
Disk identifier: 0x00000000
Disk /dev/mapper/mpathi: 1073 MB, 1073741824 bytes
Disk identifier: 0x00000000
Disk /dev/mapper/mpathj: 1073 MB, 1073741824 bytes
Disk identifier: 0x00000000
[root@server2 ~]#
```

14.5. multipath list

You can list the multipath connections and devices with **multipath -ll**.

```
[root@server2 ~]# multipath -ll
mpathj (1IET     00010001) dm-4 Reddy,VBOX HARDDISK
size=1.0G features='0' hwhandler='0' wp=rw
|-+- policy='round-robin 0' prio=1 status=active
| `- 13:0:0:1 sdh 8:112 active ready running
|-+- policy='round-robin 0' prio=1 status=enabled
| `- 12:0:0:1 sdi 8:128 active ready running
`-+- policy='round-robin 0' prio=1 status=enabled
  `- 14:0:0:1 sdm 8:192 active ready running
mpathi (1IET     00010003) dm-3 Reddy,VBOX HARDDISK
size=1.0G features='0' hwhandler='0' wp=rw
|-+- policy='round-robin 0' prio=1 status=active
| `- 13:0:0:3 sdk 8:160 active ready running
|-+- policy='round-robin 0' prio=1 status=enabled
| `- 12:0:0:3 sdn 8:208 active ready running
`-+- policy='round-robin 0' prio=1 status=enabled
  `- 14:0:0:3 sdp 8:240 active ready running
mpathh (1IET     00010002) dm-2 Reddy,VBOX HARDDISK
size=1.0G features='0' hwhandler='0' wp=rw
|-+- policy='round-robin 0' prio=1 status=active
| `- 12:0:0:2 sdl 8:176 active ready running
|-+- policy='round-robin 0' prio=1 status=enabled
| `- 13:0:0:2 sdj 8:144 active ready running
`-+- policy='round-robin 0' prio=1 status=enabled
  `- 14:0:0:2 sdo 8:224 active ready running
[root@server2 ~]#
```

The IET (iSCSI Enterprise Target) ID should match the ones you see on the Target server.

```
[root@server1 ~]# tgt-admin -s | grep -e LUN -e IET -e dev
    LUN information:
        LUN: 0
            SCSI ID: IET     00010000
        LUN: 1
            SCSI ID: IET     00010001
            Backing store path: /dev/sdb
        LUN: 2
            SCSI ID: IET     00010002
            Backing store path: /dev/sdc
        LUN: 3
            SCSI ID: IET     00010003
            Backing store path: /dev/sdd
```

14.6. using the device

The rest is standard mkfs, mkdir, mount:

```
[root@server2 ~]# mkfs.ext4 /dev/mapper/mpathi
mke2fs 1.41.12 (17-May-2010)
Filesystem label=
OS type: Linux
Block size=4096 (log=2)
Fragment size=4096 (log=2)
Stride=0 blocks, Stripe width=0 blocks
65536 inodes, 262144 blocks
13107 blocks (5.00%) reserved for the super user
First data block=0
Maximum filesystem blocks=268435456
8 block groups
32768 blocks per group, 32768 fragments per group
8192 inodes per group
Superblock backups stored on blocks:
 32768, 98304, 163840, 229376

Writing inode tables: done
Creating journal (8192 blocks): done
Writing superblocks and filesystem accounting information: done

This filesystem will be automatically checked every 38 mounts or
180 days, whichever comes first.  Use tune2fs -c or -i to override.
[root@server2 ~]# mkdir /srv/multipath
[root@server2 ~]# mount /dev/mapper/mpathi /srv/multipath/
[root@server2 ~]# df -h /srv/multipath/
Filesystem           Size  Used Avail Use% Mounted on
/dev/mapper/mpathi 1008M   34M  924M   4% /srv/multipath
```

14.7. practice: multipathing

1. Find a partner and decide who will be iSCSI Target and who will be iSCSI Initiator and Multipather. Set up Multipath as we did in the theory.

2. Uncomment the big 'defaults' section in /etc/multipath.conf and disable friendly names. Verify that multipath can work. You may need to check the manual for **/lib/dev/scsi_id** and for **multipath.conf**.

14.8. solution: multipathing

1. Find a partner and decide who will be iSCSI Target and who will be iSCSI Initiator and Multipather. Set up Multipath as we did in the theory.

```
Look in the theory...
```

2. Uncomment the big 'defaults' section in /etc/multipath.conf and disable friendly names. Verify that multipath can work. You may need to check the manual for **/lib/dev/scsi_id** and for **multipath.conf**.

```
vi multipath.conf

remove # for the big defaults section
add # for the very small one with friendly_names active
add the --replace-whitespace option to scsi_id.

defaults {
        udev_dir                    /dev
        polling_interval            10
        path_selector               "round-robin 0"
        path_grouping_policy        multibus
        getuid_callout              "/lib/udev/scsi_id --whitelisted --replace\
-whitespace --device=/dev/%n"
        prio                        const
        path_checker                readsector0
        rr_min_io                   100
        max_fds                     8192
        rr_weight                   priorities
        failback                    immediate
        no_path_retry               fail
        user_friendly_names         no
}
```

The names now (after service restart) look like:

```
root@server2 etc]# multipath -ll
1IET_00010001 dm-8 Reddy,VBOX HARDDISK
size=1.0G features='0' hwhandler='0' wp=rw
`-+- policy='round-robin 0' prio=1 status=active
  |- 17:0:0:1 sdh 8:112 active ready running
  |- 16:0:0:1 sdi 8:128 active ready running
  `- 15:0:0:1 sdn 8:208 active ready running
1IET_00010003 dm-10 Reddy,VBOX HARDDISK
size=1.0G features='0' hwhandler='0' wp=rw
`-+- policy='round-robin 0' prio=1 status=active
  |- 17:0:0:3 sdl 8:176 active ready running
  |- 16:0:0:3 sdm 8:192 active ready running
  `- 15:0:0:3 sdp 8:240 active ready running
1IET_00010002 dm-9 Reddy,VBOX HARDDISK
size=1.0G features='0' hwhandler='0' wp=rw
`-+- policy='round-robin 0' prio=1 status=active
  |- 17:0:0:2 sdj 8:144 active ready running
  |- 16:0:0:2 sdk 8:160 active ready running
  `- 15:0:0:2 sdo 8:224 active ready running
```

Did you blacklist your own devices ?

```
 vi multipath.conf
--> search for blacklist:
add
        devnode "^sd[a-g]"
```

Part III. backup management

Table of Contents

Chapter 15. backup

15.1. About tape devices

Don't forget that the name of a device strictly speaking has no meaning since the kernel will use the major and minor number to find the hardware! See the man page of **mknod** and the devices.txt file in the Linux kernel source for more info.

15.1.1. SCSI tapes

On the official Linux device list (http://www.lanana.org/docs/device-list/) we find the names for SCSI tapes (major 9 char). SCSI tape devices are located underneath **/dev/st** and are numbered starting with 0 for the first tape device.

```
/dev/st0    First tape device
/dev/st1    Second tape device
/dev/st2    Third tape device
```

To prevent **automatic rewinding of tapes**, prefix them with the letter n.

```
/dev/nst0    First no rewind tape device
/dev/nst1    Second no rewind tape device
/dev/nst2    Third no rewind tape device
```

By default, SCSI tapes on Linux will use the highest hardware compression that is supported by the tape device. To lower the compression level, append one of the letters l (low), m (medium) or a (auto) to the tape name.

```
/dev/st0l    First low compression tape device
/dev/st0m    First medium compression tape device
/dev/nst2m   Third no rewind medium compression tape device
```

15.1.2. IDE tapes

On the official Linux device list (http://www.lanana.org/docs/device-list/) we find the names for IDE tapes (major 37 char). IDE tape devices are located underneath **/dev/ht** and are numbered starting with 0 for the first tape device. No rewind and compression is similar to SCSI tapes.

```
/dev/ht0    First IDE tape device
/dev/nht0   Second no rewind IDE tape device
/dev/ht0m   First medium compression IDE tape device
```

15.1.3. mt

To manage your tapes, use **mt** (Magnetic Tape). Some examples.

To receive information about the status of the tape.

```
mt -f /dev/st0 status
```

To rewind a tape...

```
mt -f /dev/st0 rewind
```

To rewind and eject a tape...

```
mt -f /dev/st0 eject
```

To erase a tape...

```
mt -f /dev/st0 erase
```

15.2. Compression

It can be beneficial to compress files before backup. The two most popular tools for compression of regular files on Linux are **gzip/gunzip** and **bzip2/bunzip2**. Below you can see gzip in action, notice that it adds the **.gz** extension to the file.

```
paul@RHELv4u4:~/test$ ls -l allfiles.tx*
-rw-rw-r-- 1 paul paul 8813553 Feb 27 05:38 allfiles.txt
paul@RHELv4u4:~/test$ gzip allfiles.txt
paul@RHELv4u4:~/test$ ls -l allfiles.tx*
-rw-rw-r-- 1 paul paul 931863 Feb 27 05:38 allfiles.txt.gz
paul@RHELv4u4:~/test$ gunzip allfiles.txt.gz
paul@RHELv4u4:~/test$ ls -l allfiles.tx*
-rw-rw-r-- 1 paul paul 8813553 Feb 27 05:38 allfiles.txt
paul@RHELv4u4:~/test$
```

In general, gzip is much faster than bzip2, but the latter one compresses a lot better. Let us compare the two.

```
paul@RHELv4u4:~/test$ cp allfiles.txt bllfiles.txt
paul@RHELv4u4:~/test$ time gzip allfiles.txt

real    0m0.050s
user    0m0.041s
sys     0m0.009s
paul@RHELv4u4:~/test$ time bzip2 bllfiles.txt

real    0m5.968s
user    0m5.794s
sys     0m0.076s
paul@RHELv4u4:~/test$ ls -l ?llfiles.tx*
-rw-rw-r-- 1 paul paul 931863 Feb 27 05:38 allfiles.txt.gz
-rw-rw-r-- 1 paul paul 708871 May 12 10:52 bllfiles.txt.bz2
paul@RHELv4u4:~/test$
```

15.3. tar

The **tar** utility gets its name from **Tape ARchive**. This tool will receive and send files to a destination (typically a tape or a regular file). The c option is used to create a tar archive

(or tarfile), the f option to name/create the **tarfile**. The example below takes a backup of /
etc into the file /backup/etc.tar .

```
root@RHELv4u4:~# tar cf /backup/etc.tar /etc
root@RHELv4u4:~# ls -l /backup/etc.tar
-rw-r--r--  1 root root 47800320 May 12 11:47 /backup/etc.tar
root@RHELv4u4:~#
```

Compression can be achieved without pipes since tar uses the z flag to compress with gzip,
and the j flag to compress with bzip2.

```
root@RHELv4u4:~# tar czf /backup/etc.tar.gz /etc
root@RHELv4u4:~# tar cjf /backup/etc.tar.bz2 /etc
root@RHELv4u4:~# ls -l /backup/etc.ta*
-rw-r--r--  1 root root 47800320 May 12 11:47 /backup/etc.tar
-rw-r--r--  1 root root  6077340 May 12 11:48 /backup/etc.tar.bz2
-rw-r--r--  1 root root  8496607 May 12 11:47 /backup/etc.tar.gz
root@RHELv4u4:~#
```

The t option is used to **list the contents of a tar file**. Verbose mode is enabled with v (also
useful when you want to see the files being archived during archiving).

```
root@RHELv4u4:~# tar tvf /backup/etc.tar
drwxr-xr-x root/root         0 2007-05-12 09:38:21 etc/
-rw-r--r-- root/root      2657 2004-09-27 10:15:03 etc/warnquota.conf
-rw-r--r-- root/root     13136 2006-11-03 17:34:50 etc/mime.types
drwxr-xr-x root/root         0 2004-11-03 13:35:50 etc/sound/
...
```

To **list a specific file in a tar archive**, use the t option, added with the filename (without
leading /).

```
root@RHELv4u4:~# tar tvf /backup/etc.tar etc/resolv.conf
-rw-r--r-- root/root        77 2007-05-12 08:31:32 etc/resolv.conf
root@RHELv4u4:~#
```

Use the x flag to **restore a tar archive**, or a single file from the archive. Remember that by
default tar will restore the file in the current directory.

```
root@RHELv4u4:~# tar xvf /backup/etc.tar etc/resolv.conf
etc/resolv.conf
root@RHELv4u4:~# ls -l /etc/resolv.conf
-rw-r--r--  2 root root 40 May 12 12:05 /etc/resolv.conf
root@RHELv4u4:~# ls -l etc/resolv.conf
-rw-r--r--  1 root root 77 May 12 08:31 etc/resolv.conf
root@RHELv4u4:~#
```

You can **preserve file permissions** with the p flag. And you can exclude directories or file
with **--exclude**.

```
root ~# tar cpzf /backup/etc_with_perms.tgz /etc
```

```
root ~# tar cpzf /backup/etc_no_sysconf.tgz /etc --exclude /etc/sysconfig
root ~# ls -l /backup/etc_*
-rw-r--r--  1 root root 8434293 May 12 12:48 /backup/etc_no_sysconf.tgz
-rw-r--r--  1 root root 8496591 May 12 12:48 /backup/etc_with_perms.tgz
root ~#
```

You can also create a text file with names of files and directories to archive, and then supply this file to tar with the -T flag.

```
root@RHELv4u4:~# find /etc -name *.conf > files_to_archive.txt
root@RHELv4u4:~# find /home -name *.pdf >> files_to_archive.txt
root@RHELv4u4:~# tar cpzf /backup/backup.tgz -T files_to_archive.txt
```

The tar utility can receive filenames from the find command, with the help of xargs.

```
find /etc -type f -name "*.conf" | xargs tar czf /backup/confs.tar.gz
```

You can also use tar to copy a directory, this is more efficient than using cp -r.

```
(cd /etc; tar -cf - . ) | (cd /backup/copy_of_etc/; tar -xpf - )
```

Another example of tar, this copies a directory securely over the network.

```
(cd /etc;tar -cf - . )|(ssh user@srv 'cd /backup/cp_of_etc/; tar -xf - ')
```

tar can be used together with gzip and copy a file to a remote server through ssh

```
cat backup.tar | gzip | ssh bashuser@192.168.1.105 "cat - > backup.tgz"
```

Compress the tar backup when it is on the network, but leave it uncompressed at the destination.

```
cat backup.tar | gzip | ssh user@192.168.1.105 "gunzip|cat - > backup.tar"
```

Same as the previous, but let ssh handle the compression

```
cat backup.tar | ssh -C bashuser@192.168.1.105 "cat - > backup.tar"
```

15.4. Backup Types

Linux uses **multilevel incremental** backups using distinct levels. A full backup is a backup at level 0. A higher level x backup will include all changes since the last level x-1 backup.

Suppose you take a full backup on Monday (level 0) and a level 1 backup on Tuesday, then the Tuesday backup will contain all changes since Monday. Taking a level 2 on Wednesday will contain all changes since Tuesday (the last level 2-1). A level 3 backup on Thursday will contain all changes since Wednesday (the last level 3-1). Another level 3 on Friday will also contain all changes since Wednesday. A level 2 backup on Saturday would take all changes since the last level 1 from Tuesday.

15.5. dump and restore

While **dump** is similar to tar, it is also very different because it looks at the file system. Where tar receives a lists of files to backup, dump will find files to backup by itself by examining ext2. Files found by dump will be copied to a tape or regular file. In case the target is not big enough to hold the dump (end-of-media), it is broken into multiple volumes.

Restoring files that were backed up with dump is done with the **restore** command. In the example below we take a full level 0 backup of two partitions to a SCSI tape. The no rewind is mandatory to put the volumes behind each other on the tape.

```
dump 0f /dev/nst0 /boot
dump 0f /dev/nst0 /
```

Listing files in a dump archive is done with **dump -t**, and you can compare files with **dump -C**.

You can omit files from a dump by changing the dump attribute with the **chattr** command. The d attribute on ext will tell dump to skip the file, even during a full backup. In the following example, /etc/hosts is excluded from dump archives.

```
chattr +d /etc/hosts
```

To restore the complete file system with **restore**, use the -r option. This can be useful to change the size or block size of a file system. You should have a clean file system mounted and cd'd into it. Like this example shows.

```
mke2fs /dev/hda3
mount /dev/hda3 /mnt/data
cd /mnt/data
restore rf /dev/nst0
```

To extract only one file or directory from a dump, use the -x option.

```
restore -xf /dev/st0 /etc
```

15.6. cpio

Different from tar and dump is **cpio** (Copy Input and Output). It can be used to receive filenames, but copies the actual files. This makes it an easy companion with find! Some examples below.

find sends filenames to cpio, which puts the files in an archive.

```
find /etc -depth -print | cpio -oaV -O archive.cpio
```

The same, but compressed with gzip

```
find /etc -depth -print | cpio -oaV | gzip -c > archive.cpio.gz
```

Now pipe it through ssh (backup files to a compressed file on another machine)

```
find /etc -depth -print|cpio -oaV|gzip -c|ssh server "cat - > etc.cpio.gz"
```

find sends filenames to cpio | cpio sends files to ssh | ssh sends files to cpio 'cpio extracts files'

```
find /etc -depth -print | cpio -oaV | ssh user@host 'cpio -imVd'
```

the same but reversed: copy a dir from the remote host to the local machine

```
ssh user@host "find path -depth -print | cpio -oaV" | cpio -imVd
```

15.7. dd

15.7.1. About dd

Some people use **dd** to create backups. This can be very powerful, but dd backups can only be restored to very similar partitions or devices. There are however a lot of useful things possible with dd. Some examples.

15.7.2. Create a CDROM image

The easiest way to create a **.ISO file** from any CD. The if switch means Input File, of is the Output File. Any good tool can burn a copy of the CD with this .ISO file.

```
dd if=/dev/cdrom of=/path/to/cdrom.ISO
```

15.7.3. Create a floppy image

A little outdated maybe, but just in case : make an image file from a 1.44MB floppy. Blocksize is defined by bs, and count contains the number of blocks to copy.

```
dd if=/dev/floppy of=/path/to/floppy.img bs=1024 count=1440
```

15.7.4. Copy the master boot record

Use dd to copy the **MBR** (Master Boot Record) of hard disk /dev/hda to a file.

```
dd if=/dev/hda of=/MBR.img bs=512 count=1
```

15.7.5. Copy files

This example shows how dd can copy files. Copy the file summer.txt to copy_of_summer.txt .

```
dd if=~/summer.txt of=~/copy_of_summer.txt
```

15.7.6. Image disks or partitions

And who needs ghost when dd can create a (compressed) image of a partition.

```
dd if=/dev/hdb2 of=/image_of_hdb2.IMG
dd if=/dev/hdb2 | gzip > /image_of_hdb2.IMG.gz
```

15.7.7. Create files of a certain size

dd can be used to create a file of any size. The first example creates a one MEBIbyte file, the second a one MEGAbyte file.

```
dd if=/dev/zero of=file1MB count=1024 bs=1024
dd if=/dev/zero of=file1MB count=1000 bs=1024
```

15.7.8. CDROM server example

And there are of course endless combinations with ssh and bzip2. This example puts a bzip2 backup of a cdrom on a remote server.

```
dd if=/dev/cdrom |bzip2|ssh user@host "cat - > /backups/cd/cdrom.iso.bz2"
```

15.8. split

The **split** command is useful to split files into smaller files. This can be useful to fit the file onto multiple instances of a medium too small to contain the complete file. In the example below, a file of size 5000 bytes is split into three smaller files, with maximum 2000 bytes each.

```
paul@laika:~/test$ ls -l
total 8
-rw-r--r-- 1 paul paul 5000 2007-09-09 20:46 bigfile1
paul@laika:~/test$ split -b 2000 bigfile1 splitfile.
paul@laika:~/test$ ls -l
total 20
-rw-r--r-- 1 paul paul 5000 2007-09-09 20:46 bigfile1
-rw-r--r-- 1 paul paul 2000 2007-09-09 20:47 splitfile.aa
-rw-r--r-- 1 paul paul 2000 2007-09-09 20:47 splitfile.ab
-rw-r--r-- 1 paul paul 1000 2007-09-09 20:47 splitfile.ac
```

15.9. practice: backup

!! Careful with tar options and the position of the backup file, mistakes can destroy your system!!

1. Create a directory (or partition if you like) for backups. Link (or mount) it under /mnt/backup.

2a. Use tar to backup /etc in /mnt/backup/etc_date.tgz, the backup must be gzipped. (Replace date with the current date)

2b. Use tar to backup /bin to /mnt/backup/bin_date.tar.bz2, the backup must be bzip2'd.

2c. Choose a file in /etc and /bin and verify with tar that the file is indeed backed up.

2d. Extract those two files to your home directory.

3a. Create a backup directory for your neighbour, make it accessible under /mnt/ neighbourName

3b. Combine ssh and tar to put a backup of your /boot on your neighbours computer in / mnt/YourName

4a. Combine find and cpio to create a cpio archive of /etc.

4b. Choose a file in /etc and restore it from the cpio archive into your home directory.

5. Use dd and ssh to put a backup of the master boot record on your neighbours computer.

6. (On the real computer) Create and mount an ISO image of the ubuntu cdrom.

7. Combine dd and gzip to create a 'ghost' image of one of your partitions on another partition.

8. Use dd to create a five megabyte file in ~/testsplit and name it biggest. Then split this file in smaller two megabyte parts.

```
mkdir testsplit

dd if=/dev/zero of=~/testsplit/biggest count=5000 bs=1024

split -b 2000000 biggest parts
```

Part IV. mysql database

Table of Contents

Chapter 16. introduction to sql using mysql

mysql is a database server that understands Structured Query Language (**SQL**). MySQL was developed by the Swedish Company **MySQL AB**. The first release was in 1995. In 2008 MySQL AB was bought by Sun Microsystems (which is now owned by Oracle).

mysql is very popular for websites in combination with **php** and **apache** (the **m** in **lamp** servers), but **mysql** is also used in organizations with huge databases like Facebook, Flickr, Google, Nokia, Wikipedia and Youtube.

This chapter will teach you **sql** by creating and using small databases, tables, queries and a simple trigger in a local **mysql** server.

16.1. installing mysql

On Debian/Ubuntu you can use **aptitude install mysql-server** to install the **mysql server** and **client**.

```
root@ubu1204~# aptitude install mysql-server
The following NEW packages will be installed:
  libdbd-mysql-perl{a} libdbi-perl{a} libhtml-template-perl{a}
  libnet-daemon-perl{a} libplrpc-perl{a} mysql-client-5.5{a}
  mysql-client-core-5.5{a} mysql-server mysql-server-5.5{a}
  mysql-server-core-5.5{a}
0 packages upgraded, 10 newly installed, 0 to remove and 1 not upgraded.
Need to get 25.5 MB of archives. After unpacking 88.4 MB will be used.
Do you want to continue? [Y/n/?]
```

During the installation you will be asked to provide a password for the **root mysql user**, remember this password (or use **hunter2** like i do.

To verify the installed version, use **dpkg -l** on Debian/Ubuntu. This screenshot shows version 5.0 installed.

```
root@ubu1204~# dpkg -l mysql-server | tail -1 | tr -s ' ' | cut -c-72
ii mysql-server 5.5.24-0ubuntu0.12.04.1 MySQL database server (metapacka
```

Issue **rpm -q** to get version information about MySQL on Red Hat/Fedora/CentOS.

```
[paul@RHEL52 ~]$ rpm -q mysql-server
mysql-server-5.0.45-7.el5
```

You will need at least version 5.0 to work with **triggers**.

16.2. accessing mysql

16.2.1. Linux users

The installation of **mysql** creates a user account in **/etc/passwd** and a group account in **/etc/group**.

```
kevin@ubu1204:~$ tail -1 /etc/passwd
mysql:x:120:131:MySQL Server,,,:/nonexistent:/bin/false
kevin@ubu1204:~$ tail -1 /etc/group
mysql:x:131:
```

The mysql daemon **mysqld** will run with the credentials of this user and group.

```
root@ubu1204~# ps -eo uid,user,gid,group,comm | grep mysqld
  120 mysql       131 mysql    mysqld
```

16.2.2. mysql client application

You can now use mysql from the commandline by just typing **mysql -u root -p** and you'll be asked for the password (of the **mysql root** account). In the screenshot below the user typed **exit** to exit the mysql console.

```
root@ubu1204~# mysql -u root -p
Enter password:
Welcome to the MySQL monitor.  Commands end with ; or \g.
Your MySQL connection id is 43
Server version: 5.5.24-0ubuntu0.12.04.1 (Ubuntu)

Copyright (c) 2000, 2011, Oracle and/or its affiliates. All rights reserved.

Oracle is a registered trademark of Oracle Corporation and/or its
affiliates. Other names may be trademarks of their respective
owners.

Type 'help;' or '\h' for help. Type '\c' to clear the current input statement.

mysql> exit
Bye
```

You could also put the password in clear text on the command line, but that would not be very secure. Anyone with access to your bash history would be able to read your mysql root password.

```
root@ubu1204~# mysql -u root -phunter2
Welcome to the MySQL monitor.  Commands end with ; or \g.
...
```

16.2.3. ~/.my.cnf

You can save configuration in your home directory in the hidden file **.my.cnf**. In the screenshot below we put the root user and password in .my.cnf.

```
kevin@ubu1204:~$ pwd
/home/kevin
kevin@ubu1204:~$ cat .my.cnf
[client]
user=root
password=hunter2
kevin@ubu1204:~$
```

This enables us to log on as the **root mysql** user just by typing **mysql**.

```
kevin@ubu1204:~$ mysql
Welcome to the MySQL monitor.  Commands end with ; or \g.
Your MySQL connection id is 56
Server version: 5.5.24-0ubuntu0.12.04.1 (Ubuntu)
```

16.2.4. the mysql command line client

You can use the **mysql** command to take a look at the databases, and to execute SQL queries on them. The screenshots below show you how.

Here we execute the command **show databases**. Every command must be terminated by a delimiter. The default delimiter is **;** (the semicolon).

```
mysql> show databases;
+--------------------+
| Database           |
+--------------------+
| information_schema |
| mysql              |
| performance_schema |
| test               |
+--------------------+
4 rows in set (0.00 sec)
```

We will use this prompt in the next sections.

16.3. mysql databases

16.3.1. listing all databases

You can use the **mysql** command to take a look at the databases, and to execute SQL queries on them. The screenshots below show you how. First, we log on to our MySQL server and execute the command **show databases** to see which databases exist on our mysql server.

```
kevin@ubu1204:~$ mysql
Welcome to the MySQL monitor.  Commands end with ; or \g.
Your MySQL connection id is 57
Server version: 5.5.24-0ubuntu0.12.04.1 (Ubuntu)

Copyright (c) 2000, 2011, Oracle and/or its affiliates. All rights reserved.

Oracle is a registered trademark of Oracle Corporation and/or its
affiliates. Other names may be trademarks of their respective
owners.

Type 'help;' or '\h' for help. Type '\c' to clear the current input statement.

mysql> show databases;
+--------------------+
| Database           |
+--------------------+
| information_schema |
| mysql              |
| performance_schema |
| test               |
+--------------------+
4 rows in set (0.00 sec)
```

16.3.2. creating a database

You can create a new database with the **create database** command.

```
mysql> create database famouspeople;
Query OK, 1 row affected (0.00 sec)

mysql> show databases;
+--------------------+
| Database           |
+--------------------+
| information_schema |
| famouspeople       |
| mysql              |
| performance_schema |
| test               |
+--------------------+
5 rows in set (0.00 sec)
```

175

16.3.3. using a database

Next we tell **mysql** to use one particular database with the **use $database** command. This screenshot shows how to make wikidb the current database (in use).

```
mysql> use famouspeople;
Database changed
mysql>
```

16.3.4. access to a database

To give someone access to a mysql database, use the **grant** command.

```
mysql> grant all on famouspeople.* to kevin@localhost IDENTIFIED BY "hunter2";
Query OK, 0 rows affected (0.00 sec)
```

16.3.5. deleting a database

When a database is no longer needed, you can permanently remove it with the **drop database** command.

```
mysql> drop database demodb;
Query OK, 1 row affected (0.09 sec)
```

16.3.6. backup and restore a database

You can take a backup of a database, or move it to another computer using the **mysql** and **mysqldump** commands. In the screenshot below, we take a backup of the wikidb database on the computer named laika.

```
mysqldump -u root famouspeople > famouspeople.backup.20120708.sql
```

Here is a screenshot of a database restore operation from this backup.

```
mysql -u root famouspeople < famouspeople.backup.20120708.sql
```

16.4. mysql tables

16.4.1. listing tables

You can see a list of tables in the current database with the **show tables;** command. Our **famouspeople** database has no tables yet.

```
mysql> use famouspeople;
Database changed
mysql> show tables;
Empty set (0.00 sec)
```

16.4.2. creating a table

The **create table** command will create a new table.

This screenshot shows the creation of a country table. We use the **countrycode** as a **primary key** (all country codes are uniquely defined). Most country codes are two or three letters, so a **char** of three uses less space than a **varchar** of three. The **country name** and the name of the capital are both defined as **varchar**. The population can be seen as an **integer**.

```
mysql> create table country (
    -> countrycode char(3) NOT NULL,
    -> countryname varchar(70) NOT NULL,
    -> population int,
    -> countrycapital varchar(50),
    -> primary key (countrycode)
    -> );
Query OK, 0 rows affected (0.19 sec)

mysql> show tables;
+-----------------------+
| Tables_in_famouspeople |
+-----------------------+
| country               |
+-----------------------+
1 row in set (0.00 sec)

mysql>
```

You are allowed to type the **create table** command on one long line, but administrators often use multiple lines to improve readability.

```
mysql> create table country ( countrycode char(3) NOT NULL, countryname\
 varchar(70) NOT NULL, population int, countrycapital varchar(50), prim\
ary key (countrycode) );
Query OK, 0 rows affected (0.18 sec)
```

16.4.3. describing a table

To see a description of the structure of a table, issue the **describe $tablename** command as shown below.

```
mysql> describe country;
+----------------+-------------+------+-----+---------+-------+
| Field          | Type        | Null | Key | Default | Extra |
+----------------+-------------+------+-----+---------+-------+
| countrycode    | char(3)     | NO   | PRI | NULL    |       |
| countryname    | varchar(70) | NO   |     | NULL    |       |
| population     | int(11)     | YES  |     | NULL    |       |
| countrycapital | varchar(50) | YES  |     | NULL    |       |
+----------------+-------------+------+-----+---------+-------+
4 rows in set (0.00 sec)
```

16.4.4. removing a table

To remove a table from a database, issue the **drop table $tablename** command as shown below.

```
mysql> drop table country;
Query OK, 0 rows affected (0.00 sec)
```

16.5. mysql records

16.5.1. creating records

Use **insert** to enter data into the table. The screenshot shows several insert statements that insert values depending on the position of the data in the statement.

```
mysql> insert into country values ('BE','Belgium','11000000','Brussels');
Query OK, 1 row affected (0.05 sec)

mysql> insert into country values ('DE','Germany','82000000','Berlin');
Query OK, 1 row affected (0.05 sec)

mysql> insert into country values ('JP','Japan','128000000','Tokyo');
Query OK, 1 row affected (0.05 sec)
```

Some administrators prefer to use uppercase for **sql** keywords. The mysql client accepts both.

```
mysql> INSERT INTO country VALUES ('FR','France','64000000','Paris');
Query OK, 1 row affected (0.00 sec)
```

Note that you get an error when using a duplicate **primary key**.

```
mysql> insert into country values ('DE','Germany','82000000','Berlin');
ERROR 1062 (23000): Duplicate entry 'DE' for key 'PRIMARY'
```

16.5.2. viewing all records

Below an example of a simple **select** query to look at the contents of a table.

```
mysql> select * from country;
+-------------+---------------+------------+---------------+
| countrycode | countryname   | population | countrycapital |
+-------------+---------------+------------+---------------+
| BE          | Belgium       |   11000000 | Brussels      |
| CN          | China         | 1400000000 | Beijing       |
| DE          | Germany       |   82000000 | Berlin        |
| FR          | France        |   64000000 | Paris         |
| IN          | India         | 1300000000 | New Delhi     |
| JP          | Japan         |  128000000 | Tokyo         |
| MX          | Mexico        |  113000000 | Mexico City   |
| US          | United States |  313000000 | Washington    |
+-------------+---------------+------------+---------------+
8 rows in set (0.00 sec)
```

16.5.3. updating records

Consider the following **insert** statement. The capital of Spain is not Barcelona, it is Madrid.

```
mysql> insert into country values ('ES','Spain','48000000','Barcelona');
Query OK, 1 row affected (0.08 sec)
```

Using an **update** statement, the record can be updated.

```
mysql> update country set countrycapital='Madrid' where countrycode='ES';
Query OK, 1 row affected (0.07 sec)
Rows matched: 1  Changed: 1  Warnings: 0
```

We can use a **select** statement to verify this change.

```
mysql> select * from country;
+-------------+---------------+------------+----------------+
| countrycode | countryname   | population | countrycapital |
+-------------+---------------+------------+----------------+
| BE          | Belgium       |   11000000 | Brussels       |
| CN          | China         | 1400000000 | Beijing        |
| DE          | Germany       |   82000000 | Berlin         |
| ES          | Spain         |   48000000 | Madrid         |
| FR          | France        |   64000000 | Paris          |
| IN          | India         | 1300000000 | New Delhi      |
| JP          | Japan         |  128000000 | Tokyo          |
| MX          | Mexico        |  113000000 | Mexico City    |
| US          | United States |  313000000 | Washington     |
+-------------+---------------+------------+----------------+
9 rows in set (0.00 sec)
```

16.5.4. viewing selected records

Using a **where** clause in a **select** statement, you can specify which record(s) you want to see.

```
mysql> SELECT * FROM country WHERE countrycode='ES';
+-------------+-------------+------------+----------------+
| countrycode | countryname | population | countrycapital |
+-------------+-------------+------------+----------------+
| ES          | Spain       |   48000000 | Madrid         |
+-------------+-------------+------------+----------------+
1 row in set (0.00 sec)
```

Another example of the **where** clause.

```
mysql> select * from country where countryname='Spain';
+-------------+-------------+------------+----------------+
| countrycode | countryname | population | countrycapital |
+-------------+-------------+------------+----------------+
| ES          | Spain       |   48000000 | Madrid         |
+-------------+-------------+------------+----------------+
1 row in set (0.00 sec)
```

16.5.5. primary key in where clause ?

The **primary key** of a table is a field that uniquely identifies every record (every row) in the table. when using another field in the **where** clause, it is possible to get multiple rows returned.

```
mysql> insert into country values ('EG','Egypt','82000000','Cairo');
```

```
Query OK, 1 row affected (0.33 sec)

mysql> select * from country where population='82000000';
+-------------+-------------+------------+----------------+
| countrycode | countryname | population | countrycapital |
+-------------+-------------+------------+----------------+
| DE          | Germany     |   82000000 | Berlin         |
| EG          | Egypt       |   82000000 | Cairo          |
+-------------+-------------+------------+----------------+
2 rows in set (0.00 sec)
```

16.5.6. ordering records

We know that **select** allows us to see all records in a table. Consider this table.

```
mysql> select countryname,population from country;
+---------------+------------+
| countryname   | population |
+---------------+------------+
| Belgium       |   11000000 |
| China         | 1400000000 |
| Germany       |   82000000 |
| Egypt         |   82000000 |
| Spain         |   48000000 |
| France        |   64000000 |
| India         | 1300000000 |
| Japan         |  128000000 |
| Mexico        |  113000000 |
| United States |  313000000 |
+---------------+------------+
10 rows in set (0.00 sec)
```

Using the **order by** clause, we can change the order in which the records are presented.

```
mysql> select countryname,population from country order by countryname;
+---------------+------------+
| countryname   | population |
+---------------+------------+
| Belgium       |   11000000 |
| China         | 1400000000 |
| Egypt         |   82000000 |
| France        |   64000000 |
| Germany       |   82000000 |
| India         | 1300000000 |
| Japan         |  128000000 |
| Mexico        |  113000000 |
| Spain         |   48000000 |
| United States |  313000000 |
+---------------+------------+
10 rows in set (0.00 sec)
```

16.5.7. grouping records

Consider this table of people. The screenshot shows how to use the **avg** function to calculate an average.

```
mysql> select * from people;
+----------------+----------+-----------+-------------+
| Name           | Field    | birthyear | countrycode |
+----------------+----------+-----------+-------------+
| Barack Obama   | politics | 1961      | US          |
| Deng Xiaoping  | politics | 1904      | CN          |
```

```
| Guy Verhofstadt | politics   | 1953 | BE |        |
| Justine Henin   | tennis     | 1982 | BE |        |
| Kim Clijsters   | tennis     | 1983 | BE |        |
| Li Na           | tennis     | 1982 | CN |        |
| Liu Yang        | astronaut  | 1978 | CN |        |
| Serena Williams | tennis     | 1981 | US |        |
| Venus Williams  | tennis     | 1980 | US |        |
+-----------------+-----------+----------+-------------+
9 rows in set (0.00 sec)

mysql> select Field,AVG(birthyear) from people;
+----------+-------------------+
| Field    | AVG(birthyear)    |
+----------+-------------------+
| politics | 1967.111111111111 |
+----------+-------------------+
1 row in set (0.00 sec)
```

Using the **group by** clause, we can have an average per field.

```
mysql> select Field,AVG(birthyear) from people group by Field;
+-----------+--------------------+
| Field     | AVG(birthyear)     |
+-----------+--------------------+
| astronaut |               1978 |
| politics  | 1939.3333333333333 |
| tennis    |             1981.6 |
+-----------+--------------------+
3 rows in set (0.00 sec)
```

16.5.8. deleting records

You can use the **delete** to permanently remove a record from a table.

```
mysql> delete from country where countryname='Spain';
Query OK, 1 row affected (0.06 sec)

mysql> select * from country where countryname='Spain';
Empty set (0.00 sec)
```

16.6. joining two tables

16.6.1. inner join

With an **inner join** you can take values from two tables and combine them in one result. Consider the country and the people tables from the previous section when looking at this screenshot of an **inner join**.

```
mysql> select Name,Field,countryname
    -> from country
    -> inner join people on people.countrycode=country.countrycode;
+-----------------+----------+----------------+
| Name            | Field    | countryname    |
+-----------------+----------+----------------+
| Barack Obama    | politics | United States  |
| Deng Xiaoping   | politics | China          |
| Guy Verhofstadt | politics | Belgium        |
| Justine Henin   | tennis   | Belgium        |
| Kim Clijsters   | tennis   | Belgium        |
| Li Na           | tennis   | China          |
```

```
| Liu Yang          | astronaut | China         |
| Serena Williams   | tennis    | United States |
| Venus Williams    | tennis    | United States |
+-------------------+-----------+---------------+
9 rows in set (0.00 sec)
```

This **inner join** will show only records with a match on **countrycode** in both tables.

16.6.2. left join

A **left join** is different from an **inner join** in that it will take all rows from the left table, regardless of a match in the right table.

```
mysql> select Name,Field,countryname from country left join people on people.countrycode=count
+-------------------+-----------+---------------+
| Name              | Field     | countryname   |
+-------------------+-----------+---------------+
| Guy Verhofstadt   | politics  | Belgium       |
| Justine Henin     | tennis    | Belgium       |
| Kim Clijsters     | tennis    | Belgium       |
| Deng Xiaoping     | politics  | China         |
| Li Na             | tennis    | China         |
| Liu Yang          | astronaut | China         |
| NULL              | NULL      | Germany       |
| NULL              | NULL      | Egypt         |
| NULL              | NULL      | Spain         |
| NULL              | NULL      | France        |
| NULL              | NULL      | India         |
| NULL              | NULL      | Japan         |
| NULL              | NULL      | Mexico        |
| Barack Obama      | politics  | United States |
| Serena Williams   | tennis    | United States |
| Venus Williams    | tennis    | United States |
+-------------------+-----------+---------------+
16 rows in set (0.00 sec)
```

You can see that some countries are present, even when they have no matching records in the **people** table.

16.7. mysql triggers

16.7.1. using a before trigger

Consider the following **create table** command. The last field (**amount**) is the multiplication of the two fields named **unitprice** and **unitcount**.

```
mysql> create table invoices (
    -> id char(8) NOT NULL,
    -> customerid char(3) NOT NULL,
    -> unitprice int,
    -> unitcount smallint,
    -> amount int );
Query OK, 0 rows affected (0.00 sec)
```

We can let mysql do the calculation for that by using a **before trigger**. The screenshot below shows the creation of a trigger that calculates the amount by multiplying two fields that are about to be inserted.

```
mysql> create trigger total_amount before INSERT on invoices
```

```
      -> for each row set new.amount = new.unitprice * new.unitcount ;
Query OK, 0 rows affected (0.02 sec)
```

Here we verify that the trigger works by inserting a new record, without providing the total amount.

```
mysql> insert into invoices values ('20090526','ABC','199','10','');
Query OK, 1 row affected (0.02 sec)
```

Looking at the record proves that the trigger works.

```
mysql> select * from invoices;
+----------+------------+-----------+-----------+--------+
| id       | customerid | unitprice | unitcount | amount |
+----------+------------+-----------+-----------+--------+
| 20090526 | ABC        |       199 |        10 |   1990 |
+----------+------------+-----------+-----------+--------+
1 row in set (0.00 sec)
```

16.7.2. removing a trigger

When a **trigger** is no longer needed, you can delete it with the **drop trigger** command.

```
mysql> drop trigger total_amount;
Query OK, 0 rows affected (0.00 sec)
```

Part V. Introduction to Samba

Table of Contents

Chapter 17. introduction to samba

This introduction to the Samba server simply explains how to install Samba 3 and briefly mentions the SMB protocol.

17.1. verify installed version

17.1.1. .rpm based distributions

To see the version of samba installed on Red Hat, Fedora or CentOS use **rpm -q samba**.

```
[root@RHEL52 ~]# rpm -q samba
samba-3.0.28-1.el5_2.1
```

The screenshot above shows that RHEL5 has **Samba** version 3.0 installed. The last number in the Samba version counts the number of updates or patches.

Below the same command on a more recent version of CentOS with Samba version 3.5 installed.

```
[root@centos6 ~]# rpm -q samba
samba-3.5.10-116.el6_2.i686
```

17.1.2. .deb based distributions

Use **dpkg -l** or **aptitide show** on Debian or Ubuntu. Both Debian 7.0 (Wheezy) and Ubuntu 12.04 (Precise) use version 3.6.3 of the Samba server.

```
root@debian7~# aptitude show samba | grep Version
Version: 2:3.6.3-1
```

Ubuntu 12.04 is currently at Samba version 3.6.3.

```
root@ubu1204:~# dpkg -l samba | tail -1
ii samba 2:3.6.3-2ubuntu2.1 SMB/CIFS file, print, and login server for Unix
```

17.2. installing samba

17.2.1. .rpm based distributions

Samba is installed by default on Red Hat Enterprise Linux. If Samba is not yet installed, then you can use the graphical menu (Applications -- System Settings -- Add/Remove Applications) and select "Windows File Server" in the Server section. The non-graphical way is to use **rpm** or **yum**.

When you downloaded the .rpm file, you can install Samba like this.

```
[paul@RHEL52 ~]$ rpm -i samba-3.0.28-1.el5_2.1.rpm
```

When you have a subscription to RHN (Red Hat Network), then **yum** is an easy tool to use. This **yum** command works by default on Fedora and CentOS.

```
[root@centos6 ~]# yum install samba
```

17.2.2. .deb based distributions

Ubuntu and Debian users can use the **aptitude** program (or use a graphical tool like Synaptic).

```
root@debian7~# aptitude install samba
The following NEW packages will be installed:
  samba samba-common{a} samba-common-bin{a} tdb-tools{a}
0 packages upgraded, 4 newly installed, 0 to remove and 1 not upgraded.
Need to get 15.1 MB of archives. After unpacking 42.9 MB will be used.
Do you want to continue? [Y/n/?]
...
```

17.3. documentation

17.3.1. samba howto

Samba comes with excellent documentation in html and pdf format (and also as a free download from samba.org and it is for sale as a printed book).

The documentation is a separate package, so install it if you want it on the server itself.

```
[root@centos6 ~]# yum install samba-doc
...
[root@centos6 ~]# ls -l /usr/share/doc/samba-doc-3.5.10/
total 10916
drwxr-xr-x. 6 root root    4096 May  6 15:50 htmldocs
-rw-r--r--. 1 root root 4605496 Jun 14  2011 Samba3-ByExample.pdf
-rw-r--r--. 1 root root  608260 Jun 14  2011 Samba3-Developers-Guide.pdf
-rw-r--r--. 1 root root 5954602 Jun 14  2011 Samba3-HOWTO.pdf
```

This action is very similar on Ubuntu and Debian except that the pdf files are in a separate package named **samba-doc-pdf**.

```
root@ubu1204:~# aptitude install samba-doc-pdf
The following NEW packages will be installed:
  samba-doc-pdf
...
```

17.3.2. samba by example

Besides the howto, there is also an excellent book called **Samba By Example** (again available as printed edition in shops, and as a free pdf and html).

17.4. starting and stopping samba

You can start the daemons by invoking **/etc/init.d/smb start** (some systems use **/etc/init.d/ samba**) on any linux.

```
root@laika:~# /etc/init.d/samba stop
 * Stopping Samba daemons                                   [ OK ]
root@laika:~# /etc/init.d/samba start
 * Starting Samba daemons                                   [ OK ]
root@laika:~# /etc/init.d/samba restart
 * Stopping Samba daemons                                   [ OK ]
 * Starting Samba daemons                                   [ OK ]
root@laika:~# /etc/init.d/samba status
 * SMBD is running                                          [ OK ]
```

Red Hat derived systems are happy with **service smb start**.

```
[root@RHEL4b ~]# /etc/init.d/smb start
Starting SMB services:                                   [  OK  ]
Starting NMB services:                                   [  OK  ]
[root@RHEL4b ~]# service smb restart
Shutting down SMB services:                              [  OK  ]
Shutting down NMB services:                              [  OK  ]
Starting SMB services:                                   [  OK  ]
Starting NMB services:                                   [  OK  ]
[root@RHEL4b ~]#
```

17.5. samba daemons

Samba 3 consists of three daemons, they are named **nmbd**, **smbd** and **winbindd**.

17.5.1. nmbd

The **nmbd** daemon takes care of all the names and naming. It registers and resolves names, and handles browsing. According to the Samba documentation, it should be the first daemon to start.

```
[root@RHEL52 ~]# ps -C nmbd
  PID TTY          TIME CMD
 5681 ?        00:00:00 nmbd
```

17.5.2. smbd

The **smbd** daemon manages file transfers and authentication.

```
[root@RHEL52 ~]# ps -C smbd
  PID TTY          TIME CMD
 5678 ?        00:00:00 smbd
 5683 ?        00:00:00 smbd
```

17.5.3. winbindd

The **winbind daemon** (winbindd) is only started to handle Microsoft Windows domain membership.

Note that **winbindd** is started by the **/etc/init.d/winbind** script (two dd's for the daemon and only one d for the script).

```
[root@RHEL52 ~]# /etc/init.d/winbind start
Starting Winbind services:                              [  OK  ]
[root@RHEL52 ~]# ps -C winbindd
  PID TTY          TIME CMD
 5752 ?        00:00:00 winbindd
 5754 ?        00:00:00 winbindd
```

On Debian and Ubuntu, the winbindd daemon is installed via a separate package called **winbind**.

17.6. the SMB protocol

17.6.1. brief history

Development of this protocol was started by **IBM** in the early eighties. By the end of the eighties, most develpment was done by **Microsoft**. SMB is an application level protocol designed to run on top of NetBIOS/NetBEUI, but can also be run on top of tcp/ip.

In 1996 Microsoft was asked to document the protocol. They submitted CIFS (Common Internet File System) as an internet draft, but it never got final rfc status.

In 2004 the European Union decided Microsoft should document the protocol to enable other developers to write compatible software. December 20th 2007 Microsoft came to an agreement. The Samba team now has access to SMB/CIFS, Windows for Workgroups and Active Directory documentation.

17.6.2. broadcasting protocol

SMB uses the NetBIOS **service location protocol**, which is a broadcasting protocol. This means that NetBIOS names have to be unique on the network (even when you have different IP-addresses). Having duplicate names on an SMB network can seriously harm communications.

17.6.3. NetBIOS names

NetBIOS names are similar to **hostnames**, but are always uppercase and only 15 characters in length. Microsoft Windows computers and Samba servers will broadcast this name on the network.

17.6.4. network bandwidth

Having many broadcasting SMB/CIFS computers on your network can cause bandwidth issues. A solution can be the use of a **NetBIOS name server** (NBNS) like **WINS** (Windows Internet Naming Service).

17.7. practice: introduction to samba

0. !! Make sure you know your student number, anything *ANYTHING* you name must include your student number!

1. Verify that you can logon to a Linux/Unix computer. Write down the name and ip address of this computer.

2. Do the same for all the other (virtual) machines available to you.

3. Verify networking by pinging the computer, edit the appropriate hosts files so you can use names. Test the names by pinging them.

4. Make sure Samba is installed, write down the version of Samba.

5. Open the Official Samba-3 howto pdf file that is installed on your computer. How many A4 pages is this file ? Then look at the same pdf on samba.org, it is updated regularly.

6. Stop the Samba server.

Chapter 18. getting started with samba

18.1. /etc/samba/smb.conf

18.1.1. smbd -b

Samba configuration is done in the **smb.conf** file. The file can be edited manually, or you can use a web based interface like webmin or swat to manage it. The file is usually located in /etc/samba. You can find the exact location with **smbd -b**.

```
[root@RHEL4b ~]# smbd -b | grep CONFIGFILE
CONFIGFILE: /etc/samba/smb.conf
```

18.1.2. the default smb.conf

The default smb.conf file contains a lot of examples with explanations.

```
[paul@RHEL4b ~]$ ls -l /etc/samba/smb.conf
-rw-r--r--  1 root root 10836 May 30 23:08 /etc/samba/smb.conf
```

Also on Ubuntu and Debian, smb.conf is packed with samples and explanations.

```
paul@laika:~$ ls -l /etc/samba/smb.conf
-rw-r--r-- 1 root root 10515 2007-05-24 00:21 /etc/samba/smb.conf
```

18.1.3. minimal smb.conf

Below is an example of a very minimalistic **smb.conf**. It allows samba to start, and to be visible to other computers (Microsoft shows computers in Network Neighborhood or My Network Places).

```
[paul@RHEL4b ~]$ cat /etc/samba/smb.conf
[global]
workgroup = WORKGROUP
[firstshare]
path = /srv/samba/public
```

18.1.4. net view

Below is a screenshot of the **net view** command on Microsoft Windows Server 2003 sp2. It shows how a Red Hat Enterprise Linux 5.3 and a Ubuntu 9.04 Samba server, both with a minimalistic smb.conf, are visible to Microsoft computers nearby.

```
C:\Documents and Settings\Administrator>net view
Server Name            Remark
-------------------------------------------------------------------
\\LAIKA                Samba 3.3.2
\\RHEL53               Samba 3.0.33-3.7.el5
\\W2003
The command completed successfully.
```

18.1.5. long lines in smb.conf

Some parameters in smb.conf can get a long list of values behind them. You can continue a line (for clarity) on the next by ending the line with a backslash.

```
valid users = Serena, Venus, Lindsay \
```

```
        Kim, Justine, Sabine \
        Amelie, Marie, Suzanne
```

18.1.6. curious smb.conf

Curious but true: smb.conf accepts synonyms like **create mode** and **create mask**, and (sometimes) minor spelling errors like **browsable** and **browseable**. And on occasion you can even switch words, the **guest only** parameter is identical to **only guest**. And **writable = yes** is the same as **readonly = no**.

18.1.7. man smb.conf

You can access a lot of documentation when typing **man smb.conf**.

```
[root@RHEL4b samba]# apropos samba
cupsaddsmb       (8)  - export printers to samba for windows clients
lmhosts          (5)  - The Samba NetBIOS hosts file
net              (8)  - Tool for administration of Samba and remote CIFS servers
pdbedit          (8)  - manage the SAM database (Database of Samba Users)
samba            (7)  - A Windows SMB/CIFS fileserver for UNIX
smb.conf [smb]   (5)  - The configuration file for the Samba suite
smbpasswd        (5)  - The Samba encrypted password file
smbstatus        (1)  - report on current Samba connections
swat             (8)  - Samba Web Administration Tool
tdbbackup        (8)  - tool for backing up and ... of samba .tdb files
[root@RHEL4b samba]#
```

18.2. /usr/bin/testparm

18.2.1. syntax check smb.conf

To verify the syntax of the smb.conf file, you can use **testparm**.

```
[paul@RHEL4b ~]$ testparm
Load smb config files from /etc/samba/smb.conf
Processing section "[firstshare]"
Loaded services file OK.
Server role: ROLE_STANDALONE
Press enter to see a dump of your service definitions
```

18.2.2. testparm -v

An interesting option is **testparm -v**, which will output all the global options with their default value.

```
[root@RHEL52 ~]# testparm -v | head
Load smb config files from /etc/samba/smb.conf
Processing section "[pub0]"
Processing section "[global$]"
Loaded services file OK.
Server role: ROLE_STANDALONE
Press enter to see a dump of your service definitions

[global]
 dos charset = CP850
 unix charset = UTF-8
 display charset = LOCALE
 workgroup = WORKGROUP
```

```
realm =
netbios name = TEACHER0
netbios aliases =
netbios scope =
server string = Samba 3.0.28-1.el5_2.1
...
```

There were about 350 default values for smb.conf parameters in Samba 3.0.x. This number grew to almost 400 in Samba 3.5.x.

18.2.3. testparm -s

The samba daemons are constantly (once every 60 seconds) checking the smb.conf file, so it is good practice to keep this file small. But it is also good practice to document your samba configuration, and to explicitly set options that have the same default values. The **testparm -s** option allows you to do both. It will output the smallest possible samba configuration file, while retaining all your settings. The idea is to have your samba configuration in another file (like smb.conf.full) and let testparm parse this for you. The screenshot below shows you how. First the smb.conf.full file with the explicitly set option workgroup to WORKGROUP.

```
[root@RHEL4b samba]# cat smb.conf.full
[global]
workgroup = WORKGROUP

# This is a demo of a documented smb.conf
# These two lines are removed by testparm -s

server string = Public Test Server

[firstshare]
path = /srv/samba/public
```

Next, we execute testparm with the -s option, and redirect stdout to the real **smb.conf** file.

```
[root@RHEL4b samba]# testparm -s smb.conf.full > smb.conf
Load smb config files from smb.conf.full
Processing section "[firstshare]"
Loaded services file OK.
```

And below is the end result. The two comment lines and the default option are no longer there.

```
[root@RHEL4b samba]# cat smb.conf
# Global parameters
[global]
server string = Public Test Server

[firstshare]
path = /srv/samba/public
[root@RHEL4b samba]#
```

18.3. /usr/bin/smbclient

18.3.1. smbclient looking at Samba

With **smbclient** you can see browsing and share information from your smb server. It will display all your shares, your workgroup, and the name of the Master Browser. The -N switch is added to avoid having to enter an empty password. The -L switch is followed by the name of the host to check.

```
[root@RHEL4b init.d]# smbclient -NL rhel4b
Anonymous login successful
Domain=[WORKGROUP] OS=[Unix] Server=[Samba 3.0.10-1.4E.9]

Sharename       Type        Comment
---------       ----        -------
firstshare      Disk
IPC$            IPC         IPC Service (Public Test Server)
ADMIN$          IPC         IPC Service (Public Test Server)
Anonymous login successful
Domain=[WORKGROUP] OS=[Unix] Server=[Samba 3.0.10-1.4E.9]

Server                  Comment
---------               -------
RHEL4B                  Public Test Server
WINXP

Workgroup               Master
---------               -------
WORKGROUP               WINXP
```

18.3.2. smbclient anonymous

The screenshot below uses **smbclient** to display information about a remote smb server (in this case a computer with Ubuntu 11.10).

```
root@ubu1110:/etc/samba# testparm smbclient -NL 127.0.0.1
Anonymous login successful
Domain=[LINUXTR] OS=[Unix] Server=[Samba 3.5.11]

Sharename       Type        Comment
---------       ----        -------
share1          Disk
IPC$            IPC         IPC Service (Samba 3.5.11)
Anonymous login successful
Domain=[LINUXTR] OS=[Unix] Server=[Samba 3.5.11]

Server                  Comment
---------               -------

Workgroup               Master
---------               -------
LINUXTR                 DEBIAN6
WORKGROUP               UBU1110
```

18.3.3. smbclient with credentials

Windows versions after xp sp2 and 2003 sp1 do not accept guest access (the NT_STATUS_ACCESS_DENIED error). This example shows how to provide credentials with **smbclient**.

```
[paul@RHEL53 ~]$ smbclient -L w2003 -U administrator%stargate
Domain=[W2003] OS=[Windows Server 2003 3790 Service Pack 2] Server=...

Sharename       Type        Comment
---------       ----        -------
C$              Disk        Default share
```

```
IPC$            IPC       Remote IPC
ADMIN$          Disk      Remote Admin
...
```

18.4. /usr/bin/smbtree

Another useful tool to troubleshoot Samba or simply to browse the SMB network is **smbtree**. In its simplest form, smbtree will do an anonymous browsing on the local subnet. displaying all SMB computers and (if authorized) their shares.

Let's take a look at two screenshots of smbtree in action (with blank password). The first one is taken immediately after booting four different computers (one MS Windows 2000, one MS Windows xp, one MS Windows 2003 and one RHEL 4 with Samba 3.0.10).

```
[paul@RHEL4b ~]$ smbtree
Password:
WORKGROUP
PEGASUS
 \\WINXP
 \\RHEL4B                              Pegasus Domain Member Server
Error connecting to 127.0.0.1 (Connection refused)
cli_full_connection: failed to connect to RHEL4B<20> (127.0.0.1)
 \\HM2003
[paul@RHEL4b ~]$
```

The information displayed in the previous screenshot looks incomplete. The browsing elections are still ongoing, the browse list is not yet distributed to all clients by the (to be elected) browser master. The next screenshot was taken about one minute later. And it shows even less.

```
[paul@RHEL4b ~]$ smbtree
Password:
WORKGROUP
 \\W2000
[paul@RHEL4b ~]$
```

So we wait a while, and then run **smbtree** again, this time it looks a lot nicer.

```
[paul@RHEL4b ~]$ smbtree
Password:
WORKGROUP
 \\W2000
PEGASUS
 \\WINXP
 \\RHEL4B                       Pegasus Domain Member Server
  \\RHEL4B\ADMIN$                IPC Service (Pegasus Domain Member Server)
  \\RHEL4B\IPC$                  IPC Service (Pegasus Domain Member Server)
  \\RHEL4B\domaindata            Active Directory users only
 \\HM2003
[paul@RHEL4b ~]$ smbtree --version
Version 3.0.10-1.4E.9
[paul@RHEL4b ~]$
```

I added the version number of **smbtree** in the previous screenshot, to show you the difference when using the latest version of smbtree (below a screenshot taken from Ubuntu Feisty Fawn). The latest version shows a more complete overview of machines and shares.

```
paul@laika:~$ smbtree --version
Version 3.0.24
```

```
paul@laika:~$ smbtree
Password:
WORKGROUP
 \\W2000
  \\W2000\firstshare
  \\W2000\C$              Default share
  \\W2000\ADMIN$          Remote Admin
  \\W2000\IPC$            Remote IPC
PEGASUS
 \\WINXP
cli_rpc_pipe_open: cli_nt_create failed on pipe \srvsvc to machine WINXP.
Error was NT_STATUS_ACCESS_DENIED
  \\RHEL4B                       Pegasus Domain Member Server
   \\RHEL4B\ADMIN$               IPC Service (Pegasus Domain Member Server)
   \\RHEL4B\IPC$                 IPC Service (Pegasus Domain Member Server)
   \\RHEL4B\domaindata           Active Directory users only
  \\HM2003
cli_rpc_pipe_open: cli_nt_create failed on pipe \srvsvc to machine HM2003.
Error was NT_STATUS_ACCESS_DENIED
paul@laika:~$
```

The previous screenshot also provides useful errors on why we cannot see shared info on computers winxp and w2003. Let us try the old **smbtree** version on our RHEL server, but this time with Administrator credentials (which are the same on all computers).

```
[paul@RHEL4b ~]$ smbtree -UAdministrator%Stargate1
WORKGROUP
 \\W2000
PEGASUS
 \\WINXP
  \\WINXP\C$              Default share
  \\WINXP\ADMIN$          Remote Admin
  \\WINXP\share55
  \\WINXP\IPC$            Remote IPC
 \\RHEL4B                 Pegasus Domain Member Server
  \\RHEL4B\ADMIN$         IPC Service (Pegasus Domain Member Server)
  \\RHEL4B\IPC$           IPC Service (Pegasus Domain Member Server)
  \\RHEL4B\domaindata     Active Directory users only
 \\HM2003
  \\HM2003\NETLOGON       Logon server share
  \\HM2003\SYSVOL         Logon server share
  \\HM2003\WSUSTemp       A network share used by Local Publishing ...
  \\HM2003\ADMIN$         Remote Admin
  \\HM2003\tools
  \\HM2003\IPC$           Remote IPC
  \\HM2003\WsusContent    A network share to be used by Local ...
  \\HM2003\C$             Default share
[paul@RHEL4b ~]$
```

As you can see, this gives a very nice overview of all SMB computers and their shares.

18.5. server string

The comment seen by the **net view** and the **smbclient** commands is the default value for the **server string** option. Simply adding this value to the global section in **smb.conf** and restarting samba will change the option.

```
[root@RHEL53 samba]# testparm -s 2>/dev/null | grep server
 server string = Red Hat Server in Paris
```

After a short while, the changed option is visible on the Microsoft computers.

```
C:\Documents and Settings\Administrator>net view
Server Name            Remark

-------------------------------------------------------------------------
\\LAIKA                Ubuntu 9.04 server in Antwerp
\\RHEL53               Red Hat Server in Paris
\\W2003
```

18.6. Samba Web Administration Tool (SWAT)

Samba comes with a web based tool to manage your samba configuration file. **SWAT** is accessible with a web browser on port 901 of the host system. To enable the tool, first find out whether your system is using the **inetd** or the **xinetd** superdaemon.

```
[root@RHEL4b samba]# ps fax | grep inet
 15026 pts/0    S+     0:00                        \_ grep inet
  2771 ?        Ss     0:00 xinetd -stayalive -pidfile /var/run/xinetd.pid
[root@RHEL4b samba]#
```

Then edit the **inetd.conf** or change the disable = yes line in **/etc/xinetd.d/swat** to disable = no.

```
[root@RHEL4b samba]# cat /etc/xinetd.d/swat
# default: off
# description: SWAT is the Samba Web Admin Tool. Use swat \
#              to configure your Samba server. To use SWAT, \
#              connect to port 901 with your favorite web browser.
service swat
{
 port            = 901
 socket_type     = stream
 wait            = no
 only_from       = 127.0.0.1
 user            = root
 server          = /usr/sbin/swat
 log_on_failure  += USERID
 disable         = no
}
[root@RHEL4b samba]# /etc/init.d/xinetd restart
Stopping xinetd:                                        [  OK  ]
Starting xinetd:                                        [  OK  ]
[root@RHEL4b samba]#
```

Change the **only from** value to enable swat from remote computers. This examples shows how to provide swat access to all computers in a /24 subnet.

```
[root@RHEL53 xinetd.d]# grep only /etc/xinetd.d/swat
 only_from  = 192.168.1.0/24
```

Be careful when using SWAT, it erases all your manually edited comments in smb.conf.

18.7. practice: getting started with samba

1. Take a backup copy of the original smb.conf, name it smb.conf.orig

2. Enable SWAT and take a look at it.

3. Stop the Samba server.

4. Create a minimalistic smb.conf.minimal and test it with testparm.

5. Use tesparm -s to create /etc/samba/smb.conf from your smb.conf.minimal .

6. Start Samba with your minimal smb.conf.

7. Verify with smbclient that your Samba server works.

8. Verify that another (Microsoft) computer can see your Samba server.

9. Browse the network with net view, smbtree and with Windows Explorer.

10. Change the "Server String" parameter in smb.conf. How long does it take before you see the change (net view, smbclient, My Network Places,...) ?

11. Will restarting Samba after a change to smb.conf speed up the change ?

12. Which computer is the master browser master in your workgroup ? What is the master browser ?

13. If time permits (or if you are waiting for other students to finish this practice), then install a sniffer (wireshark) and watch the browser elections.

18.8. solution: getting started with samba

1. Take a backup copy of the original smb.conf, name it smb.conf.orig

```
cd /etc/samba ; cp smb.conf smb.conf.orig
```

2. Enable SWAT and take a look at it.

```
on Debian/Ubuntu: vi /etc/inetd.conf (remove # before swat)
```

```
on RHEL/Fedora: vi /etc/xinetd.d/swat (set disable to no)
```

3. Stop the Samba server.

```
/etc/init.d/smb stop (Red Hat)
```

```
/etc/init.d/samba stop (Debian)
```

4. Create a minimalistic smb.conf.minimal and test it with testparm.

```
cd /etc/samba ; mkdir my_smb_confs ; cd my_smb_confs
```

```
vi smb.conf.minimal
```

```
testparm smb.conf.minimal
```

5. Use tesparm -s to create /etc/samba/smb.conf from your smb.conf.minimal .

```
testparm -s smb.conf.minimal > ../smb.conf
```

6. Start Samba with your minimal smb.conf.

```
/etc/init.d/smb restart (Red Hat)
```

```
/etc/init.d/samba restart (Debian)
```

7. Verify with smbclient that your Samba server works.

```
smbclient -NL 127.0.0.1
```

8. Verify that another computer can see your Samba server.

```
smbclient -NL 'ip-address' (on a Linux)
```

9. Browse the network with net view, smbtree and with Windows Explorer.

```
on Linux: smbtree
```

```
on Windows: net view (and WindowsKey ı e)
```

10. Change the "Server String" parameter in smb.conf. How long does it take before you see the change (net view, smbclient, My Network Places,...) ?

```
vi /etc/samba/smb.conf
```

```
(should take only seconds when restarting samba)
```

11. Will restarting Samba after a change to smb.conf speed up the change ?

```
yes
```

12. Which computer is the master browser master in your workgroup ? What is the master browser ?

```
The computer that won the elections.
```

```
This machine will make the list of computers in the network
```

13. If time permits (or if you are waiting for other students to finish this practice), then install a sniffer (wireshark) and watch the browser elections.

```
On ubuntu: sudo aptitude install wireshark
```

```
then: sudo wireshark, select interface
```

Chapter 19. a read only file server

19.1. Setting up a directory to share

Let's start with setting up a very simple read only file server with Samba. Everyone (even anonymous guests) will receive read access.

The first step is to create a directory and put some test files in it.

```
[root@RHEL52 ~]# mkdir -p /srv/samba/readonly
[root@RHEL52 ~]# cd /srv/samba/readonly/
[root@RHEL52 readonly]# echo "It is cold today." > winter.txt
[root@RHEL52 readonly]# echo "It is hot today." > summer.txt
[root@RHEL52 readonly]# ls -l
total 8
-rw-r--r-- 1 root root 17 Jan 21 05:49 summer.txt
-rw-r--r-- 1 root root 18 Jan 21 05:49 winter.txt
[root@RHEL52 readonly]#
```

19.2. configure the share

19.2.1. smb.conf [global] section

In this example the samba server is a member of WORKGROUP (the default workgroup). We also set a descriptive server string, this string is visible to users browsing the network with net view, windows explorer or smbclient.

```
[root@RHEL52 samba]# head -5 smb.conf
[global]
 workgroup = WORKGROUP
 server string = Public Anonymous File Server
 netbios name = TEACHER0
 security = share
```

You might have noticed the line with **security = share**. This line sets the default security mode for our samba server. Setting the security mode to **share** will allow clients (smbclient, any windows, another Samba server, ...) to provide a password for each share. This is one way of using the SMB/CIFS protocol. The other way (called **user mode**) will allow the client to provide a username/password combination, before the server knows which share the client wants to access.

19.2.2. smb.conf [share] section

The share is called pubread and the path is set to our newly created directory. Everyone is allowed access (**guest ok = yes**) and security is set to read only.

```
[pubread]
path = /srv/samba/readonly
comment = files to read
read only = yes
guest ok = yes
```

Here is a very similar configuration on Ubuntu 11.10.

```
root@ubu1110:~# cat /etc/samba/smb.conf
[global]
workgroup = LINUXTR
netbios name = UBU1110
security = share
[roshare1]
path = /srv/samba/readonly
read only = yes
guest ok = yes
```

It doesn't really matter which Linux distribution you use. Below the same config on Debian 6, as good as identical.

```
root@debian6:~# cat /etc/samba/smb.conf
[global]
workgroup = LINUXTR
netbios name = DEBIAN6
security = share
[roshare1]
path = /srv/samba/readonly
read only = yes
guest ok = yes
```

19.3. restart the server

After testing with **testparm**, restart the samba server (so you don't have to wait).

```
[root@RHEL4b readonly]# service smb restart
Shutting down SMB services:                        [  OK  ]
Shutting down NMB services:                        [  OK  ]
Starting SMB services:                             [  OK  ]
Starting NMB services:                             [  OK  ]
```

19.4. verify the share

19.4.1. verify with smbclient

You can now verify the existence of the share with **smbclient**. Our **pubread** is listed as the fourth share.

```
[root@RHEL52 samba]# smbclient -NL 127.0.0.1
Domain=[WORKGROUP] OS=[Unix] Server=[Samba 3.0.33-3.7.el5]

    Sharename       Type      Comment
    ---------       ----      -------
    IPC$            IPC       IPC Service (Public Anonymous File Server)
    global$         Disk
    pub0            Disk
    pubread         Disk      files to read
Domain=[WORKGROUP] OS=[Unix] Server=[Samba 3.0.33-3.7.el5]

    Server              Comment
    ---------           -------
    TEACHER0            Samba 3.0.33-3.7.el5
    W2003EE

    Workgroup           Master
    ---------           -------
    WORKGROUP           W2003EE
```

19.4.2. verify on windows

The final test is to go to a Microsoft windows computer and read a file on the Samba server. First we use the **net use** command to mount the pubread share on the driveletter k.

```
C:\>net use K: \\teacher0\pubread
The command completed successfully.
```

Then we test looking at the contents of the share, and reading the files.

```
C:\>dir k:
 Volume in drive K is pubread
 Volume Serial Number is 0C82-11F2

 Directory of K:\

21/01/2009  05:49    <DIR>          .
21/01/2009  05:49    <DIR>          ..
21/01/2009  05:49                17 summer.txt
21/01/2009  05:49                18 winter.txt
               2 File(s)             35 bytes
               2 Dir(s)   13.496.242.176 bytes free
```

Just to be on the safe side, let us try writing.

```
K:\>echo very cold > winter.txt
Access is denied.

K:\>
```

Or you can use windows explorer...

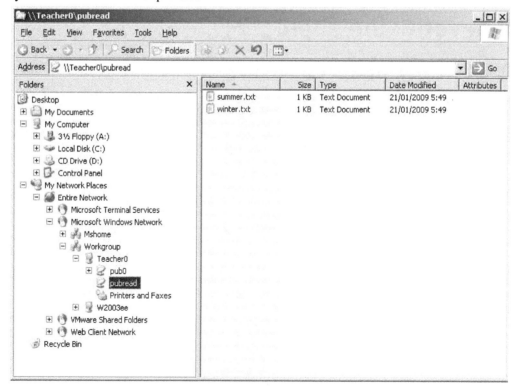

19.5. a note on netcat

The Windows command line screenshot is made in a Linux console, using **netcat** as a pipe to a Windows command shell.

The way this works, is by enabling netcat to listen on the windows computer to a certain port, executing cmd.exe when a connection is received. Netcat is similar to cat, in the way that cat does nothing, only netcat does nothing over the network.

To enable this connection, type the following on the windows computer (after downloading netcat for windows).

```
nc -l -p 23 -t -e cmd.exe
```

And then connect to this machine with netcat from any Linux computer. You end up with a cmd.exe prompt inside your Linux shell.

```
paul@laika:~$ nc 192.168.1.38 23
Microsoft Windows [Version 5.2.3790]
(C) Copyright 1985-2003 Microsoft Corp.

C:\>net use k: /delete
net use k: /delete
k: was deleted successfully.
```

19.6. practice: read only file server

1. Create a directory in a good location (FHS) to share files for everyone to read.

2. Make sure the directory is owned properly and is world accessible.

3. Put a textfile in this directory.

4. Share the directory with Samba.

5. Verify from your own and from another computer (smbclient, net use, ...) that the share is accessible for reading.

6. Make a backup copy of your smb.conf, name it smb.conf.ReadOnlyFileServer.

19.7. solution: read only file server

1. Create a directory in a good location (FHS) to share files for everyone to read.

```
choose one of these...

mkdir -p /srv/samba/readonly

mkdir -p /home/samba/readonly

/home/paul/readonly is wrong!!

/etc/samba/readonly is wrong!!

/readonly is wrong!!
```

2. Make sure the directory is owned properly and is world accessible.

```
chown root:root /srv/samba/readonly

chmod 755 /srv/samba/readonly
```

3. Put a textfile in this directory.

```
echo Hello World > hello.txt
```

4. Share the directory with Samba.

```
You smb.conf.readonly could look like this:
[global]
 workgroup = WORKGROUP
 server string = Read Only File Server
 netbios name = STUDENTx
 security = share

[readonlyX]
 path = /srv/samba/readonly
 comment = read only file share
 read only = yes
 guest ok = yes


test with testparm before going in production!
```

5. Verify from your own and from another computer (smbclient, net use, ...) that the share is accessible for reading.

```
On Linux: smbclient -NL 127.0.0.1

On Windows Explorer: browse to My Network Places

On Windows cmd.exe: net use L: //studentx/readonly
```

6. Make a backup copy of your smb.conf, name it smb.conf.ReadOnlyFileServer.

```
cp smb.conf smb.conf.ReadOnlyFileServer
```

Chapter 20. a writable file server

20.1. set up a directory to share

In this second example, we will create a share where everyone can create files and write to files. Again, we start by creating a directory

```
[root@RHEL52 samba]# mkdir -p /srv/samba/writable
[root@RHEL52 samba]# chmod 777 /srv/samba/writable/
```

20.2. share section in smb.conf

There are two parameters to make a share writable. We can use **read only** or **writable**. This example shows how to use **writable** to give write access to a share.

```
writable = yes
```

And this is an example of using the **read only** parameter to give write access to a share.

```
read only = no
```

20.3. configure the share

Then we simply add a share to our file server by editing **smb.conf**. Below the check with testparm. (We could have changed the description of the server...)

```
[root@RHEL52 samba]# testparm
Load smb config files from /etc/samba/smb.conf
Processing section "[pubwrite]"
Processing section "[pubread]"
Loaded services file OK.
Server role: ROLE_STANDALONE
Press enter to see a dump of your service definitions

[global]
 netbios name = TEACHER0
 server string = Public Anonymous File Server
 security = SHARE

[pubwrite]
 comment = files to write
 path = /srv/samba/writable
 read only = No
 guest ok = Yes

[pubread]
 comment = files to read
 path = /srv/samba/readonly
 guest ok = Yes
```

20.4. test connection with windows

We can now test the connection on a windows 2003 computer. We use the **net use** for this.

```
C:\>net use L: \\teacher0\pubwrite
net use L: \\teacher0\pubwrite
The command completed successfully.
```

20.5. test writing with windows

We mounted the **pubwrite** share on the L: drive in windows. Below we test that we can write to this share.

```
L:\>echo hoi > hoi.txt

L:\>dir
 Volume in drive L is pubwrite
 Volume Serial Number is 0C82-272A

 Directory of L:\

21/01/2009  06:11    <DIR>          .
21/01/2009  06:11    <DIR>          ..
21/01/2009  06:16                 6 hoi.txt
               1 File(s)              6 bytes
               2 Dir(s)   13.496.238.080 bytes free
```

20.6. How is this possible ?

Linux (or any Unix) always needs a user account to gain access to a system. The windows computer did not provide the samba server with a user account or a password. Instead, the Linux owner of the files created through this writable share is the Linux guest account (usually named nobody).

```
[root@RHEL52 samba]# ls -l /srv/samba/writable/
total 4
-rwxr--r-- 1 nobody nobody 6 Jan 21 06:16 hoi.txt
```

So this is not the cleanest solution. We will need to improve this.

20.7. practice: writable file server

1. Create a directory and share it with Samba.

2. Make sure everyone can read and write files, test writing with smbclient and from a Microsoft computer.

3. Verify the ownership of files created by (various) users.

20.8. solution: writable file server

1. Create a directory and share it with Samba.

```
mkdir /srv/samba/writable

chmod 777 /srv/samba/writable


the share section in smb.conf can look like this:

[pubwrite]
 path = /srv/samba/writable
 comment = files to write
 read only = no
 guest ok = yes
```

2. Make sure everyone can read and write files, test writing with smbclient and from a Microsoft computer.

```
to test writing with smbclient:


echo one > count.txt
echo two >> count.txt
echo three >> count.txt
smbclient //localhost/pubwrite
Password:
smb: \> put count.txt
```

3. Verify the ownership of files created by (various) users.

```
ls -l /srv/samba/writable
```

Chapter 21. samba first user account

21.1. creating a samba user

We will create a user for our samba file server and make this user the owner of the directory and all of its files. This anonymous user gets a clear description, but does not get a login shell.

```
[root@RHEL52 samba]# useradd -s /bin/false sambanobody
[root@RHEL52 samba]# usermod -c "Anonymous Samba Access" sambanobody
[root@RHEL52 samba]# passwd sambanobody
Changing password for user sambanobody.
New UNIX password:
Retype new UNIX password:
passwd: all authentication tokens updated successfully.
```

21.2. ownership of files

We can use this user as owner of files and directories, instead of using the root account. This approach is clear and more secure.

```
[root@RHEL52 samba]# chown -R sambanobody:sambanobody /srv/samba/
[root@RHEL52 samba]# ls -al /srv/samba/writable/
total 12
drwxrwxrwx 2 sambanobody sambanobody 4096 Jan 21 06:11 .
drwxr-xr-x 6 sambanobody sambanobody 4096 Jan 21 06:11 ..
-rwxr--r-- 1 sambanobody sambanobody    6 Jan 21 06:16 hoi.txt
```

21.3. /usr/bin/smbpasswd

The sambanobody user account that we created in the previous examples is not yet used by samba. It just owns the files and directories that we created for our shares. The goal of this section is to force ownership of files created through the samba share to belong to our sambanobody user. Remember, our server is still accessible to everyone, nobody needs to know this user account or password. We just want a clean Linux server.

To accomplish this, we first have to tell Samba about this user. We can do this by adding the account to **smbpasswd**.

```
[root@RHEL52 samba]# smbpasswd -a sambanobody
New SMB password:
Retype new SMB password:
Added user sambanobody.
```

21.4. /etc/samba/smbpasswd

To find out where Samba keeps this information (for now), use **smbd -b**. The PRIVATE_DIR variable will show you where the smbpasswd database is located.

```
[root@RHEL52 samba]# smbd -b | grep PRIVATE
   PRIVATE_DIR: /etc/samba
[root@RHEL52 samba]# ls -l smbpasswd
-rw------- 1 root root 110 Jan 21 06:19 smbpasswd
```

You can use a simple cat to see the contents of the **smbpasswd** database. The sambanobody user does have a password (it is secret).

```
[root@RHEL52 samba]# cat smbpasswd
```

```
sambanobody:503:AE9 ... 9DB309C528E540978:[U        ]:LCT-4976B05B:
```

21.5. passdb backend

Note that recent versions of Samba have **tdbsam** as default for the **passdb backend** paramater.

```
root@ubu1110:~# testparm -v 2>/dev/null| grep 'passdb backend'

 passdb backend = tdbsam
```

21.6. forcing this user

Now that Samba knows about this user, we can adjust our writable share to force the ownership of files created through it. For this we use the **force user** and **force group** options. Now we can be sure that all files in the Samba writable share are owned by the same sambanobody user.

Below is the renewed definition of our share in smb.conf.

```
[pubwrite]
 path = /srv/samba/writable
 comment = files to write
 force user = sambanobody
 force group = sambanobody
 read only = no
 guest ok = yes
```

When you reconnect to the share and write a file, then this sambanobody user will own the newly created file (and nobody needs to know the password).

21.7. practice: first samba user account

1. Create a user account for use with samba.

2. Add this user to samba's user database.

3. Create a writable shared directory and use the "force user" and "force group" directives to force ownership of files.

4. Test the working of force user with smbclient, net use and Windows Explorer.

21.8. solution: first samba user account

1. Create a user account for use with samba.

```
useradd -s /bin/false smbguest

usermod -c 'samba guest'

passwd smbguest
```

2. Add this user to samba's user database.

```
smbpasswd -a smbguest
```

3. Create a writable shared directory and use the "force user" and "force group" directives to force ownership of files.

```
[userwrite]
 path = /srv/samba/userwrite
 comment = everyone writes files owned by smbguest
 read only = no
 guest ok = yes
 force user = smbguest
 force group = smbguest
```

4. Test the working of force user with smbclient, net use and Windows Explorer.

```
ls -l /srv/samba/userwrite (and verify ownership)
```

Chapter 22. samba authentication

22.1. creating the users on Linux

The goal of this example is to set up a file share accessible to a number of different users. The users will need to authenticate with their password before access to this share is granted. We will first create three randomly named users, each with their own password. First we add these users to Linux.

```
[root@RHEL52 ~]# useradd -c "Serena Williams" serena
[root@RHEL52 ~]# useradd -c "Justine Henin" justine
[root@RHEL52 ~]# useradd -c "Martina Hingis" martina
[root@RHEL52 ~]# passwd serena
Changing password for user serena.
New UNIX password:
Retype new UNIX password:
passwd: all authentication tokens updated successfully.
[root@RHEL52 ~]# passwd justine
Changing password for user justine.
New UNIX password:
Retype new UNIX password:
passwd: all authentication tokens updated successfully.
[root@RHEL52 ~]# passwd martina
Changing password for user martina.
New UNIX password:
Retype new UNIX password:
passwd: all authentication tokens updated successfully.
```

22.2. creating the users on samba

Then we add them to the **smbpasswd** file, with the same password.

```
[root@RHEL52 ~]# smbpasswd -a serena
New SMB password:
Retype new SMB password:
Added user serena.
[root@RHEL52 ~]# smbpasswd -a justine
New SMB password:
Retype new SMB password:
Added user justine.
[root@RHEL52 ~]# smbpasswd -a martina
New SMB password:
Retype new SMB password:
Added user martina.
```

22.3. security = user

Remember that we set samba's security mode to share with the **security = share** directive in the [global] section ? Since we now require users to always provide a userid and password for access to our samba server, we will need to change this. Setting **security = user** will require the client to provide samba with a valid userid and password before giving access to a share.

Our [global] section now looks like this.

```
[global]
 workgroup = WORKGROUP
 netbios name = TEACHER0
 server string = Samba File Server
 security = user
```

22.4. configuring the share

We add the following [share] section to our smb.conf (and we do not forget to create the directory /srv/samba/authwrite).

```
[authwrite]
path = /srv/samba/authwrite
comment = authenticated users only
read only = no
guest ok = no
```

22.5. testing access with net use

After restarting samba, we test with different users from within Microsoft computers. The screenshots use the **net use**First serena from Windows XP.

```
C:\>net use m: \\teacher0\authwrite stargate /user:serena
The command completed successfully.

C:\>m:

M:\>echo greetings from Serena > serena.txt
```

The next screenshot is martina on a Windows 2000 compulter, she succeeds in writing her files, but fails to overwrite the file from serena.

```
C:\>net use k: \\teacher0\authwrite stargate /user:martina
The command completed successfully.

C:\>k:

K:\>echo greetings from martina > Martina.txt

K:\>echo test overwrite > serena.txt
Access is denied.
```

22.6. testing access with smbclient

You can also test connecting with authentication with **smbclient**. First we test with a wrong password.

```
[root@RHEL52 samba]# smbclient //teacher0/authwrite -U martina wrongpass
session setup failed: NT_STATUS_LOGON_FAILURE
```

Then we test with the correct password, and verify that we can access a file on the share.

```
[root@RHEL52 samba]# smbclient //teacher0/authwrite -U martina stargate
Domain=[TEACHER0] OS=[Unix] Server=[Samba 3.0.33-3.7.el5]
smb: \> more serena.txt
getting file \serena.txt of size 14 as /tmp/smbmore.QQfmSN (6.8 kb/s)
one
two
three
smb: \> q
```

22.7. verify ownership

We now have a simple standalone samba file server with authenticated access. And the files in the shares belong to their proper owners.

```
[root@RHEL52 samba]# ls -l /srv/samba/authwrite/
total 8
-rwxr--r-- 1 martina martina  0 Jan 21 20:06 martina.txt
-rwxr--r-- 1 serena  serena  14 Jan 21 20:06 serena.txt
-rwxr--r-- 1 serena  serena   6 Jan 21 20:09 ser.txt
```

22.8. common problems

22.8.1. NT_STATUS_BAD_NETWORK_NAME

You can get **NT_STATUS_BAD_NETWORK_NAME** when you forget to create the target directory.

```
[root@RHEL52 samba]# rm -rf /srv/samba/authwrite/
[root@RHEL52 samba]# smbclient //teacher0/authwrite -U martina stargate
Domain=[TEACHER0] OS=[Unix] Server=[Samba 3.0.33-3.7.el5]
tree connect failed: NT_STATUS_BAD_NETWORK_NAME
```

22.8.2. NT_STATUS_LOGON_FAILURE

You can get **NT_STATUS_LOGON_FAILURE** when you type the wrong password or when you type an unexisting username.

```
[root@RHEL52 samba]# smbclient //teacher0/authwrite -U martina STARGATE
session setup failed: NT_STATUS_LOGON_FAILURE
```

22.8.3. usernames are (not) case sensitive

Remember that usernames om Linux are case sensitive.

```
[root@RHEL52 samba]# su - MARTINA
su: user MARTINA does not exist
```

```
[root@RHEL52 samba]# su - martina
[martina@RHEL52 ~]$
```

But usernames on Microsoft computers are not case sensitive.

```
[root@RHEL52 samba]# smbclient //teacher0/authwrite -U martina stargate
Domain=[TEACHER0] OS=[Unix] Server=[Samba 3.0.33-3.7.el5]
smb: \> q
[root@RHEL52 samba]# smbclient //teacher0/authwrite -U MARTINA stargate
Domain=[TEACHER0] OS=[Unix] Server=[Samba 3.0.33-3.7.el5]
smb: \> q
```

22.9. practice : samba authentication

0. Make sure you have properly named backups of your smb.conf of the previous practices.

1. Create three users (on the Linux and on the samba), remember their passwords!

2. Set up a shared directory that is only accessible to authenticated users.

3. Use smbclient and a windows computer to access your share, use more than one user account (windows requires a logoff/logon for this).

4. Verify that files created by these users belong to them.

5. Try to change or delete a file from another user.

22.10. solution: samba authentication

1. Create three users (on the Linux and on the samba), remember their passwords!

```
useradd -c 'SMB user1' userx

passwd userx
```

2. Set up a shared directory that is only accessible to authenticated users.

```
The shared section in smb.conf could look like this:
```

```
[authwrite]
 path = /srv/samba/authwrite
 comment = authenticated users only
 read only = no
 guest ok = no
```

3. Use smbclient and a windows computer to access your share, use more than one user account (windows requires a logoff/logon for this).

```
on Linux: smbclient //studentX/authwrite -U user1 password

on windows net use p: \\studentX\authwrite password /user:user2
```

4. Verify that files created by these users belong to them.

```
ls -l /srv/samba/authwrite
```

5. Try to change or delete a file from another user.

```
you should not be able to change or overwrite files from others.
```

Chapter 23. samba securing shares

23.1. security based on user name

23.1.1. valid users

To restrict users per share, you can use the **valid users** parameter. In the example below, only the users listed as valid will be able to access the tennis share.

```
[tennis]
path = /srv/samba/tennis
comment = authenticated and valid users only
read only = No
guest ok = No
valid users = serena, kim, venus, justine
```

23.1.2. invalid users

If you are paranoia, you can also use **invalid users** to explicitely deny the listed users access. When a user is in both lists, the user has no access!

```
[tennis]
path = /srv/samba/tennis
read only = No
guest ok = No
valid users = kim, serena, venus, justine
invalid users = venus
```

23.1.3. read list

On a writable share, you can set a list of read only users with the **read list** parameter.

```
[football]
path = /srv/samba/football
read only = No
guest ok = No
read list = martina, roberto
```

23.1.4. write list

Even on a read only share, you can set a list of users that can write. Use the **write list** parameter.

```
[football]
path = /srv/samba/golf
read only = Yes
guest ok = No
write list = eddy, jan
```

23.2. security based on ip-address

23.2.1. hosts allow

The **hosts allow** or **allow hosts** parameter is one of the key advantages of Samba. It allows access control of shares on the ip-address level. To allow only specific hosts to access a share, list the hosts, separated by comma's.

```
allow hosts = 192.168.1.5, 192.168.1.40
```

Allowing entire subnets is done by ending the range with a dot.

```
allow hosts = 192.168.1.
```

Subnet masks can be added in the classical way.

```
allow hosts = 10.0.0.0/255.0.0.0
```

You can also allow an entire subnet with exceptions.

```
hosts allow = 10. except 10.0.0.12
```

23.2.2. hosts deny

The **hosts deny** or **deny hosts** parameter is the logical counterpart of the previous. The syntax is the same as for hosts allow.

```
hosts deny = 192.168.1.55, 192.168.1.56
```

23.3. security through obscurity

23.3.1. hide unreadable

Setting **hide unreadable** to yes will prevent users from seeing files that cannot be read by them.

```
hide unreadable = yes
```

23.3.2. browsable

Setting the **browseable = no** directive will hide shares from My Network Places. But it will not prevent someone from accessing the share (when the name of the share is known).

Note that **browsable** and **browseable** are both correct syntax.

```
[pubread]
 path = /srv/samba/readonly
 comment = files to read
 read only = yes
 guest ok = yes
 browseable = no
```

23.4. file system security

23.4.1. create mask

You can use **create mask** and **directory mask** to set the maximum allowed permissions for newly created files and directories. The mask you set is an AND mask (it takes permissions away).

```
[tennis]
 path = /srv/samba/tennis
 read only = No
```

```
guest ok = No
create mask = 640
directory mask = 750
```

23.4.2. force create mode

Similar to **create mask**, but different. Where the mask from above was a logical AND, the mode you set here is a logical OR (so it adds permissions). You can use the **force create mode** and **force directory mode** to set the minimal required permissions for newly created files and directories.

```
[tennis]
path = /srv/samba/tennis
read only = No
guest ok = No
force create mode = 444
force directory mode = 550
```

23.4.3. security mask

The **security mask** and **directory security mask** work in the same way as **create mask** and **directory mask**, but apply only when a windows user is changing permissions using the windows security dialog box.

23.4.4. force security mode

The **force security mode** and **force directory security mode** work in the same way as **force create mode** and **force directory mode**, but apply only when a windows user is changing permissions using the windows security dialog box.

23.4.5. inherit permissions

With **inherit permissions = yes** you can force newly created files and directories to inherit permissions from their parent directory, overriding the create mask and directory mask settings.

```
[authwrite]
path = /srv/samba/authwrite
comment = authenticated users only
read only = no
guest ok = no
create mask = 600
directory mask = 555
inherit permissions = yes
```

23.5. practice: securing shares

1. Create a writable share called sales, and a readonly share called budget. Test that it works.

2. Limit access to the sales share to ann, sandra and veronique.

3. Make sure that roberto cannot access the sales share.

4. Even though the sales share is writable, ann should only have read access.

5. Even though the budget share is read only, sandra should also have write access.

6. Limit one shared directory to the 192.168.1.0/24 subnet, and another share to the two computers with ip-addresses 192.168.1.33 and 172.17.18.19.

7. Make sure the computer with ip 192.168.1.203 cannot access the budget share.

8. Make sure (on the budget share) that users can see only files and directories to which they have access.

9. Make sure the sales share is not visible when browsing the network.

10. All files created in the sales share should have 640 permissions or less.

11. All directories created in the budget share should have 750 permissions or more.

12. Permissions for files on the sales share should never be set more than 664.

13. Permissions for files on the budget share should never be set less than 500.

14. If time permits (or if you are waiting for other students to finish this practice), then combine the "read only" and "writable" statements to check which one has priority.

15. If time permits then combine "read list", "write list", "hosts allow" and "hosts deny". Which of these has priority ?

23.6. solution: securing shares

1. Create a writable share called sales, and a readonly share called budget. Test that it works.

```
see previous solutions on how to do this...
```

2. Limit access to the sales share to ann, sandra and veronique.

```
valid users = ann, sandra, veronique
```

3. Make sure that roberto cannot access the sales share.

```
invalid users = roberto
```

4. Even though the sales share is writable, ann should only have read access.

```
read list = ann
```

5. Even though the budget share is read only, sandra should also have write access.

```
write list = sandra
```

6. Limit one shared directory to the 192.168.1.0/24 subnet, and another share to the two computers with ip-addresses 192.168.1.33 and 172.17.18.19.

```
hosts allow = 192.168.1.
hosts allow = 192.168.1.33, 172.17.18.19
```

7. Make sure the computer with ip 192.168.1.203 cannot access the budget share.

```
hosts deny = 192.168.1.203
```

8. Make sure (on the budget share) that users can see only files and directories to which they have access.

```
hide unreadable = yes
```

9. Make sure the sales share is not visible when browsing the network.

```
browsable = no
```

10. All files created in the sales share should have 640 permissions or less.

```
create mask = 640
```

11. All directories created in the budget share should have 750 permissions or more.

```
force directory mode = 750
```

12. Permissions for files on the sales share should never be set more than 664.

```
security mask = 750
```

13. Permissions for files on the budget share should never be set less than 500.

```
force security directory mask = 500
```

14. If time permits (or if you are waiting for other students to finish this practice), then combine the "read only" and "writable" statements to check which one has priority.

15. If time permits then combine "read list", "write list", "hosts allow" and "hosts deny". Which of these has priority ?

Chapter 24. samba domain member

24.1. changes in smb.conf

24.1.1. workgroup

The **workgroup** option in the global section should match the netbios name of the Active Directory domain.

```
workgroup = STARGATE
```

24.1.2. security mode

Authentication will not be handled by samba now, but by the Active Directory domain controllers, so we set the **security** option to domain.

```
security = Domain
```

24.1.3. Linux uid's

Linux requires a user account for every user accessing its file system, we need to provide Samba with a range of uid's and gid's that it can use to create these user accounts. The range is determined with the **idmap uid** and the **idmap gid** parameters. The first Active Directory user to connect will receive Linux uid 20000.

```
idmap uid = 20000-22000
idmap gid = 20000-22000
```

24.1.4. winbind use default domain

The **winbind use default domain** parameter makes sure winbind also operates on users without a domain component in their name.

```
winbind use default domain = yes
```

24.1.5. [global] section in smb.conf

Below is our new global section in **smb.conf**.

```
[global]
 workgroup = STARGATE
 security = Domain
 server string = Stargate Domain Member Server
 idmap uid = 20000-22000
 idmap gid = 20000-22000
 winbind use default domain = yes
```

24.1.6. realm in /etc/krb5.conf

To connect to a Windows 2003 sp2 (or later) you will need to adjust the kerberos realm in **/etc/krb5.conf** and set both lookup statements to true.

```
[libdefaults]
 default_realm = STARGATE.LOCAL
 dns_lookup_realm = true
 dns_lookup_kdc = true
```

24.1.7. [share] section in smb.conf

Nothing special is required for the share section in smb.conf. Remember that we do not manually create users in smbpasswd or on the Linux (/etc/passwd). Only Active Directory users are allowed access.

```
[domaindata]
 path = /srv/samba/domaindata
 comment = Active Directory users only
 read only = No
```

24.2. joining an Active Directory domain

While the Samba server is stopped, you can use **net rpc join** to join the Active Directory domain.

```
[root@RHEL52 samba]# service smb stop
Shutting down SMB services:                          [  OK  ]
Shutting down NMB services:                          [  OK  ]
[root@RHEL52 samba]# net rpc join -U Administrator
Password:
Joined domain STARGATE.
```

We can verify in the aduc (Active Directory Users and Computers) that a computer account is created for this samba server.

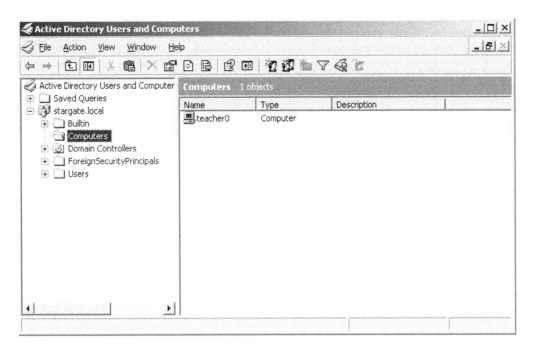

24.3. winbind

24.3.1. adding winbind to nsswitch.conf

The **winbind daemon** is talking with the Active Directory domain.

We need to update the **/etc/nsswitch.conf** file now, so user group and host names can be resolved against the winbind daemon.

```
[root@RHEL52 samba]# vi /etc/nsswitch.conf
[root@RHEL52 samba]# grep winbind /etc/nsswitch.conf
passwd:        files winbind
group:         files winbind
hosts:         files dns winbind
```

24.3.2. starting samba and winbindd

Time to start Samba followed by **winbindd**.

```
[root@RHEL4b samba]# service smb start
Starting SMB services:                              [  OK  ]
Starting NMB services:                              [  OK  ]
[root@RHEL4b samba]# service winbind start
Starting winbindd services:                         [  OK  ]
[root@RHEL4b samba]#
```

24.4. wbinfo

24.4.1. verify the trust

You can use **wbinfo -t** to verify the trust between your samba server and Active Directory.

```
[root@RHEL52 ~]# wbinfo -t
checking the trust secret via RPC calls succeeded
```

24.4.2. list all users

We can obtain a list of all user with the **wbinfo -u** command. The domain is not shown when the **winbind use default domain** parameter is set.

```
[root@RHEL52 ~]# wbinfo -u
TEACHER0\serena
TEACHER0\justine
TEACHER0\martina
STARGATE\administrator
STARGATE\guest
STARGATE\support_388945a0
STARGATE\pol
STARGATE\krbtgt
STARGATE\arthur
STARGATE\harry
```

24.4.3. list all groups

We can obtain a list of all domain groups with the **wbinfo -g** command. The domain is not shown when the **winbind use default domain** parameter is set.

```
[root@RHEL52 ~]# wbinfo -g
BUILTIN\administrators
BUILTIN\users
BATMAN\domain computers
BATMAN\domain controllers
BATMAN\schema admins
BATMAN\enterprise admins
BATMAN\domain admins
BATMAN\domain users
BATMAN\domain guests
BATMAN\group policy creator owners
BATMAN\dnsupdateproxy
```

24.4.4. query a user

We can use **wbinfo -a** to verify authentication of a user against Active Directory. Assuming a user account **harry** with password **stargate** is just created on the Active Directory, we get the following screenshot.

```
[root@RHEL52 ~]# wbinfo -a harry%stargate
plaintext password authentication succeeded
challenge/response password authentication succeeded
```

24.5. getent

We can use **getent** to verify that winbindd is working and actually adding the Active directory users to /etc/passwd.

```
[root@RHEL52 ~]# getent passwd harry
harry:*:20000:20008:harry potter:/home/BATMAN/harry:/bin/false
[root@RHEL52 ~]# getent passwd arthur
arthur:*:20001:20008:arthur dent:/home/BATMAN/arthur:/bin/false
[root@RHEL52 ~]# getent passwd bilbo
bilbo:*:20002:20008:bilbo baggins:/home/BATMAN/bilbo:/bin/false
```

If the user already exists locally, then the local user account is shown. This is because winbind is configured in **/etc/nsswitch.conf** after **files**.

```
[root@RHEL52 ~]# getent passwd paul
paul:x:500:500:Paul Cobbaut:/home/paul:/bin/bash
```

All the Active Directory users can now easily connect to the Samba share. Files created by them, belong to them.

24.6. file ownership

```
[root@RHEL4b samba]# ll /srv/samba/domaindata/
total 0
-rwxr--r--  1 justine 20000 0 Jun 22 19:54 create_by_justine_on_winxp.txt
-rwxr--r--  1 venus   20000 0 Jun 22 19:55 create_by_venus.txt
-rwxr--r--  1 maria   20000 0 Jun 22 19:57 Maria.txt
```

24.7. practice : samba domain member

1. Verify that you have a working Active Directory (AD) domain.

2. Add the domain name and domain controller to /etc/hosts. Set the AD-DNS in /etc/resolv.conf.

3. Setup Samba as a member server in the domain.

4. Verify the creation of a computer account in AD for your Samba server.

5. Verify the automatic creation of AD users in /etc/passwd with wbinfo and getent.

6. Connect to Samba shares with AD users, and verify ownership of their files.

Chapter 25. samba domain controller

25.1. about Domain Controllers

25.1.1. Windows NT4

Windows NT4 works with single master replication domain controllers. There is exactly one PDC (Primary Domain Controller) in the domain, and zero or more BDC's (Backup Domain Controllers). Samba 3 has all features found in Windows NT4 PDC and BDC, and more. This includes file and print serving, domain control with single logon, logon scripts, home directories and roaming profiles.

25.1.2. Windows 200x

With Windows 2000 came Active Directory. AD includes multimaster replication and group policies. Samba 3 can only be a member server in Active Directory, it cannot manage group policies. Samba 4 can do this (in beta).

25.1.3. Samba 3

Samba 3 can act as a domain controller in its own domain. In a Windows NT4 domain, with one Windows NT4 PDC and zero or more BDC's, Samba 3 can only be a member server. The same is valid for Samba 3 in an Active Directory Domain. In short, a Samba 3 domain controller can not share domain control with Windows domain controllers.

25.1.4. Samba 4

Samba 4 can be a domain controller in an Active Directory domain, including managing group policies. As of this writing, Samba 4 is not released for production!

25.2. About security modes

25.2.1. security = share

The 'Windows for Workgroups' way of working, a client requests connection to a share and provides a password for that connection. Aanyone who knows a password for a share can access that share. This security model was common in Windows 3.11, Windows 95, Windows 98 and Windows ME.

25.2.2. security = user

The client will send a userid + password before the server knows which share the client wants to access. This mode should be used whenever the samba server is in control of the user database. Both for standalone and samba domain controllers.

25.2.3. security = domain

This mode will allow samba to verify user credentials using NTLM in Windows NT4 and in all Active Directory domains. This is similar to Windows NT4 BDC's joining a native Windows 2000/3 Active Directory domain.

25.2.4. security = ads

This mode will make samba use Kerberos to connect to the Active Directory domain.

25.2.5. security = server

This mode is obsolete, it can be used to forward authentication to another server.

25.3. About password backends

The previous chapters all used the **smbpasswd** user database. For domain control we opt for the **tdbsam** password backend. Another option would be to use LDAP. Larger domains will benefit from using LDAP instead of the not so scalable tdbsam. When you need more than one Domain Controller, then the Samba team advises to not use tdbsam.

25.4. [global] section in smb.conf

Now is a good time to start adding comments in your smb.conf. First we will take a look at the naming of our domain and server in the **[global]** section, and at the domain controlling parameters.

25.4.1. security

The security must be set to user (which is the default). This mode will make samba control the user accounts, so it will allow samba to act as a domain controller.

```
security = user
```

25.4.2. os level

A samba server is the most stable computer in the network, so it should win all browser elections (**os level** above 32) to become the **browser master**

```
os level = 33
```

25.4.3. passdb backend

The **passdb backend** parameter will determine whether samba uses **smbpasswd, tdbsam** or ldap.

```
passdb backend = tdbsam
```

25.4.4. preferred master

Setting the **preferred master** parameter to yes will make the nmbd daemon force an election on startup.

```
preferred master = yes
```

25.4.5. domain logons

Setting the **domain logons** parameter will make this samba server a domain controller.

```
domain logons = yes
```

25.4.6. domain master

Setting the **domain master** parameter can cause samba to claim the **domain master browser** role for its workgroup. Don't use this parameter in a workgroup with an active NT4 PDC.

```
domain master = yes
```

25.4.7. [global] section

The screenshot below shows a sample [global] section for a samba domain controller.

```
[global]
# names
 workgroup = SPORTS
 netbios name = DCSPORTS
 server string = Sports Domain Controller
# domain control parameters
 security = user
 os level = 33
 preferred master = Yes
 domain master = Yes
 domain logons = Yes
```

25.5. netlogon share

Part of the microsoft definition for a domain controller is that it should have a **netlogon share**. This is the relevant part of smb.conf to create this netlogon share on Samba.

```
[netlogon]
comment = Network Logon Service
path = /srv/samba/netlogon
admin users = root
guest ok = Yes
browseable = No
```

25.6. other [share] sections

We create some sections for file shares, to test the samba server. Users can all access the general sports file share, but only group members can access their own sports share.

```
[sports]
comment = Information about all sports
path = /srv/samba/sports
valid users = @ntsports
read only = No

[tennis]
comment = Information about tennis
path = /srv/samba/tennis
valid users = @nttennis
read only = No
```

```
[football]
comment = Information about football
path = /srv/samba/football
valid users = @ntfootball
read only = No
```

25.7. Users and Groups

To be able to use users and groups in the samba domain controller, we can first set up some groups on the Linux computer.

```
[root@RHEL52 samba]# groupadd ntadmins
[root@RHEL52 samba]# groupadd ntsports
[root@RHEL52 samba]# groupadd ntfootball
[root@RHEL52 samba]# groupadd nttennis
```

This enables us to add group membership info to some new users for our samba domain. Don't forget to give them a password.

```
[root@RHEL52 samba]# useradd -m -G ntadmins Administrator
[root@RHEL52 samba]# useradd -m -G ntsports,nttennis venus
[root@RHEL52 samba]# useradd -m -G ntsports,nttennis kim
[root@RHEL52 samba]# useradd -m -G ntsports,nttennis jelena
[root@RHEL52 samba]# useradd -m -G ntsports,ntfootball figo
[root@RHEL52 samba]# useradd -m -G ntsports,ntfootball ronaldo
[root@RHEL52 samba]# useradd -m -G ntsports,ntfootball pfaff
```

It is always safe to verify creation of users, groups and passwords in /etc/passwd, /etc/shadow and /etc/group.

```
[root@RHEL52 samba]# tail -11 /etc/group
ntadmins:x:507:Administrator
ntsports:x:508:venus,kim,jelena,figo,ronaldo,pfaff
ntfootball:x:509:figo,ronaldo,pfaff
nttennis:x:510:venus,kim,jelena
Administrator:x:511:
venus:x:512:
kim:x:513:
jelena:x:514:
figo:x:515:
ronaldo:x:516:
pfaff:x:517:
```

25.8. tdbsam

Next we must make these users known to samba with the smbpasswd tool. When you add the first user to **tdbsam**, the file **/etc/samba/passdb.tdb** will be created.

```
[root@RHEL52 samba]# smbpasswd -a root
New SMB password:
```

```
Retype new SMB password:
tdbsam_open: Converting version 0 database to version 3.
Added user root.
```

Adding all the other users generates less output, because tdbsam is already created.

```
[root@RHEL4b samba]# smbpasswd -a root
New SMB password:
Retype new SMB password:
Added user root.
```

25.9. about computer accounts

Every NT computer (Windows NT, 2000, XP, Vista) can become a member of a domain. Joining the domain (by right-clicking on My Computer) means that a computer account will be created in the domain. This computer account also has a password (but you cannot know it) to prevent other computers with the same name from accidentally becoming member of the domain. The computer account created by Samba is visible in the **/etc/passwd** file on Linux. Computer accounts appear as a normal user account, but end their name with a dollar sign. Below a screenshot of the windows 2003 computer account, created by Samba 3.

```
[root@RHEL52 samba]# tail -5 /etc/passwd
jelena:x:510:514::/home/jelena:/bin/bash
figo:x:511:515::/home/figo:/bin/bash
ronaldo:x:512:516::/home/ronaldo:/bin/bash
pfaff:x:513:517::/home/pfaff:/bin/bash
w2003ee$:x:514:518::/home/nobody:/bin/false
```

To be able to create the account, you will need to provide credentials of an account with the permission to create accounts (by default only root can do this on Linux). And we will have to tell Samba how to to this, by adding an **add machine script** to the global section of smb.conf.

```
add machine script = /usr/sbin/useradd -s /bin/false -d /home/nobody %u
```

You can now join a Microsoft computer to the sports domain (with the root user). After reboot of the Microsoft computer, you will be able to logon with Administrator (password Stargate1), but you will get an error about your roaming profile. We will fix this in the next section.

When joining the samba domain, you have to enter the credentials of a Linux account that can create users (usually only root can do this). If the Microsoft computer complains with **The parameter is incorrect**, then you possibly forgot to add the **add machine script**.

25.10. local or roaming profiles

For your information, if you want to force local profiles instead of roaming profiles, then simply add the following two lines to the global section in smb.conf.

```
logon home =
logon path =
```

Microsoft computers store a lot of User Metadata and application data in a user profile. Making this profile available on the network will enable users to keep their Desktop and Application settings across computers. User profiles on the network are called **roaming profiles** or **roving profiles**. The Samba domain controller can manage these profiles. First we need to add the relevant section in smb.conf.

```
[Profiles]
 comment = User Profiles
 path = /srv/samba/profiles
 readonly = No
 profile acls = Yes
```

Besides the share section, we also need to set the location of the profiles share (this can be another Samba server) in the global section.

```
logon path = \\%L\Profiles\%U
```

The **%L** variable is the name of this Samba server, the **%U** variable translates to the username. After adding a user to smbpasswd and letting the user log on and off, the profile of the user will look like this.

```
[root@RHEL4b samba]# ll /srv/samba/profiles/Venus/
total 568
drwxr-xr-x  4 Venus Venus   4096 Jul  5 10:03 Application Data
drwxr-xr-x  2 Venus Venus   4096 Jul  5 10:03 Cookies
drwxr-xr-x  3 Venus Venus   4096 Jul  5 10:03 Desktop
drwxr-xr-x  3 Venus Venus   4096 Jul  5 10:03 Favorites
drwxr-xr-x  4 Venus Venus   4096 Jul  5 10:03 My Documents
drwxr-xr-x  2 Venus Venus   4096 Jul  5 10:03 NetHood
-rwxr--r--  1 Venus Venus 524288 Jul  5  2007 NTUSER.DAT
-rwxr--r--  1 Venus Venus   1024 Jul  5  2007 NTUSER.DAT.LOG
-rw-r--r--  1 Venus Venus    268 Jul  5 10:03 ntuser.ini
drwxr-xr-x  2 Venus Venus   4096 Jul  5 10:03 PrintHood
drwxr-xr-x  2 Venus Venus   4096 Jul  5 10:03 Recent
drwxr-xr-x  2 Venus Venus   4096 Jul  5 10:03 SendTo
drwxr-xr-x  3 Venus Venus   4096 Jul  5 10:03 Start Menu
drwxr-xr-x  2 Venus Venus   4096 Jul  5 10:03 Templates
```

25.11. Groups in NTFS acls

We have users on Unix, we have groups on Unix that contain those users.

```
[root@RHEL4b samba]# grep nt /etc/group
...
ntadmins:x:506:Administrator
ntsports:x:507:Venus,Serena,Kim,Figo,Pfaff
nttennis:x:508:Venus,Serena,Kim
ntfootball:x:509:Figo,Pfaff
```

```
[root@RHEL4b samba]#
```

We already added Venus to the **tdbsam** with **smbpasswd**.

```
smbpasswd -a Venus
```

Does this mean that Venus can access the tennis and the sports shares ? Yes, all access works fine on the Samba server. But the nttennis group is not available on the windows machines. To make the groups available on windows (like in the ntfs security tab of files and folders), we have to map unix groups to windows groups. To do this, we use the **net groupmap** command.

```
[root@RHEL4b samba]# net groupmap add ntgroup="tennis" unixgroup=nttennis type=d
No rid or sid specified, choosing algorithmic mapping
Successully added group tennis to the mapping db
[root@RHEL4b samba]# net groupmap add ntgroup="football" unixgroup=ntfootball type=d
No rid or sid specified, choosing algorithmic mapping
Successully added group football to the mapping db
[root@RHEL4b samba]# net groupmap add ntgroup="sports" unixgroup=ntsports type=d
No rid or sid specified, choosing algorithmic mapping
Successully added group sports to the mapping db
[root@RHEL4b samba]#
```

Now you can use the Samba groups on all NTFS volumes on members of the domain.

25.12. logon scripts

Before testing a logon script, make sure it has the proper carriage returns that DOS files have.

```
[root@RHEL4b netlogon]# cat start.bat
net use Z: \\DCSPORTS0\SPORTS
[root@RHEL4b netlogon]# unix2dos start.bat
unix2dos: converting file start.bat to DOS format ...
[root@RHEL4b netlogon]#
```

Then copy the scripts to the netlogon share, and add the following parameter to smb.conf.

```
logon script = start.bat
```

25.13. practice: samba domain controller

1. Setup Samba as a domain controller.

2. Create the shares salesdata, salespresentations and meetings. Salesdata must be accessible to all sales people and to all managers. SalesPresentations is only for all sales people. Meetings is only accessible to all managers. Use groups to accomplish this.

3. Join a Microsoft computer to your domain. Verify the creation of a computer account in /etc/passwd.

4. Setup and verify the proper working of roaming profiles.

5. Find information about home directories for users, set them up and verify that users receive their home directory mapped under the H:-drive in MS Windows Explorer.

6. Use a couple of samba domain groups with members to set acls on ntfs. Verify that it works!

7. Knowing that the %m variable contains the computername, create a separate log file for every computer(account).

8. Knowing that %s contains the client operating system, include a smb.%s.conf file that contains a share. (The share will only be visible to clients with that OS).

9. If time permits (or if you are waiting for other students to finish this practice), then combine "valid users" and "invalid users" with groups and usernames with "hosts allow" and "hosts deny" and make a table of which get priority over which.

Chapter 26. a brief look at samba 4

26.1. Samba 4 alpha 6

A quick view on Samba 4 alpha 6 (January 2009). You can also follow this guide http://wiki.samba.org/index.php/Samba4/HOWTO

Remove old Samba from Red Hat

```
yum remove samba
```

set a fix ip address (Red Hat has an easy GUI)

download and untar

```
samba.org, click 'download info', choose mirror, dl samba4 latest alpha
```

once untarred, enter the directory and read the howto4.txt

```
cd samba-4.0.0alpha6/

more howto4.txt
```

first we have to configure, compile and install samba4

```
cd source4/

./configure

make

make install
```

Then we can use the provision script to setup our realm. I used booi.schot as domain name (instead of example.com).

```
./setup/provision --realm=BOOI.SCHOT --domain=BOOI --adminpass=stargate \
--server-role='domain controller'
```

i added a simple share for testing

```
vi /usr/local/samba/etc/smb.conf
```

then i started samba

```
cd /usr/local/samba/sbin/

./samba
```

I tested with smbclient, it works

```
smbclient //localhost/test -Uadministrator%stargate
```

I checked that bind (and bind-chroot) were installed (yes), so copied the srv records

```
cp booi.schot.zone /var/named/chroot/etc/
```

then appended to named.conf

```
cat named.conf >> /var/named/chroot/etc/named.conf
```

I followed these steps in the howto4.txt

```
vi /etc/init.d/named  [added two export lines right after start()]
chmod a+r /usr/local/samba/private/dns.keytab
cp krb5.conf /etc/
vi /var/named/chroot/etc/named.conf
 --> remove a lot, but keep allow-update { any; };
```

restart bind (named!), then tested dns with dig, this works (stripped screenshot!)

```
[root@RHEL52 private]# dig _ldap._tcp.dc._msdcs.booi.schot SRV @localhost

; (1 server found)
;; global options:  printcmd
;; Got answer:
;; -HEADER- opcode: QUERY, status: NXDOMAIN, id: 58186
;; flags: qr rd ra; QUERY: 1, ANSWER: 0, AUTHORITY: 1, ADDITIONAL: 0

;; QUESTION SECTION:
;_ldap._tcp.dc._msdcs.booi.schot. IN SRV

;; AUTHORITY SECTION:
.   10800 IN SOA A.ROOT-SERVERS.NET....

;; Query time: 54 msec
;; SERVER: 127.0.0.1#53(127.0.0.1)
;; WHEN: Tue Jan 27 20:57:05 2009
;; MSG SIZE  rcvd: 124

[root@RHEL52 private]#
```

made sure /etc/resolv.conf points to himself

```
[root@RHEL52 private]# cat /etc/resolv.conf
search booi.schot
nameserver 127.0.0.1
```

start windows 2003 server, enter the samba4 as DNS!

ping the domain, if it doesn't work, then add your redhats hostname and your realm to windows/system32/drivers/etc/hosts

join the windows computer to the domain

reboot the windows

log on with administrator stargate

start run dsa.msc to manage samba4

create an OU, a user and a GPO, test that it works

Part VI. Appendix

Table of Contents

Appendix A. License

GNU Free Documentation License

Version 1.3, 3 November 2008

Copyright © 2000, 2001, 2002, 2007, 2008 Free Software Foundation, Inc.

Everyone is permitted to copy and distribute verbatim copies of this license document, but changing it is not allowed.

0. PREAMBLE

The purpose of this License is to make a manual, textbook, or other functional and useful document "free" in the sense of freedom: to assure everyone the effective freedom to copy and redistribute it, with or without modifying it, either commercially or noncommercially. Secondarily, this License preserves for the author and publisher a way to get credit for their work, while not being considered responsible for modifications made by others.

This License is a kind of "copyleft", which means that derivative works of the document must themselves be free in the same sense. It complements the GNU General Public License, which is a copyleft license designed for free software.

We have designed this License in order to use it for manuals for free software, because free software needs free documentation: a free program should come with manuals providing the same freedoms that the software does. But this License is not limited to software manuals; it can be used for any textual work, regardless of subject matter or whether it is published as a printed book. We recommend this License principally for works whose purpose is instruction or reference.

1. APPLICABILITY AND DEFINITIONS

This License applies to any manual or other work, in any medium, that contains a notice placed by the copyright holder saying it can be distributed under the terms of this License. Such a notice grants a world-wide, royalty-free license, unlimited in duration, to use that work under the conditions stated herein. The "Document", below, refers to any such manual or work. Any member of the public is a licensee, and is addressed as "you". You accept the license if you copy, modify or distribute the work in a way requiring permission under copyright law.

A "Modified Version" of the Document means any work containing the Document or a portion of it, either copied verbatim, or with modifications and/or translated into another language.

A "Secondary Section" is a named appendix or a front-matter section of the Document that deals exclusively with the relationship of the publishers or authors of the Document to the Document's overall subject (or to related matters) and contains nothing that could fall directly within that overall subject. (Thus, if the Document is in part a textbook of mathematics, a Secondary Section may not explain any mathematics.) The relationship could be a matter of historical connection with the subject or with related matters, or of legal, commercial, philosophical, ethical or political position regarding them.

The "Invariant Sections" are certain Secondary Sections whose titles are designated, as being those of Invariant Sections, in the notice that says that the Document is released under this License. If a section does not fit the above definition of Secondary then it is not allowed to be designated as Invariant. The Document may contain zero Invariant Sections. If the Document does not identify any Invariant Sections then there are none.

The "Cover Texts" are certain short passages of text that are listed, as Front-Cover Texts or Back-Cover Texts, in the notice that says that the Document is released under this License. A Front-Cover Text may be at most 5 words, and a Back-Cover Text may be at most 25 words.

A "Transparent" copy of the Document means a machine-readable copy, represented in a format whose specification is available to the general public, that is suitable for revising the document straightforwardly with generic text editors or (for images composed of pixels) generic paint programs or (for drawings) some widely available drawing editor, and that is suitable for input to text formatters or for automatic translation to a variety of formats suitable for input to text formatters. A copy made in an otherwise Transparent file format whose markup, or absence of markup, has been arranged to thwart or discourage subsequent modification by readers is not Transparent. An image format is not Transparent if used for any substantial amount of text. A copy that is not "Transparent" is called "Opaque".

Examples of suitable formats for Transparent copies include plain ASCII without markup, Texinfo input format, LaTeX input format, SGML or XML using a publicly available DTD, and standard-conforming simple HTML, PostScript or PDF designed for human modification. Examples of transparent image formats include PNG, XCF and JPG. Opaque formats include proprietary formats that can be read and edited only by proprietary word processors, SGML or XML for which the DTD and/or processing tools are not generally available, and the machine-generated HTML, PostScript or PDF produced by some word processors for output purposes only.

The "Title Page" means, for a printed book, the title page itself, plus such following pages as are needed to hold, legibly, the material this License requires to appear in the title page. For works in formats which do not have any title page as such, "Title Page" means the text near the most prominent appearance of the work's title, preceding the beginning of the body of the text.

The "publisher" means any person or entity that distributes copies of the Document to the public.

A section "Entitled XYZ" means a named subunit of the Document whose title either is precisely XYZ or contains XYZ in parentheses following text that translates XYZ in another language. (Here XYZ stands for a specific section name mentioned below, such as "Acknowledgements", "Dedications", "Endorsements", or "History".) To "Preserve the Title" of such a section when you modify the Document means that it remains a section "Entitled XYZ" according to this definition.

The Document may include Warranty Disclaimers next to the notice which states that this License applies to the Document. These Warranty Disclaimers are considered to be included by reference in this License, but only as regards disclaiming warranties: any other implication that these Warranty Disclaimers may have is void and has no effect on the meaning of this License.

2. VERBATIM COPYING

You may copy and distribute the Document in any medium, either commercially or noncommercially, provided that this License, the copyright notices, and the license notice saying this License applies to the Document are reproduced in all copies, and that you add no other conditions whatsoever to those of this License. You may not use technical measures to obstruct or control the reading or further copying of the copies you make or distribute. However, you may accept compensation in exchange for copies. If you distribute a large enough number of copies you must also follow the conditions in section 3.

You may also lend copies, under the same conditions stated above, and you may publicly display copies.

3. COPYING IN QUANTITY

If you publish printed copies (or copies in media that commonly have printed covers) of the Document, numbering more than 100, and the Document's license notice requires Cover Texts, you must enclose the copies in covers that carry, clearly and legibly, all these Cover Texts: Front-Cover Texts on the front cover, and Back-Cover Texts on the back cover. Both covers must also clearly and legibly identify you as the publisher of these copies. The front cover must present the full title with all words of the title equally prominent and visible. You may add other material on the covers in addition. Copying with changes limited to the covers, as long as they preserve the title of the Document and satisfy these conditions, can be treated as verbatim copying in other respects.

If the required texts for either cover are too voluminous to fit legibly, you should put the first ones listed (as many as fit reasonably) on the actual cover, and continue the rest onto adjacent pages.

If you publish or distribute Opaque copies of the Document numbering more than 100, you must either include a machine-readable Transparent copy along with each Opaque copy, or state in or with each Opaque copy a computer-network location from which the general network-using public has access to download using public-standard network protocols a complete Transparent copy of the Document, free of added material. If you use the latter option, you must take reasonably prudent steps, when you begin distribution of Opaque copies in quantity, to ensure that this Transparent copy will remain thus accessible at the stated location until at least one year after the last time you distribute an Opaque copy (directly or through your agents or retailers) of that edition to the public.

It is requested, but not required, that you contact the authors of the Document well before redistributing any large number of copies, to give them a chance to provide you with an updated version of the Document.

4. MODIFICATIONS

You may copy and distribute a Modified Version of the Document under the conditions of sections 2 and 3 above, provided that you release the Modified Version under precisely this License, with the Modified Version filling the role of the Document, thus licensing distribution and modification of the Modified Version to whoever possesses a copy of it. In addition, you must do these things in the Modified Version:

   * A. Use in the Title Page (and on the covers, if any) a title distinct from that of the Document, and from those of previous versions (which should, if there were any, be listed in the History section of the Document). You may use the same title as a previous version if the original publisher of that version gives permission.

* B. List on the Title Page, as authors, one or more persons or entities responsible for authorship of the modifications in the Modified Version, together with at least five of the principal authors of the Document (all of its principal authors, if it has fewer than five), unless they release you from this requirement.
* C. State on the Title page the name of the publisher of the Modified Version, as the publisher.
* D. Preserve all the copyright notices of the Document.
* E. Add an appropriate copyright notice for your modifications adjacent to the other copyright notices.
* F. Include, immediately after the copyright notices, a license notice giving the public permission to use the Modified Version under the terms of this License, in the form shown in the Addendum below.
* G. Preserve in that license notice the full lists of Invariant Sections and required Cover Texts given in the Document's license notice.
* H. Include an unaltered copy of this License.
* I. Preserve the section Entitled "History", Preserve its Title, and add to it an item stating at least the title, year, new authors, and publisher of the Modified Version as given on the Title Page. If there is no section Entitled "History" in the Document, create one stating the title, year, authors, and publisher of the Document as given on its Title Page, then add an item describing the Modified Version as stated in the previous sentence.
* J. Preserve the network location, if any, given in the Document for public access to a Transparent copy of the Document, and likewise the network locations given in the Document for previous versions it was based on. These may be placed in the "History" section. You may omit a network location for a work that was published at least four years before the Document itself, or if the original publisher of the version it refers to gives permission.
* K. For any section Entitled "Acknowledgements" or "Dedications", Preserve the Title of the section, and preserve in the section all the substance and tone of each of the contributor acknowledgements and/or dedications given therein.
* L. Preserve all the Invariant Sections of the Document, unaltered in their text and in their titles. Section numbers or the equivalent are not considered part of the section titles.
* M. Delete any section Entitled "Endorsements". Such a section may not be included in the Modified Version.
* N. Do not retitle any existing section to be Entitled "Endorsements" or to conflict in title with any Invariant Section.
* O. Preserve any Warranty Disclaimers.

If the Modified Version includes new front-matter sections or appendices that qualify as Secondary Sections and contain no material copied from the Document, you may at your option designate some or all of these sections as invariant. To do this, add their titles to the list of Invariant Sections in the Modified Version's license notice. These titles must be distinct from any other section titles.

You may add a section Entitled "Endorsements", provided it contains nothing but endorsements of your Modified Version by various parties—for example, statements of peer review or that the text has been approved by an organization as the authoritative definition of a standard.

You may add a passage of up to five words as a Front-Cover Text, and a passage of up to 25 words as a Back-Cover Text, to the end of the list of Cover Texts in the Modified Version. Only one passage of Front-Cover Text and one of Back-Cover Text may be added by (or through arrangements made by) any one entity. If the Document already includes a cover text for the same cover, previously added by you or by arrangement made by the same entity you are acting on behalf of, you may not add another; but you may replace the old one, on explicit permission from the previous publisher that added the old one.

The author(s) and publisher(s) of the Document do not by this License give permission to use their names for publicity for or to assert or imply endorsement of any Modified Version.

5. COMBINING DOCUMENTS

You may combine the Document with other documents released under this License, under the terms defined in section 4 above for modified versions, provided that you include in the combination all of the Invariant Sections of all of the original documents, unmodified, and list them all as Invariant Sections of your combined work in its license notice, and that you preserve all their Warranty Disclaimers.

The combined work need only contain one copy of this License, and multiple identical Invariant Sections may be replaced with a single copy. If there are multiple Invariant Sections with the same name but different contents, make the title of each such section unique by adding at the end of it, in parentheses, the name of the original author or publisher of that section if known, or else a unique number. Make the same adjustment to the section titles in the list of Invariant Sections in the license notice of the combined work.

In the combination, you must combine any sections Entitled "History" in the various original documents, forming one section Entitled "History"; likewise combine any sections Entitled "Acknowledgements", and any sections Entitled "Dedications". You must delete all sections Entitled "Endorsements".

6. COLLECTIONS OF DOCUMENTS

You may make a collection consisting of the Document and other documents released under this License, and replace the individual copies of this License in the various documents with a single copy that is included in the collection, provided that you follow the rules of this License for verbatim copying of each of the documents in all other respects.

You may extract a single document from such a collection, and distribute it individually under this License, provided you insert a copy of this License into the extracted document, and follow this License in all other respects regarding verbatim copying of that document.

7. AGGREGATION WITH INDEPENDENT WORKS

A compilation of the Document or its derivatives with other separate and independent documents or works, in or on a volume of a storage or distribution medium, is called an "aggregate" if the copyright resulting from the compilation is not used to limit the legal rights of the compilation's users beyond what the individual works permit. When the Document is included in an aggregate, this License does not apply to the other works in the aggregate which are not themselves derivative works of the Document.

If the Cover Text requirement of section 3 is applicable to these copies of the Document, then if the Document is less than one half of the entire aggregate, the Document's Cover Texts may be placed on covers that bracket the Document within the aggregate, or the electronic equivalent of covers if the Document is in electronic form. Otherwise they must appear on printed covers that bracket the whole aggregate.

8. TRANSLATION

Translation is considered a kind of modification, so you may
distribute translations of the Document under the terms of section 4.
Replacing Invariant Sections with translations requires special
permission from their copyright holders, but you may include
translations of some or all Invariant Sections in addition to the
original versions of these Invariant Sections. You may include a
translation of this License, and all the license notices in the
Document, and any Warranty Disclaimers, provided that you also include
the original English version of this License and the original versions
of those notices and disclaimers. In case of a disagreement between
the translation and the original version of this License or a notice
or disclaimer, the original version will prevail.

If a section in the Document is Entitled "Acknowledgements",
"Dedications", or "History", the requirement (section 4) to Preserve
its Title (section 1) will typically require changing the actual
title.

9. TERMINATION

You may not copy, modify, sublicense, or distribute the Document
except as expressly provided under this License. Any attempt otherwise
to copy, modify, sublicense, or distribute it is void, and will
automatically terminate your rights under this License.

However, if you cease all violation of this License, then your license
from a particular copyright holder is reinstated (a) provisionally,
unless and until the copyright holder explicitly and finally
terminates your license, and (b) permanently, if the copyright holder
fails to notify you of the violation by some reasonable means prior to
60 days after the cessation.

Moreover, your license from a particular copyright holder is
reinstated permanently if the copyright holder notifies you of the
violation by some reasonable means, this is the first time you have
received notice of violation of this License (for any work) from that
copyright holder, and you cure the violation prior to 30 days after
your receipt of the notice.

Termination of your rights under this section does not terminate the
licenses of parties who have received copies or rights from you under
this License. If your rights have been terminated and not permanently
reinstated, receipt of a copy of some or all of the same material does
not give you any rights to use it.

10. FUTURE REVISIONS OF THIS LICENSE

The Free Software Foundation may publish new, revised versions of the
GNU Free Documentation License from time to time. Such new versions
will be similar in spirit to the present version, but may differ in
detail to address new problems or concerns. See
http://www.gnu.org/copyleft/.

Each version of the License is given a distinguishing version number.
If the Document specifies that a particular numbered version of this
License "or any later version" applies to it, you have the option of
following the terms and conditions either of that specified version or
of any later version that has been published (not as a draft) by the
Free Software Foundation. If the Document does not specify a version
number of this License, you may choose any version ever published (not
as a draft) by the Free Software Foundation. If the Document specifies

that a proxy can decide which future versions of this License can be used, that proxy's public statement of acceptance of a version permanently authorizes you to choose that version for the Document.

11. RELICENSING

"Massive Multiauthor Collaboration Site" (or "MMC Site") means any World Wide Web server that publishes copyrightable works and also provides prominent facilities for anybody to edit those works. A public wiki that anybody can edit is an example of such a server. A "Massive Multiauthor Collaboration" (or "MMC") contained in the site means any set of copyrightable works thus published on the MMC site.

"CC-BY-SA" means the Creative Commons Attribution-Share Alike 3.0 license published by Creative Commons Corporation, a not-for-profit corporation with a principal place of business in San Francisco, California, as well as future copyleft versions of that license published by that same organization.

"Incorporate" means to publish or republish a Document, in whole or in part, as part of another Document.

An MMC is "eligible for relicensing" if it is licensed under this License, and if all works that were first published under this License somewhere other than this MMC, and subsequently incorporated in whole or in part into the MMC, (1) had no cover texts or invariant sections, and (2) were thus incorporated prior to November 1, 2008.

The operator of an MMC Site may republish an MMC contained in the site under CC-BY-SA on the same site at any time before August 1, 2009, provided the MMC is eligible for relicensing.

Index

Symbols

A

B

C

D

E

F